THE RIGHT TO HAVE RIGHTS

The Right to Have Rights: Citizenship, Humanity, and International Law

ALISON KESBY

OXFORD

UNIVERSITY PRESS

OXFORD
UNIVERSITY PRESS

Great Clarendon Street, Oxford OX2 6DP

Oxford University Press is a department of the University of Oxford.
It furthers the University's objective of excellence in research, scholarship,
and education by publishing worldwide in

Oxford New York

Auckland Cape Town Dar es Salaam Hong Kong Karachi
Kuala Lumpur Madrid Melbourne Mexico City Nairobi
New Delhi Shanghai Taipei Toronto

With offices in

Argentina Austria Brazil Chile Czech Republic France Greece
Guatemala Hungary Italy Japan Poland Portugal Singapore
South Korea Switzerland Thailand Turkey Ukraine Vietnam

Oxford is a registered trade mark of Oxford University Press
in the UK and in certain other countries

Published in the United States
by Oxford University Press Inc., New York

British Library Cataloguing in Publication Data

Data available

Library of Congress Cataloging in Publication Data
Library of Congress Control Number: 2011939860

Typeset by Newgen Imaging Systems (P) Ltd, Chennai, India
Printed in Great Britain
on acid-free paper by
CPI Group (UK) Ltd, Croydon, CR0 4yy

ISBN 978-0-19-960082-3

1 3 5 7 9 10 8 6 4 2

For Chris, Kit, and Keith

Acknowledgements

I would like to express my deep gratitude to Susan Marks for her nurturing of the PhD dissertation that was to be the seed of this project. I could not have asked for a more inspiring, generous, and encouraging mentor and colleague, and I owe her a great debt. I am thankful to my dissertation examiners Matthew Craven and Martti Koskenniemi for providing perceptive and valuable comments, and to Daniel Joyce, Jan Klabbers, Panu Minkkinen, Jacqueline Mowbray, Guglielmo Verdirame, and the anonymous reviewers from Oxford University Press who offered insightful comments and encouragement at key points in the project. The reflections of one reviewer in particular were of enormous assistance in revising the typescript for publication, and opened up several new lines of inquiry. In addition, my thinking has been greatly enriched by the conversations and contributions of colleagues at the University of Cambridge and beyond. I would also like to record my sincere thanks to Kenneth Watkin for his generosity and thoroughness in proofreading the text, and to Merel Alstein, Anthony Hinton, David Lewis, John Louth, and Cheryl Prophett at Oxford University Press for their encouragement and warm professionalism.

This project has benefited from generous funding from several institutions. St John's College, Cambridge; the Commonwealth Scholarship Commission in the United Kingdom; and the Cambridge Commonwealth Trust funded my original research. It has been a great joy to continue at St John's as a Research Fellow, and not only participate in College life but have the opportunity to pursue my research and complete this book. I am indebted to the Master and Fellows of St John's for their generous support and for making being part of the College community such a pleasure.

Throughout the time of writing this book I have been blessed with a circle of cherished friends in Cambridge and around the globe whose support I acknowledge here with heartfelt thanks.

Words cannot express my profound gratitude to all of my family, and especially to my parents, Kit and Keith, whose self-sacrificial love knows no bounds. Above all, my thanks go to my husband, Chris, without whom this book would never have been completed, and whose unconditional love points me daily to the one 'full of grace and truth'.

Fragments of Chapter 1 were previously published in 'The Shifting and Multiple Border and International Law' (2007) 27(1) *OJLS* 101 and 'International Law and the Right to have Rights', *Select Proceedings of the European Society of International law*, Vol 2, 2008 (Oxford: Hart, 2010) 133, and fragments of Chapter 4 in 'Internal Borders and Immigration Control: New Prospects and Challenges' [2010] *European Human Rights Law Review* 176. They are reproduced here with thanks to the publishers and reviewers.

Contents

Table of Cases

INTER-AMERICAN COURT OF HUMAN RIGHTS

INTERNATIONAL COURT OF JUSTICE

OTHER INTERNATIONAL CASES

DOMESTIC CASES

Australia

Canada

UNITED NATIONS

Committee against Torture

Committee on the Elimination of Racial Discrimination

Human Rights Committee

Table of Treaties, Declarations, and Other Instruments

List of Abbreviations

1954 Statelessness Convention	Convention relating to the Status of Stateless Persons (New York, 28 September 1954, entered into force 6 June 1960, 360 *UNTS* 117)
ACHR	American Convention on Human Rights (San José, 22 November 1969, entered into force 18 July 1978, 1144 *UNTS* 144)
African Charter or ACHPR	African Charter on Human and Peoples' Rights (Nairobi, 27 June 1981, entered into force 21 October 1986, 1520 *UNTS* 217)
Arab Charter on Human Rights or ArabCHR	(Tunis, 23 May 2004, entered into force 15 March 2008)
CAT	Convention against Torture and Other Cruel, Inhuman or Degrading Treatment or Punishment (New York, 10 December 1984, entered into force 26 June 1987, 1465 *UNTS* 85)
CEDAW	Convention on the Elimination of All Forms of Discrimination against Women (New York, 18 December 1979, entered into force 3 September 1981, 1249 *UNTS* 13)
CERD	Committee on the Elimination of Racial Discrimination
CESCR	Committee on Economic, Social and Cultural Rights
CRC	Convention on the Rights of the Child (New York, 20 November 1989, entered into force 2 September 1990, 1577 *UNTS* 3)
ECHR or European Convention	Convention for the Protection of Human Rights and Fundamental Freedoms (European Convention on Human Rights) (Rome, 4 November 1950, entered into force 3 September 1953, 213, ETS No 5, *UNTS* 221)
ECtHR	European Court of Human Rights
HRC	Human Rights Committee
IACHR	Inter-American Commission on Human Rights
IACtHR	Inter-American Court of Human Rights
ICCPR	International Covenant on Civil and Political Rights (New York, 16 December 1966, entered into force 23 March 1976, 999 *UNTS* 171)

ICERD	International Convention on the Elimination of All Forms of Racial Discrimination (New York, 21 December 1965, entered into force 4 January 1969, 660 *UNTS* 195)
ICESCR	International Covenant on Economic, Social and Cultural Rights (New York, 16 December 1966, entered into force 3 January 1976, 993 *UNTS* 3)
ICJ	International Court of Justice
ICRMW or Migrant Workers Convention	International Convention on the Protection of the Rights of All Migrant Workers and Members of their Families (New York, 18 December 1990, entered into force 1 July 2003, 2220 *UNTS* 3)
ILA	International Law Association
ILC	International Law Commission
OHCHR	Office of the United Nations High Commissioner for Human Rights
PCIJ	Permanent Court of International Justice
Refugee Convention	Convention relating to the Status of Refugees (Geneva, 28 July 1951, entered into force 22 April 1954, 189 *UNTS* 137) as amended by the Protocol relating to the Status of Refugees (New York, 31 January 1967, entered into force 4 October 1967, 606 *UNTS* 267)
UDHR or Universal Declaration	Universal Declaration of Human Rights (10 December 1948, UN GA Res 217A(III))
UN	United Nations
UNHCR	United Nations High Commissioner for Refugees

Introduction

The situation is routine, almost banal. The state in which a woman is born and resides refuses to issue her with a birth certificate or any other document by which she can prove her right to a nationality. Without such documents she lives under the constant threat of expulsion from the only state she has ever known and is unable to obtain health care, participate in elections, or even acquire and transfer property. Her most basic rights are denied. Question: what has happened to her?

In being refused a nationality, has she lost the 'right to have rights'? If her right to a nationality were recognized would her 'right to have rights' be restored? Surely with the advent of international human rights law, a person holds rights irrespective of their nationality status such that an 'illegal' migrant is also a legitimate rights-bearer. Do we enjoy the right to have rights by virtue of our humanity alone? What then of the significance of citizenship as a political concept for right-bearing? Do we recognize one another's rights by virtue of our membership of the political community? Or is it more apt to dispense with notions of nationality, humanity, and citizenship, however conceived, and grapple with the politics of human rights: the right to have rights as the vulnerable and excluded taking up and enacting the rights they have been denied and constituting themselves as the subject of rights?

Writing in the immediate aftermath of the Second World War, and with personal experience of statelessness, the political theorist Hannah Arendt (1906–1975) pointed to the existence of a 'right to have rights'. Human rights, she argued, had proved impotent at the moment of their greatest need. In being deprived of a political community willing and able to guarantee their rights, stateless people had been left entirely without rights. They lost not only their distinct rights as citizens, but all human rights. Citizenship, therefore, remained an essential basis of rights, and the right to have rights was the right to citizenship—to membership of a political community. Since then, and especially in recent years, theorists have continued to grapple with the meaning of the right to have rights. In the context of enduring statelessness, mass migration, people flows, and the contested nature of democratic politics, the question of the right to have rights remains of pressing concern for writers and advocates across the disciplines, and indeed for all concerned with the complex question of the protection of human rights in the contemporary context. From international relations scholars[1] to sociologists,[2] from deliberative democracy

---

[1] See P Owens, *Between War and Politics: International Relations and the Thought of Hannah Arendt* (Oxford: Oxford University Press, 2007) Chapter 6 and B Cotter, 'Hannah Arendt and "The Right to have Rights"' in A F Lang and J Williams, *Hannah Arendt and International Relations: Reading across the Lines* (New York: Palgrave Macmillan, 2005) 95.

[2] M R Somers, *Genealogies of Citizenship: Markets, Statelessness, and the Right to have Rights* (New York: Cambridge University Press, 2008).

theorists[3] to French philosophers,[4] the concept of the 'right to have rights' has captured the imagination of theorists and advocates alike. For many, it raises no less fundamental a question than the subject of rights. While Arendt's work has figured as a 'source for inspiration'[5] in the work of an ever-increasing number of international legal scholars,[6] to date no one has engaged in an in-depth examination of the right to have rights in the context of the international protection of human rights. In seeking to remedy this lack, the present volume explores two overarching questions. First, how do different and competing conceptions of the right to have rights shed light on right-bearing in the contemporary context, and in particular on concepts and relationships central to the protection of human rights in public international law? How, for example, does the political concept of citizenship relate to concepts of humanity and nationality in international law? Secondly, given the contested and competing conceptions of the right to have rights, how is the right to have rights to be understood in the context of international law? What is the significance of this intriguing concept for international legal thought and practice today?

1. Arendt and the right to have rights

The starting point of my exploration of the right to have rights is the work of Hannah Arendt. For the eighteen years spanning Arendt's flight from Germany in 1933 to her obtaining American citizenship in 1951, she was stateless.[7] Her writing bears the stamp of the events she experienced and the opinions she formed during those turbulent years. Arendt's primary discussion of the 'right to have rights' appears in chapter 9 of *The Origins of Totalitarianism* entitled 'The Decline of the Nation-State and the End of the Rights of Man'.[8] Taking the plight of stateless people in

[3] S Benhabib, *The Rights of Others: Aliens, Residents and Citizens* (Cambridge: Cambridge University Press, 2004).

[4] J Rancière, 'Who is the Subject of the Rights of Man?' (2004) 103(2/3) *South Atlantic Quarterly* 297 and É Balibar, *We, the People of Europe?: Reflections on Transnational Citizenship*, J Swenson (trans) (Princeton: Princeton University Press, 2004).

[5] J Klabbers, 'Possible Islands of Predictability: The Legal Thought of Hannah Arendt' (2007) 20(1) *LJIL* 1, 23.

[6] See ibid; J Bhabha, 'Arendt's Children: Do Today's Migrant Children have a Right to have Rights?' (2009) 31(2) *Hum Rts Q* 410; and M Osiel, *Mass Atrocity, Ordinary Evil, and Hannah Arendt: Criminal Consciousness in Argentina's Dirty War* (New Haven: Yale University Press, 2001).

[7] See E Young-Bruehl, *Hannah Arendt: For Love of the World* (2nd edn) (New Haven: Yale University Press, 2004) 113, 115–63.

[8] H Arendt, *The Origins of Totalitarianism* (revised edn) (New York: Harcourt, [1973]) 267. Excerpts from that chapter first appeared in Arendt's article, ' "The Rights of Man" What are They?' (1949) 3(1) *Modern Review* (New York) 24. *Origins* consists of three parts, dealing respectively with anti-Semitism, imperialism, and totalitarianism. Chapter 9 appears in part two, dealing with imperialism. Arendt identifies totalitarianism as an entirely novel form of government which combined hubris—the belief that everything is possible—with obedience to the strict logic of the laws of nature or of history. She seeks to understand how totalitarian regimes were able to reduce humans to what she terms 'superfluous' beings. She is concerned with how anti-Semitism and imperialism unleashed phenomena such as social rootlessness, statelessness, expansion for expansion's sake, and the decline of the nation state and of political life which 'crystallized into totalitarianism'. (See H Arendt, 'A Reply to Eric Voegelin' in H Arendt, *Essays in Understanding 1930–1954: Formation, Exile, and*

the inter-war period as a test case, Arendt provides a devastating critique of human rights. Stateless people, she maintains, became the anomaly for which the law did not provide, and were therefore 'outlaws', exposed to arbitrary power, and at the mercy of the police and illegal acts.[9] The only 'country' the world had to offer the stateless was the 'internment camp', as Arendt herself had experienced.[10] The treatment of stateless people revealed what she terms the 'perplexities' of human rights:[11] rights are not a given by virtue of an individual's abstract 'humanity', rather they are an artefact associated with membership of a political community. As Arendt famously remarked: '[t]he world found nothing sacred in the abstract nakedness of being human'.[12] Stripped of the legal and political status of their former citizenship, and thus reduced to the status of 'a human being in general',[13] the stateless found themselves to have lost all human rights—to be rightless. The loss of their human rights coincided with their reduction to the very status for which human rights—those inalienable rights which are said to be independent of government—are supposed to provide. The issue was not the loss of 'specific rights' (which are the rights of citizens) 'but the loss of a community willing and able to guarantee any rights whatsoever'.[14] Arendt asserts that the French Revolution, in declaring the rights of man and yet demanding national sovereignty, contained a contradiction which ensured that human rights were protected and enforced only as national rights. The 'people' and not the individual became the 'image of man'.[15] Ironically, the rights of man therefore became dependent upon, rather than independent of, governments.[16] This became evident in the inter-war period as growing numbers of people emerged who, in lacking citizenship of any sovereign state, found that their seemingly 'inalienable' human rights had been rendered meaningless.

Thus Arendt argues that the stateless point to the existence of a 'right to have rights'. If human rights flow from membership of a political community, the one true human right is the right to belong to such a community—the right to have rights:

We became aware of the existence of a right to have rights (and that means to live in a framework where one is judged by one's actions and opinions) and a right to belong to some kind of organized community, only when millions of people emerged who had lost and could not regain these rights because of the new global political situation.[17]

The conundrum with which, for Arendt, the world was faced was that the right to have rights could only be guaranteed by humanity, and yet in a world of sovereign

Totalitarianism, J Kohn (ed) (New York: Schocken Books, 1994) 401, 403 and H Arendt, 'On the Nature of Totalitarianism: An Essay in Understanding' in Arendt, *Essays in Understanding*, 328.) That is to say, the issue for her is how political and social ties linking people could be dissolved, resulting in the atomization and loneliness which facilitated the total domination of individuals by totalitarian regimes.

[9] Arendt, *Origins*, 283–4.

[10] In 1940, Arendt was interned along with other 'enemy aliens' in a camp at Gurs in France which she was able to leave in the chaos following the fall of France. Tragically, those who remained were later transported to German extermination camps. Young-Bruehl, *Hannah Arendt: For Love of the World*, 152–5.

[11] Arendt, *Origins*, 290.

[12] Ibid, 299.   [13] Ibid, 302.   [14] Ibid, 297.   [15] Ibid, 291.

[16] Ibid, 291–2.   [17] Ibid, 296–7.

states, it was 'by no means certain whether this [were] possible'.[18] A 'law above nations' was required which would be concerned with the rights of man, with the 'one right that transcends [a person's] various rights as a citizen: the right never to be excluded from the rights granted by his community'.[19]

Arendt's articulation of the right to have rights is strongly influenced by her republican conception of politics. Like Aristotle, she conceived of man as a political being, who derives his dignity from speech and action in community. For Arendt, freedom consists in acting. To act is to be free: it is to begin something new and initiate change.[20] For action to be significant and not merely another 'form of achievement among others',[21] it must reveal something of the actor and be the means by which a person 'inserts' him- or herself into the world.[22] Thus action is dependent upon speech. Arendt writes: '[i]n acting and speaking, men show who they are, reveal actively their unique personal identities and thus make their appearance in the human world'.[23] In Arendt's framework of thought, action and speech are what make a person distinctly human. To be human is to live in community and in relation with others. Arendt maintained that a life without speech and without action is 'dead to the world'. It 'has ceased to be a human life because it is no longer lived among men'.[24] Action and speech bind people together because they deal with interests we hold in common with others. They do not take place in isolation but within the '"web" of human relationships'.[25] As conceived by Arendt, action is 'the political activity par excellence':[26] it 'found[s] and preserve[s] political bodies'.[27]

Arendt's conception of action undergirds her understanding of the right to have rights. As articulated by Arendt, the right to have rights expresses the need to guarantee to each individual 'a *place in the world* which makes opinions significant and actions effective'[28] (my emphasis)—where he or she can live, act, and contribute to public life as of right and not out of charity. The 'fundamental deprivation of human rights' was manifested 'first and above all' in the deprivation of such a 'place'.[29] Only membership of a political community, Arendt asserted, gives a person a distinct political status[30] by which she can have a voice in shaping the laws of the community, claim their protection, and above all, bring her own unique individuality to bear in building a 'common world, together with [her] equals'.[31] For Arendt, the polity and community are sources of agency and equality. While the private sphere is the sphere of differentiation, the political sphere is the sphere of equality. In Arendt's words, we are not born equal but become so through 'human organization'[32] 'as members of a group on the strength of our decision to guarantee ourselves mutually equal rights'.[33] Without a political status and legal personality, the stateless are expelled from the public sphere of equality and left with only those

[18] Ibid, 298.
[19] H Arendt, *The Burden of Our Time* (London: Secker and Warburg, 1951) (British title of the 1st edition of *The Origins of Totalitarianism*) 436–7.
[20] H Arendt, *The Human Condition* (2nd edn) (Chicago: University of Chicago Press, 1998) 9, 177.
[21] Ibid, 180.
[22] Ibid, 176–7.   [23] Ibid, 179.   [24] Ibid, 176.   [25] Ibid, 183.   [26] Ibid, 9.
[27] Ibid, 8–9.   [28] Arendt, *Origins*, 296.   [29] Ibid.   [30] Ibid, 301.
[31] Ibid.
[32] Ibid.   [33] Ibid.

characteristics which can be expressed in the private sphere[34]—characteristics which bring to the fore differences between people and thus arouse 'dumb hatred, mistrust, and discrimination'.[35] For Arendt this was a paradoxical situation. She maintained:

> The paradox involved in the loss of human rights is that such loss coincides with the instant when a person becomes a human being in general—without a profession, without a citizenship, without an opinion, without a deed by which to identify and specify himself—*and* different in general, representing nothing but his own absolutely unique individuality which, deprived of expression within and action upon a common world, loses all significance.[36]

To summarize, Arendt believed that human rights flow from citizenship such that the right to have rights becomes the right to citizenship. Reversing most constitutional formulae which found the rights of the citizen on the rights of man, and citizenship on humanity, for Arendt human rights are not the foundation but the outcome of politics. To be excluded from a political community is to be excluded from the sphere of rights—to have no voice in their content and no chance of claiming their protection—and ultimately to become an 'anomaly' for which the law does not provide. It is to be deprived of a community in which people can bring their distinct individuality to bear productively. She contrasted the rootedness of the rights-bearing citizen with the rightlessness of the stateless, and stressed the importance of each individual having a community to which to belong.

The concept of the right to have rights has attracted the interest of scholars from a variety of disciplinary backgrounds and with a range of theoretical orientations. While some see it as poorly conceived and lacking any coherent theoretical foundation, others find in it a rich tool of critique which can be reinterpreted in the light of contemporary challenges. For those coming to Arendt from a cosmopolitan perspective, the right to have rights is deeply problematic. Seyla Benhabib, for example, maintains that the concept is philosophically and normatively ungrounded.[37] According to Benhabib, Arendt's 'moral cosmopolitanism founders on [her] legal and civic particularism'.[38] Other scholars, such as Margaret Canovan, emphasize Arendt's republican framework of thought. They argue that a foundation for, and means of realizing the right to have rights, can be found in Arendt's principle of plurality. Rights are not a given but rather need to be articulated and guaranteed together with others in community. They are the product of human action—in particular action in political community.[39] As will be discussed in Chapter 5, other theorists (Jacques Rancière prominent among them) still go beyond Arendt

[34] Ibid.
[35] Ibid. Arendt for example, wrote: 'If a [black person] in a white community is considered [black] and nothing else, he loses along with his right to equality that freedom of action which is specifically human; all his deeds are now explained as "necessary" consequences of some "[black]" qualities; he has become some specimen of an animal species, called man.' Ibid, 301–2.
[36] Ibid, 302 (original emphasis).
[37] S Benhabib, *The Reluctant Modernism of Hannah Arendt* (Oxford: Rowman & Littlefield Publishers, 2000) 82.
[38] Benhabib, *The Rights of Others*, 66.
[39] M Canovan, *Hannah Arendt: A Reinterpretation of Her Political Thought* (Cambridge: Cambridge University Press, 1994) 191 and S Parekh, 'A Meaningful Place in the World: Hannah Arendt on the Nature of Human Rights' (2004) 3(1) *Journal of Human Rights* 41.

and indeed argue that the paradox of human rights, and the conundrum of the right to have rights she posits, is the outworking of the limitations of Arendt's own conceptual framework.

My aim here, however, is not to resolve these debates about Arendt's work, nor to provide an Arendtian conception of the right to have rights. Arendt provides the starting point of my analysis, but I think with and beyond Arendt to reach my own understanding of the right to have rights and its significance for public international law. My analysis is not shackled by Arendt's conceptual framework, nor by that of contemporary theorists who have sought to reconceive the right to have rights. Moreover, the object of my analysis is not merely the right to have rights, but the right to have rights as an analytical tool to illuminate concepts and relationships central to the protection of human rights.

2. Structure of the book

In dialoguing my way to a fresh understanding of the right to have rights, I first examine five different and at times competing interpretations of the right to have rights (Chapters 1 to 5). Each chapter in turn explores the question of the right to have rights along two related axes: the right to have rights in terms of 'a place in the world' and the right to have rights in terms of the subject of rights. These two questions form a unifying thread across the chapters.

2.1 A 'place in the world'

My first point of entry in examining the right to have rights is Arendt's statement that the right to have rights means having 'a *place in the world* which makes opinions significant and actions effective' (my emphasis). With this in mind, 'place' is an idea which is foregrounded in each chapter. What does it mean to have a 'place in the world'? Clearly, this phrase had a particular meaning in Arendt's work—not least referring to the importance of individuals through their speech and action bringing their unique singularity and opinions to bear on a world held in common with a plurality of people. Having a place in the world meant having a voice and agency and above all a political status. While drawing on Arendt, my analysis of a 'place in the world' is not limited to her conceptual framework. Chapter 1 adopts the most tangible and straightforward conception of a place in the world—namely a place of lawful residence. There has to be somewhere in the world, some state, where a person has the right to enter and reside. In Chapters 2 to 5, the phrase a 'place in the world' is more explicitly concerned with the question of whether a person is recognized and included as a rights-holder.

'Place' is a particularly rich concept for examining the right to have rights for it not only raises the question of the site or sphere of right-holding, but crucially also a person's status or means of recognition as a rights-bearer within it, and the resultant level of protection of human rights afforded. With these layered meanings in mind, a recurring question across the chapters is 'what does it mean to be "in place" within the international legal system' and 'who is "out of place" '?[40] It will be seen that each articulation of the right to have rights sheds light on one aspect of what it means to be 'in place' in the international system. Let me elaborate these inter-related aspects of a place in the world as used in the following chapters.

The sphere or site of right-bearing

'Place' raises the issue of the sphere of right-bearing. This may refer to the site or location of right-holding. For example, a particular conception of the right to have rights may privilege the national and/or international level. From another perspective however, 'place' may raise the issue of how the sphere of right-bearing is conceived. Is it, for example, the sphere of the political community and, if so, how is the political community itself to be understood? Thus, one aspect of the analysis in Chapters 1 to 5 is to probe different spheres and sites of right-bearing. Related to this is the role of international law in constituting or hindering the constitution of a particular sphere or site.

Recognition as a rights-bearer

Crucially, a 'place in the world' also raises the question of the basis of 'belonging' and 'recognition' of rights. What is the means of emplacement—of acquiring a place and being in place? And what does it mean to 'have' a place in the world? For example, is this achieved through the conferral of a legal status (and/or politi-cal status), and if so which? Or is recognition as a rights-holder something which needs to be fought for and conferred upon oneself through a politics of human rights? This aspect of a place in the world directly overlaps with that of the right to have rights examined from the perspective of the 'subject of rights' discussed below. I nevertheless retain the language of a 'place in the world' for it brings to the surface aspects of right-bearing, and of what is at stake, more clearly than the more muted, and seemingly objective, or even distancing, language of the sub-ject of rights. It underscores that there is an evaluative or judgement-conferring aspect to subjectivity.[41] Being a subject is related to conceptions of who is con-sidered to be 'in place' and who is 'out of place'. We begin to focus on the relation between right-bearing and belonging, right-bearing and 'visibility', right-bearing and recognition.

International law and emplacement as a rights-bearer

Finally, a central concern of each chapter is how legal analyses emplace or misplace the most vulnerable as rights-holders. How does the articulation of the right to have rights in any given chapter illuminate how international law (as presently conceived and articulated) facilitates and negates the recognition and protection of the human rights of the most vulnerable, marginalized, or otherwise stigmatized?

---

[40] This idea was prompted by T Cresswell, *In Place/Out of Place: Geography, Ideology, and Transgression* (Minneapolis: University of Minnesota Press, 1996) and A Brysk and G Shafir (eds), *People Out of Place: Globalization, Human Rights, and the Citizenship Gap* (New York: Routledge, 2004).

[41] Again, I draw here on Cresswell, *In Place/Out of Place: Geography, Ideology, and Transgression.*

At the same time, I examine the emancipatory potential and limits of the given conceptions of the right to have rights, and in varying degrees, how they might be rearticulated or reoriented.

2.2 The subject of rights

If the right to have rights can be examined in terms of having a 'place in the world' then a closely related, and indeed central question it poses, is that of the subject of rights. Four different subjects emerge from the analysis: the subject as the national, the citizen, the human, and the subject of politics. What is the significance of nationality, citizenship, humanity, and politics for right-bearing? These are each highly contested terms which I do not attempt to define for the purposes of this introduction for their meaning is one aspect of the analysis in the ensuing chapters. Not only does the question of the right to have rights bring these concepts into focus, but it also raises the question of their interrelation. How, for example, does the international legal status of nationality stand in relation to humanity of international human rights law? Or what is the relationship of citizenship as a political concept to holding human rights? Then again, how might the contested concepts of nationality and citizenship stand in relation to one another? This is not to suggest that there is only one possible configuration of the relationship in each instance. Clearly there are as many configurations as conceptions of the individual terms themselves.

At this point, let me clarify what this book is not about. It is not an analysis of international legal personality or of the individual in international law.[42] Although my analysis clearly touches on these issues, its focus lies elsewhere, namely with the concepts of citizenship, nationality, humanity, and politics, the connections between them, and their significance for right-bearing. At times, the very deferral of analyses to the 'international level' or to within the 'international legal order' may be symptomatic of a politics of the denial of rights and thus precisely what needs to be put in question.

2.3 Chapter descriptions

My aim in Chapters 1 to 5 is to examine five different and often competing conceptions of the right to have rights. I map the contours of the given articulation of the right to have rights, and its strengths and weaknesses, while simultaneously examining how the given conception of the right to have rights sheds light on the capacity and incapacity, as the case may be, of international law to find a place for the most vulnerable, excluded, and stigmatized within the international legal system, thought, and practice. In light of this overarching aim, the analysis of any

---

[42] On international legal personality see F Johns (ed), *International Legal Personality* (Farnham: Ashgate, 2010) and R Portmann, *Legal Personality in International Law* (Cambridge: Cambridge University Press, 2010). As to the position of the individual in international law, see K Parlett, *The Individual in the International Legal System: Continuity and Change in International Law* (Cambridge: Cambridge University Press, 2011).

given conception of the right to have rights (and the law relevant to that conception) does not intend or purport to be exhaustive. Chapters 1 and 2 approach the concept of the right to have rights from the perspective of public international law, focusing in particular on the international legal status of nationality. It is primarily in Chapters 3 to 5 that the question of the 'having' of the right to *have* rights comes to the fore, taking the form of membership of a political community (Chapter 3), entitlement to rights under international human rights law (Chapter 4), and most pertinently, the politics of human rights (Chapter 5) respectively.

Chapter 1 commences with perhaps the most tangible conception of 'a place in the world', namely a place of lawful residence. In the international system of sovereign states it is essential that a person has the right to enter and reside in at least one state. The context in which the right to have rights is examined in this chapter is thus the movement of people across borders. It is shown how international law is integral to the construction of the present international legal order of sovereign states and posits two primary legal statuses or means by which an individual may attain the right to enter and reside in a state, namely the international legal status of nationality, and exceptionally, humanity of international human rights law as asserted in rights such as the right to respect for family and private life. At one level, if the national is in place then a stateless person is out of place and at risk of being shunted between states. At another level, however, I argue that this picture is patently simplistic for in the context of the movement of people across borders, distinctions are not only drawn between nationals and non-nationals but also within these categories—distinctions which international law in part facilitates. For example, non-nationals lacking the requisite social status and substantive citizenship may be contained within their state of nationality and denied the right to leave and enter a third state such that their state of nationality becomes what I term the 'non-place' of containment. Notwithstanding evident discrepancies in the rights attaching to any given nationality, I argue that the legal status of nationality remains a prized possession in the present international legal order.

Having examined the significance of the legal status of nationality for admission and residence in states, Chapter 2 considers one of the central conceptions of the right to have rights by public international lawyers—namely the right to have rights as the right to a nationality. If statelessness remains an acutely vulnerable condition, then it is argued by some that it is to be addressed through the conferral of the right to a nationality. What, however, does this right to a nationality entail? If the right to a nationality were secured, what would be the protection afforded? I explore four different articulations of the right to a nationality which I term the formal, human rights, democratic governance, and the substantive belonging approaches. The site of right-bearing, and the protection afforded—the place in the world conferred—differs on each articulation as does the given conception of statelessness and the 'need' which the right to a nationality is to address. I argue that if the full vulnerability of the condition of statelessness is to be addressed, then the right to a nationality is to be reconceived in terms of the substantive belonging approach, such that it is oriented towards the individual holding a rich, multifaceted place in the world which embraces nationality as an international and domestic legal status, but which also connotes political agency, and substantive inclusion. In examining the right to have rights in terms of the right to a nationality, the chapter also explores the complex relationship between the legal status of nationality and the legal and political status of citizenship, and between nationality of public international law and humanity of international human rights law (that is, between nationality and the protection of human rights). Drawing on Arendt, for example, the analysis draws the link between participatory political communities founded on plurality on the one hand, and protection against arbitrary deprivation of nationality and statelessness on the other. It is also shown that whichever conception of this articulation of the right to have rights is adopted, nationality risks usurping or even cannibalizing humanity such that the subject of rights becomes the national alone, thereby exacerbating the vulnerability of the inevitable remainder of stateless people denied the right to a nationality.

If, for certain public international lawyers, the right to have rights is founded on the international legal status of nationality, for political theorists such as Arendt it brings into focus the political status of citizenship and the relationship of citizenship to humanity. Taking Arendt's conception of citizenship as the starting point for the analysis, at issue in Chapter 3 is the construction of the subject-as-citizen: the right to have rights is citizenship due to the equality of status conferred—and the political participation secured—by membership of the political community. The human is not the abstract human of human rights, but the situated human who holds rights among her equals in the political community. The lens through which I examine this conception of the right to have rights is the denial to convicted prisoners of the right to vote. While by no means exhausting the meaning of citizenship or of this conception of the right to have rights, the right to vote is a powerful symbol of inclusion. The analysis illustrates the strengths and limitations of this conception of the right to have rights on the one hand, and of the 'citizenship' which emerges from international legal analyses in this context on the other. It is argued that the political equality of prisoners posited by international law remains tenuous. International law embraces two arguably conflicting conceptions of citizenship—namely citizenship as a privilege and citizenship as a status of equality conferred on all without differentiation. The denial of the right to vote also raises the issue of overlapping grounds of exclusion from the equality of citizenship, namely of criminality, 'race', and social exclusion. In exploring these issues, and in calling into question legal and Arendtian analyses which privilege political membership and inclusion for the protection and recognition of rights, I draw on the work of the sociologists Loïc Wacquant and Margaret Somers. While international human rights analyses may acknowledge the disproportionate effect of disenfranchisement laws on ethnic minorities, the link between disenfranchisement and social exclusion remains elusive. If the right to have rights is citizenship, it is a precarious citizenship of potential internal exiles.

Arendt's articulation of the human-as-citizen—the subject-as-citizen—stands in direct opposition to the claims of international human rights law which form the focus of Chapter 4. On what might be termed an orthodox or standard interpretation of international human rights law,[43] the human is the subject of rights.

[43] See M-B Dembour, *Who Believes in Human Rights?: Reflections on the European Convention* (Cambridge: Cambridge University Press, 2006) 243–7, 253–6.

Rights are held by virtue of being a person as such and irrespective of the legal status of nationality or citizenship. A person's place in the world is that which their humanity confers upon them. While noting claims that the individual is now a subject of rights at the international level, at issue in this chapter is the protection international human rights norms afford non-citizens (in particular the stateless and undocumented) within a state's territory. Certain postnational citizenship theorists, for example, cite international human rights law as an example of rights being delinked from nationality or citizenship status and being based on person-hood. The context in which I explore this conception of the right to have rights (the right to have rights as humanity, the subject of rights as the human) is the practice of certain states of interpreting human rights on the basis of immigration status, which I argue is an example of the institution of what might be termed an 'internal border'. A non-national may be physically present in a state's territory, but exclusion is secured through the interpretation of rights on the basis of immigra-tion status. At times, international human rights norms may challenge these inter-nal borders (as evidenced by a case involving an undocumented migrant's right to marry). Yet international human rights law may equally be the means by which internal borders are fostered as in the case of the Migrant Workers Convention. Finally, the chapter explores the border between international and national law: an indefinitely detained stateless person may be entitled to protection from arbitrary detention in international human rights law, and yet as a non-national be denied that right under national law. I conclude that humanity at times incorporates and at times overcomes the exclusions of the territorial border and the construction of the rights-bearer on the basis of immigration status. In sum, humanity is not the answer to the right to have rights but the site of its contestation.

If a stateless person may be entitled to the right to liberty of the person under international human rights law, but be denied the enjoyment of that right under national law, are human rights the rights of the rightless, or is the putative conun-drum the impetus for yet again reconceiving who is the subject of rights. In Chapter 5, taking the French political theorist Jacques Rancière as my guide, I examine the right to have rights in terms of the politics of human rights such that the subject of rights is the subject of politics. The focus here is on a performative understanding of the 'having' of the right to have rights and of a place in the world. Rancière's work is illuminating for it takes issue with the paradox of rights Arendt poses, while also positing a novel conception of the subject of rights and of the relationship between man and the citizen. Human rights, Rancière contends, are not as per Arendt, the rights of the citizen (the rights of those who have rights) or the rights of the rightless (abstract man who is denied rights) but the rights of the ever-fluctuating subject of politics. Here the relationship of humanity and citizen-ship is not framed in terms of an identification (the human is the citizen) but is rearticulated as an interval or gap: rights are not possessed by definite, predeter-mined subjects (the national, citizen, or the human) but by the political subject who emerges in the gap between man and the citizen and lodges a dispute as to whom is included in their terms. Man and the citizen—or the human and the citizen—are political predicates. The subject of rights is whoever takes up, enacts, and demonstrates their capacity to hold the very rights they have been denied. The subject is the collective subject who engages in dissensual politics, asserts and then verifies or demonstrates their equality. Recognition as a rights-holder is not conferred from above, but claimed by the excluded themselves. In this way they confer a place in the world on themselves and simultaneously reconfigure that place by challenging who is considered to count as a member of the political community. While Rancière's analysis does not suffer from the overt exclusions of the subject as the national, the citizen, or the human, exclusion still persists as it is only those who demonstrate their capacity to hold the rights they have been denied who, on Rancière's analysis, 'have' them. Finally, I examine the implications of Rancière's work for international human rights law. While he helpfully underscores the limits of international human rights law—not least its pacifying effect and potential to transform the subject of rights into the victim—we cannot simply escape from the law into a Rancièrian politics for if the rightless are indeed to 'have' rights then alongside a dissensual politics, the emancipatory potential within the law must also be exploited.

Finally, having come to the limits of nationality, citizenship, humanity, and politics, how is the right to have rights to be understood in the context of international legal thought and practice? In the Conclusion I outline my understanding of the right to have rights and its significance for international law. At this point, however, I merely pose the following question: will the different articulations of the right to have rights discussed in Chapters 1 to 5 suggest that a new subject of rights is needed, or is the very attempt to name the subject in fact the problem which must be addressed?

1

The Right to have Rights as a 'Place in the World'

Arendt's experience of statelessness and her study of the fate of the stateless impressed upon her the importance of securing for each person a place in the world where he or she can reside as of right. According to Arendt, the first loss which the stateless suffered was the loss of their home, that is, the loss of the 'entire social texture into which they were born' and 'a distinct place in the world' recognized and guaranteed by others.[1] Having lost this place they were unable to secure another. Wherever the stateless travelled, they were met with border controls, the impossibility of securing visas, the constant threat of expulsion, and the denial of the right to reside. For Arendt, the fate of stateless people was linked to the structure of the international system. In a system of states, to be stateless was to be an 'anomaly' for which the international system and international law did not provide. To be expelled from one state without having the right to enter another was to be 'thrown out of the family of nations altogether'.[2] Without the legal status of nationality there was nowhere left for the stateless person to reside, leaving them perilously exposed.

Thinking with and beyond Arendt, the articulation of the right to have rights explored in this chapter is the right to enter and reside in a state. In the present international system of states, it is imperative that each person has a 'place in the world' in the sense of a place of lawful residence and is not constantly shunted between states. At this moment, each one of us is situated at some point on the globe. Yet some of us will be, or be considered to be, 'in place' and others 'out of place'.[3] We are not only located physically, but legally, because how our physical presence is characterized turns on our legal status. This chapter examines how international law constructs the need for a 'place in the world' and the legal statuses by which individuals are emplaced (or misplaced) within it. The first section explores nationality as the primary status of admission and residence and the enduring vulnerability of stateless people in the present international legal order. The second section then turns to practices by which non-nationals are contained within their state of nationality and excluded from third states. How, I ask, might

---

[1] H Arendt, *The Origins of Totalitarianism* (revised edn) (New York: Harcourt, [1973]) 293.
[2] Ibid, 294.
[3] This idea was prompted by T Cresswell, *In Place/Out of Place: Geography, Ideology, and Transgression* (Minneapolis: University of Minnesota Press, 1996) and A Brysk and G Shafir (eds), *People Out of Place: Globalization, Human Rights, and the Citizenship Gap* (New York: Routledge, 2004).

probing what it means to be 'out of place' further illuminate the sense of being 'in place' in the context of the movement of people across borders? Finally, I examine the contribution of international human rights law to emplacing non-nationals within a state.

Before addressing these questions, let me briefly return to the concept of 'place'. In this chapter, I am referring to place as a given: at one level, it is the territory of the state. More broadly, a 'place in the world' as used in this chapter concerns the relation between physical and legal space—a place of lawful residence. This is clearly a static and one-dimensional conception, whereas in the social sciences place is a contested and multifaceted concept.[4] In contrast to the passive conception of place I have employed here, writers across the disciplines argue that places emerge when space is 'produced'.[5] Places are not given but are socially produced in that the meaning we attribute to a 'space' is shaped by societal and political relations. Edward Soya explains as follows: '[s]pace in itself may be primordially given, but the organization, and meaning of space is a product of social translation, transformation, and experience'.[6] On a performative conception of place, a person is not merely the passive recipient of a 'place in the world' in the sense of possessing and exercising the right to reside in a territory, but comes to 'have' a place and to constitute places through their action, to which I return in Chapter 5. Places are never fully constituted but always in the process of becoming. To a limited extent, the contingent and produced nature of places is taken into account in section 3 below in that the characterization of the place where a person lives (a place of rights to which entry is sought or the non-place of containment from which egress is impeded) is a product of acts of placement and/or containment. While cognizant of the rich conceptions of place noted above, the focus of the present chapter largely lies elsewhere, namely on territorial conceptions of place, on the importance in an international system of sovereign territorial states of having the right to enter and reside in a state. Such an approach is a more passive conception of place. I am here concerned with notions of being emplaced, 'in place' and 'out of place', which is not to imply that there is anything natural or inevitable about the present legal, political, and territorial configuration of space and consequent categorization of people, but to seek to probe the implications of that configuration and whom it excludes.[7]

---

[4] I am indebted to one of the anonymous OUP reviewers who highlighted this point.

[5] Most notably, see H Lefebvre, *The Production of Space*, D Nicholson-Smith (trans) (Oxford: Blackwell Publishing, 1991).

[6] E W Soya, *Postmodern Geographies: The Reassertion of Space in Critical Social Theory* (London: Verso, 1989) 79–80. Of course, these ideas have also been taken up by critical legal geographers. See, for example, N Blomley, *Law, Space, and the Geographies of Power* (New York: Guilford Press, 1994); N Blomley, D Delaney, and R T Ford (eds), *The Legal Geographies Reader: Law, Power, and Space* (Oxford: Blackwell, 2001); and J Holder and C Harrison (eds), *Law and Geography*, Current Legal Issues 5 (Oxford: Oxford University Press, 2003).

[7] Indeed, it was not until the late nineteenth and early twentieth centuries that states' governance of territory came to incorporate control of the movement of people across borders. The First World War was a key turning point marking the end of the era of relatively free movement across borders. See J Torpey, *The Invention of the Passport: Surveillance, Citizenship and the State* (Cambridge: Cambridge University Press, 2000) 111–21.

1. Nationality and emplacement: a 'place in the world' and the international legal order

As stated above, in the present international system, it is imperative that a person possesses the right to enter and reside within the territory of at least one state. This imperative stems from the present legal and political configuration of global space. With few exceptions,[8] there are no 'non-governed spaces'. The territory of the globe is governed, administered, with international law being integral to this administration of space. For example, international law constitutes the 'spaces on a map'[9] as 'territory' of a state subject to its jurisdiction—its governance and control. In international law, the border is the means of delineating the territory over which a state exercises sovereignty. The borders of a state's territory have been described as 'the imaginary lines on the surface of the earth which separate the territory of one state from that of another, or from unappropriated territory, or from the open sea'.[10] Although international law does not require the borders of a state to be fully delimited in order for that state to exist,[11] several consequences follow from such a delimitation. Borders, for example, demarcate the internal territory over which a state exercises its exclusive authority, that is, its territorial sovereignty.[12] Within the limits of its borders, a state is said to have 'exclusive territorial control',[13] and on crossing a state's border all individuals and property fall under the territorial authority of that state.[14] Through being bordered, space/territory comes under the control and title of the state. In the words of one writer, '[b]oundaries have pulled territory into a statist paradigm making it available for administration'.[15] Borders, however, not only bring territory, but also people, under the statist paradigm. Indeed it is in relation to borders that people are categorized. The legal status of the national or the 'illegal' migrant only has meaning in relation to 'bounded spaces'.[16] Given this administration of the territory of the world, it is essential that there is a 'place' (here, a state) in relation to which a person possesses the requisite legal status for entry and residence. To cite Catherine Dauvergne, 'the geography of the globe is "nationalized". There is no empty, non-national space where people can live beyond the reach of [a] nation'.[17]

---

[8] See V Prescott and G D Triggs, *International Frontiers and Boundaries: Law, Politics and Geography* (Leiden: Martinus Nijhoff Publishers, 2008) 148.

[9] I am drawing here on terminology used by Vasuki Nesiah in 'Placing International Law: White Spaces on a Map' (2003) 16(1) *LJIL* 1, although the context in which I am doing so clearly differs.

[10] R Jennings and A Watts (eds), *Oppenheim's International Law* (9th edn) (Harlow: Longman, 1992) 661 (para 226).

[11] Ibid, 121 (para 34).

[12] Ibid, 382 (para 117).   [13] *Corfu Channel Case* ICJ Rep 1949, 4, 18.

[14] Jennings and Watts, *Oppenheim's International Law*, 384 (para 118).

[15] Nesiah, 'Placing International Law', 30.

[16] N Blomley, D Delaney, and R T Ford, 'Preface: Where is Law?' in Blomley, Delaney, and Ford, *The Legal Geographies Reader*, xiii, xviii.

[17] C Dauvergne, *Making People Illegal: What Globalization Means for Migration and Law* (New York: Cambridge University Press, 2008) 44. Dauvergne notes that the high seas and Antarctica are limited exceptions to this.

In this section the focus is on nationality as the legal status which enables a person to be physically and legally emplaced (in the sense of acquiring a place of lawful residence) in the international system of states with all the consequent legal ramifications for the enjoyment of rights. It is the national who has the right to enter and reside in the state of nationality and who therefore enjoys a 'place in the world' to live. Both the articulation and interpretation of the right to enter in international law tie admission to nationality.

1.1 Entry as the national's return

In customary international law, and in international human rights law, admission to a state primarily depends upon a person's nationality. A state's duty to admit its nationals (and allow them to reside within the state of nationality) is said to be of the essence of nationality.[18] This customary legal duty is the product of the system of territorially sovereign states. For a state to refuse admission to its nationals is to violate the 'territorial supremacy' of the expelling state.[19] Similarly, the state of nationality is under a duty not to expel its nationals. Therefore under customary international law, a state's duty to admit its nationals is owed not to the individual national him- or herself, but rather to whichever other state wishes to expel that individual.[20] Accordingly, no such duty lies in relation to non-nationals. In their case, admission is a matter of state discretion[21] subject to countervailing international legal obligations[22] not least under international human rights and refugee law.[23] In international human rights law, a state's duty to admit its nationals becomes the individual's right to enter and reside free from expulsion in his or her 'own country' or country of nationality.[24] Though today articulated as a right of the individual, rather than only a duty of the state of nationality to another state, nationality remains the axis on which admission turns. The presupposition of international human rights law is that an individual possesses a state of nationality, or 'his own country', so that what is in question is his or her freedom of movement in relation to that state.[25]

---

[18] H F van Panhuys, *The Rôle of Nationality in International Law: An Outline* (Leiden: Sijthoff, 1959) 56.
[19] P Weis, *Nationality and Statelessness in International Law* (2nd edn) (Alphen aan den Rijn: Sijthoff & Noordhoff, 1979) 47.
[20] See Jennings and Watts, *Oppenheim's International Law*, 857–8 (para 379).
[21] Ibid, 897–8 (para 400). For challenges to the traditional position see J Nafziger, 'The General Admission of Aliens Under International Law' (1983) 77(4) *AJIL* 804 and S Juss, 'Free Movement and the World Order' (2004) 16(3) *IJRL* 289.
[22] See further ILC, 'Third Report on the Expulsion of Aliens' (Special Rapporteur M Kamto), UN Doc A/CN.4/581 (19 April 2007) paras 6–23.
[23] See further section 2 below.
[24] For example, a national's freedom from expulsion is explicitly protected in ECHR, Fourth Protocol, art 3(1) and ACHR, art 22(5) and is implicit in the right to enter one's 'own country': ICCPR, art 12(4). See HRC, General Comment No 27, 'Freedom of Movement', adopted 2 November 1999, UN Doc CCPR/C/21/Rev.1/Add.9 (2 November 1999) para 19.
[25] The ILC's Special Rapporteur on the expulsion of aliens has posited that states may exceptionally refuse to admit nationals (see ILC, 'Third Report on the Expulsion of Aliens', paras 50–7), however, the unconditional nature of a national's freedom from expulsion was emphasized by several

That the right to enter was originally conceived in terms of the national's right to leave and return to his or her state of nationality is reflected in article 13(2) of the Universal Declaration which provides that 'everyone has the right to leave any country, including his own, and to return to his country'. The right to return was added as a means of strengthening the right to leave; in effect, what was contemplated was thus a right of re-entry.[26] In terms of the ICCPR, an initial proposal referred to the individual's right 'to return to the country of which he is a national'. 'Return' was later changed to 'enter' to take into account nationals who were born elsewhere and had never actually lived in their country of nationality. At the same time, the phrase 'country of which he is a national' became 'his own country' so as to incorporate permanent residents.[27] Several human rights instruments retain the language of 'return' or limit admission to nationals. For example, ICERD and the African Charter refer to 'the right to return to [one's] country',[28] while the ECHR and the ACHR articulate the right of a national to enter the state of nationality.[29] Vincent Chetail therefore aptly concludes that the right of admission is primarily conceived as a right 'concentrated on the state of origin'.[30] Indeed, in the words of John Torpey, the very enunciation of the right to leave and to return 'indicates the extent to which states and the state system have expropriated and monopolized the legitimate means of movement in our time'.[31]

The original conception of the right to enter as the right of the national continues to inform the interpretation of article 12(4) of the ICCPR which provides that '[n]o one shall be arbitrarily deprived of the right to enter his own country'. In principle, one's 'own country' is not limited to a person's country of nationality. According to the HRC, it 'embraces, at the very least, an individual who, because of his or her special ties to or claims in relation to a given country, cannot be considered to be a mere alien'.[32] While it may extend to 'categories of long-term residents',[33] the Committee's interpretation of one's 'own country' suggests that it involves cases where nationality would have been conferred but for the arbitrary acts of the state in question. For example, it would extend to 'stateless persons arbitrarily deprived of the right to

ILC members: 'Report of the International Law Commission on the Work of its Fifty-ninth Session (7 May–5 June and 9 July–10 August 2007)', UN Doc A/62/10 (2007) para 229.

[26] V Chetail, 'Freedom of Movement and Transnational Migrations: A Human Rights Perspective' in T A Aleinikoff and V Chetail (eds), *Migration and International Legal Norms* (The Hague: TMC Asser Press, 2003) 47, 57.

[27] M Bossuyt, *Guide to the 'Travaux Préparatoires' of the International Covenant on Civil and Political Rights* (Dordrecht: Martinus Nijhoff Publishers, 1987) 261 and S Jagerskiold, 'The Freedom of Movement' in L Henkin (ed), *The International Bill of Rights: The Covenant on Civil and Political Rights* (New York: Columbia University Press, 1981) 166, 180.

[28] ICERD, art 5(d)(ii) and African Charter, art 12(2).

[29] ECHR, Fourth Protocol, art 3(2) and ACHR, art 22(5). The *Declaration on the Right to Leave and the Right to Return* 1972 (a declaration adopted by the Uppsala Colloquium, Sweden, 21 June 1972) is even more explicit, referring to every person's entitlement 'to return to the country of which he is a national' (art 9). See H Hannum, *The Right to Leave and Return in International Law and Practice* (Dordrecht: Martinus Nijhoff, 1987) 150–3.

[30] Chetail, 'Freedom of Movement and Transnational Migrations', 59.

[31] Torpey, *The Invention of the Passport*, 159.   [32] HRC, General Comment No 27, para 20.

[33] Ibid.

acquire the nationality of the country of... residence'.[34] In the Committee's view, a failure to adopt a country's nationality when there are no obstacles preventing such a step demonstrates the intention to remain a non-national such that a person cannot call the country in question 'his own'. One's 'place in the world', in the sense of the state where a person has the right to reside, primarily remains the state of nationality. The primary community of importance is the community of the state of nationality. *Stewart v Canada* before the Committee involved a UK national who faced deportation from Canada due to conviction for petty crimes.[35] Although he had resided in Canada since the age of seven and had dependants in Canada, the Committee reasoned that Canada had not become the author's 'own country'. It deemed that as he had opted to remain a non-national in Canada in circumstances where Canada did not impose restrictions on the grant of nationality, he had to bear the consequences of that decision.[36] Despite having lived in Canada from the age of seven, on this analysis, the UK constituted the applicant's 'country'—his place in the world. Similar reasoning has been applied by the Committee in further communications.[37] Here, a place in the world is the territorial state entry to which is gained and guaranteed via the legal status of nationality. The legal status of nationality—or of de facto nationality where nationality has been arbitrarily denied—forms the link between a person and entry and residence in a state. It is the formal tie of nationality, or the arbitrary deprivation of that tie, which has purchase—in other words: is recognized—as gaining entry to the state, and thus which in this sense emplaces the individual within the international system of states.

With the advent of multiple nationality that place may no longer be a single state, but the point remains that it is the formal legal status of nationality which is the key to admission and the right to reside in the state's territory. The importance of nationality for a right to enter and reside in a state is most clearly demonstrated by the plight of stateless persons. Unlike nationals, there is no state a stateless person may enter and remain in as of right.[38] A striking deficiency of the 1954 Convention relating to the Status of Stateless Persons[39] is the omission of the right of stateless people to enter and remain in the territory of state parties. The non-penalization provision for

---

[34] Ibid. The Committee did go on to acknowledge that '[s]ince other factors may in certain circumstances result in the establishment of close and enduring connections between a person and a country, States parties should include in their reports information on the rights of permanent residents to return to their country of residence' (para 20). As noted by David Martin, this is 'modestly suggestive' but 'quite cautious' language. D A Martin, 'The Authority and Responsibility of States' in T A Aleinikoff and V Chetail (eds), *Migration and International Legal Norms* (The Hague: TMC Asser Press, 2003) 31, 42 (fn 39).

[35] UN Doc CCPR/C/58/D/538/1993 (views adopted 1 November 1996).

[36] Ibid, para 12.8.

[37] See *Canepa v Canada*, UN Doc CCPR/C/59/D/558/1993 (views adopted 3 April 1997) para 11.3 and *Francesco Madafferi v Australia*, UN Doc CCPR/C/81/D/1011/2001 (views adopted 26 July 2004) para 9.6.

[38] However, the HRC's interpretation of one's 'own country' in art 12(4) of the ICCPR may be of benefit to certain categories of stateless people: see L van Waas, *Nationality Matters: Statelessness under International Law* (Antwerp: Intersentia, 2008) 260–1.

[39] New York, 28 September 1954, entered into force 6 June 1960, 360 *UNTS* 117 (hereafter '1954 Statelessness Convention').

unlawful entry contained in the Refugee Convention[40] is not reproduced, nor does the Convention provide for the regularization of a stateless person's immigration status.[41] Indeed, the 1954 Statelessness Convention only provides protection from expulsion for a stateless person lawfully on the territory of a state party (subject to the exceptions of expulsion on the grounds of national security or public order)[42] leaving unaddressed the plight of the unlawfully resident stateless person.[43] Even where a stateless person is habitually resident in a state, his residence has been said to be a mere 'state of affairs rather than something that confers rights'.[44] As stated by Audrey Macklin such an approach assimilates the position of the stateless to that of non-nationals in general. It fails to grasp that unlike non-nationals who possess a nationality, stateless people have nowhere else to go. They have no other state in which they may reside as of right.[45] Indeed the 'powerlessness' of stateless people derives in large part from the absence of freedom of movement in relation to at least one state thereby exposing them to the vulnerable existence flowing from illegal entry.[46]

Modise v Botswana[47] before the African Commission on Human and Peoples' Rights is a striking example of how expulsion from one state without the right to enter another relegates a person to a no man's land of arbitrary treatment. Though Mr Modise was a Botswanan citizen, Botswana refused to acknowledge his nationality status (rendering him stateless) and deported him to South Africa four times. Each time he was rejected by the South African authorities. As summarized by the Commission, Mr Modise was forced to live for seven years in the 'homeland' of Bophuthatswana, and then for several weeks in 'no man's land', a border strip between the former South African 'homeland' of Bophuthatswana and Botswana.[48] The Commission accepted his submission that these acts exposed him to personal suffering and indignity in violation of the right to freedom from cruel, inhuman

---

[40] Art 31(1). A further omission is the principle of *non-refoulement*: Refugee Convention, art 33.

[41] However, note art 32 on naturalization. See further van Waas, *Nationality Matters*, 248–9.

[42] Art 31(1).

[43] See ILC, 'Third Report on the Expulsion of Aliens', paras 86–96. As noted by Kamto, in reproducing the corresponding provision in the Refugee Convention, the 1954 Statelessness Convention fails to address the particular vulnerability of stateless people. While Kamto advocates a progressive development of the law in relation to the expulsion of stateless persons, as presently drafted, the ILC's article on the non-expulsion of stateless persons is ambiguous as to whether the article extends to unlawfully present stateless people (para 96).

[44] *MT (Palestinian Territories) v Secretary of State for the Home Department* [2008] EWCA Civ 1149, para 50 (Scott Baker LJ). As noted by Stefanie Grant, however, readmission agreements 'increasingly include an obligation to readmit third country nationals and stateless persons coming from or having resided in the country concerned'. S Grant, 'The Legal Protection of Stranded Migrants' in R Cholewinski, R Perruchoud, and E MacDonald (eds), *International Migration Law* (The Hague: TMC Asser Press, 2007) 29, 39.

[45] A Macklin, 'Who is the Citizen's Other? Considering the Heft of Citizenship' (2007) 8(2) *Theoretical Inq L* 333, 344.

[46] M S McDougal, H D Lasswell, and L Chen, 'Nationality and Human Rights: The Protection of the Individual in External Arenas' (1973) 83(5) *Yale LJ* 900, 961.

[47] *John K Modise v Botswana*, Communication No 97/93, 'Fourteenth Annual Activity Report of the African Commission on Human and Peoples' Rights 2000–2001', AHG/229(XXXVII) 28.

[48] There is a large discrepancy in the case report as to the time frames in question. See ibid, para 5 (seven years in the 'homeland' of Bophuthatswana and five weeks in no man's land) and para 87 (eight years in the 'homeland' of Bophuthatswana and seven years in no man's land).

or degrading treatment guaranteed under article 5 of the African Charter,[49] and deprived him of his family, and his family of his support, in violation of article 18(1) of the Charter.[50] The deportations also violated Mr Modise's right to leave and to return to his country (article 12(2) of the Charter).[51] The case affirms the link between nationality on the one hand, and admission to, and the right to reside within a state's territory on the other[52] and the vulnerability of stateless people unlawfully present in the host state. In being relegated to the no man's land border strip, Mr Modise's plight also illustrates Arendt's assertion that the international order consists of a closed system of states such that to be expelled from one, without having any right to enter another, is to be expelled from the sphere of rights itself.[53]

So essential is a national's right to enter his or her own state for the enjoyment of other rights that it has been argued that to deny such a right may constitute persecution under the Refugee Convention when done for a Convention reason. To exclude a national is said to 'cu[t] him off from enjoyment of all those benefits and rights enjoyed by citizens and duties owed by a state to its citizens'.[54] Similarly, the HRC has argued that the violation of a person's right to remain in, return to and reside in his own country 'necessarily has a negative impact on [their] enjoyment of the other rights ensured under the Covenant'.[55] Thus, while article 12(4) of the ICCPR provides that 'no one shall be arbitrarily deprived of the right to enter his own country', the HRC maintains that 'there are few, if any, circumstances in which deprivation of [that] right... could be reasonable'.[56]

In the case of stateless people, the right to enter the territory of a state party to the 1954 Statelessness Convention may also be crucial as the conferral of many rights in the Convention is conditional on 'physical, lawful or even durable access to the territory of the contracting state'.[57] Most crucially, unlawful entry compels a stateless person or other non-national to 'lead an illegal existence, avoiding all contact with the authorities and living under the constant threat of discovery and expulsion'[58] such that he does not claim any rights to which he may be entitled under international human rights law within a state's territory. Having lost the

---

[49] Ibid, para 91. The European Commission of Human Rights has also stated that constant expulsion to a country where admission is not guaranteed may violate art 3 of the ECHR: see *Harabi v The Netherlands*, Application No 10798/84, decision of 5 March 1986.

[50] *Modise v Botswana*, para 92.   [51] Ibid, para 93.

[52] Clearly the case also raises the issue of the arbitrary deprivation of nationality and the right to a nationality discussed in Chapter 2.

[53] Arendt, *Origins*, 293–4.

[54] *Adan v Secretary of State for the Home Department* [1997] 1 WLR 1107, 1126 (Hutchison LJ obiter). See also *EB (Ethiopia) v Secretary of State for the Home Department* [2009] QB 1, 18–21 (paras 64–72) (Longmore LJ).

[55] *Luis Asdrúbal Jiménez Vaca v Colombia*, UN Doc CCPR/C/74/D/859/1999 (views adopted 25 March 2002) para 7.4.

[56] HRC, General Comment No 27, para 21. The effect of restrictions of movement (both internal movement and the right to enter from abroad) on the exercise of a range of rights is perhaps most clearly demonstrated in the context of Palestine. See United Nations Fact-Finding Mission on the Gaza Conflict, 'Human Rights in Palestine and other Occupied Arab Territories', UN Doc A/HRC/12/48 (25 September 2009) para 1543.

[57] See van Waas, *Nationality Matters*, 246, 229–31.

[58] UN, 'A Study of Statelessness', UN Doc E/1112;E/1112/Add.1 (August 1949) 14.

'place in the world' where he or she can reside as of right, a person unable to secure another such place becomes exposed to arbitrary treatment. This link between lawful residence and the enjoyment of rights within a state is examined further in Chapter 4 but it is crucial to bear it in mind here for it underscores the importance of the right to enter and reside in a state not only for a physical place to live but for the enjoyment of rights per se.

From the discussion above, it can be seen that, at the present time, nationality remains the principal international legal status by which access to a state's territory is achieved. It is the national who has the right to enter and reside in the state of nationality and who therefore enjoys a 'place in the world' to live. There is a place, here a state, in which nationals can live and reside as of right without the constant threat of expulsion. The prevailing assumption of the international legal system is that an individual will possess the nationality of at least one state.

1.2 Questioning the national's place: not all nationals are 'in place'

So far I have noted the importance of possessing the right to enter and reside in a state and have argued that the legal status of nationality is the key instrument of admission. However, we need to beware of reifying nationality. Clearly, the value of the right to enter and remain in the state of nationality differs among states and even between nationals. Not every state is a refuge. A national may possess the right to enter and reside in a state but be unwilling to avail himself of that state's protection for fear of persecution as is the premise of international refugee law. Recognizing this, the IACtHR has held that the right to enter and reside is denied where an exiled population is unable to return for fear that their rights—in particular their right to life and personal integrity—will be violated.[59] Even if a person's life may not be threatened through persecution or war, the place one enters also varies in terms of the rights the national enjoys whether civil, political, economic, or social. As argued by Macklin, the value of the right to enter a state 'is conditioned by the quality of social citizenship available generally and in particular to an individual. Returning to one's country of citizenship may represent the restoration of state protection, or consignment to an abyss'.[60] A person may be a national in law and yet be politically, socially, or economically 'absent' or superfluous. I return to this issue in Chapter 2.

Finally, the reverse side of nationality also comes to the fore when we consider restrictions on nationals' right to leave their state of nationality. Nationality is not only the trigger permitting admission to the state of nationality, but may also be the basis for effectively 'imprisoning' the national within that state. While the practice of states imprisoning their entire population within their territory (a practice which prevailed during the Cold War) has been held to violate the right to leave,[61]

---

[59] *Case of the Moiwana Community v Suriname*, Petition No 11,821/97, judgment of the IACtHR of 15 June 2005, Series C, No 124, paras 119–20.
[60] Macklin, 'Who is the Citizen's Other?', 356.
[61] *Streletz v Germany* (2001) 33 EHRR 31, paras 98–101.

this right—including (although not limited to) the state of nationality—may be restricted on grounds such as national security, public order, and public health.[62] One of the most evident examples of this is where the right to leave is denied to a national due to his failure to perform military service. According to one study on the movement of persons across borders, such a restriction is 'founded on the bond of nationality that exists between an individual and a State which gives rise to certain duties and obligations on the part of both the individual and the State'.[63] The national's duty to the state reciprocates the state's duty to admit nationals and provide them with diplomatic protection while abroad.[64] To date, the views of the HRC on this issue have been inconsistent. Relying on the *travaux préparatoires* of the ICCPR, the Committee has maintained that restrictions on the freedom of movement of individuals who have not yet performed their military service are in principle to be considered necessary for the protection of national security and public order,[65] and therefore fall within the ambit of the exceptions in article 12(3) of the Covenant. On other occasions, however, the Committee has expressed its regret at a state's imposition of restrictions on the right to leave for failure to perform military service.[66]

In general, however restrictions on the right to leave have been construed narrowly. For example, the removal of a passport pending a trial may serve the legitimate aim of the maintenance of public order, but the right to leave will be violated where that ban continues without review so as to become indefinite.[67] This need for a narrow interpretation is particularly acute in the context of the national security exception to the right to leave[68] as evidenced by cases before the African Commission on Human and Peoples' Rights concerning political activists or members of the opposition who have been prevented from leaving the state in question's territory due to their criticism of government practices.[69] Similarly, both the ECtHR[70] and

---

[62] ICCPR, art 12(2) and (3); ECHR, Fourth Protocol, art 2(2) and (3); ACHR, art 22(2) and (3); ACHPR, art 12(2); and ArabCHR, art 27(1).

[63] L B Sohn and T Buergenthal (eds), *The Movement of Persons across Borders*, A Part of the Joint Project on the Governing Rules of International Law of The American Society of International Law, The John D and Catherine T MacArthur Foundation, Studies in Transnational Legal Policy No 23, The American Society of International Law, October 1992, 78.

[64] See further Chapter 2.

[65] *Peltonen v Finland*, UN Doc CCPR/C/51/D/492/1992 (views adopted 21 July 1994) paras 8.2–8.4.

[66] See, for example, the Committee's Concluding Observations on the Russian Federation in which the Committee 'regretted' the imposition of restrictions on the right to leave for failure to complete national service. UN Doc A/50/40 Vol I (1995), 65 (para 381).

[67] *Hajlik v Hungary* (2008) 47 EHRR 11. An automatic travel ban for failure to pay taxes is also a disproportionate measure: *Riener v Bulgaria* (2007) 45 EHRR 32 and *A E v Poland*, Application No 14480/04, judgment of the ECtHR of 31 March 2009.

[68] See M Nowak, *UN Covenant on Civil and Political Rights CCPR Commentary* (Kehl am Rhein: N P Engel, 1993) 214 and R Higgins, 'The Right in International Law of an Individual to Enter, Stay in and Leave a Country' (1973) 49(3) *International Affairs* 341, 353.

[69] See *Burkinabé des Droits de l'Homme et des Peuples v Burkina Faso*, Communication No 204/97 (2001), 'Fourteenth Annual Activity Report of the African Commission on Human and Peoples' Rights 2000–2001', AHG/229(XXXVII) 78, 85 (para 47) and in the context of the ACHR, *Canese v Paraguay*, Petition No 12,032, judgment of IACtHR, 31 August 2004, Series C, No 111.

[70] *Bartik v Russia*, Application No 55565/00, judgment of the ECtHR of 21 December 2006, para 49.

the HRC[71] have determined that the requirements of necessity and proportionality will not be met by the mere fact that a person holds state secrets. A contested issue, however, remains travel bans imposed on individuals designated as being associated with a terrorist organization.[72] The approach of the HRC is that it remains obliged to consider the extent to which obligations imposed on a state party under UN Security Council resolutions may justify the infringement of the right to liberty of movement protected under the ICCPR. The facts of the individual case have to be examined to determine whether the restriction on the right to leave is indeed necessary on the grounds of national security or public order and thus comes within the legitimate exceptions to the right provided in article 12(3) of the Covenant.[73]

Whereas in the context in which Arendt articulated the right to have rights, departure was due to an act of coercion, as in the case of expulsion or flight from persecution, international human rights law concerns itself with the possibilities for voluntary departure, and articulates the right to leave. But the right to leave is not an absolute or unqualified right; in the case of nationals, it may be restricted on the grounds of failure to perform military service or, for example, for reasons to do with national security. Nationality may not only open the door to admission, but potentially also seal it against departure. In exercising the right to leave a state, the non-national may therefore be in a privileged position as contrasted with the national. So if nationality is the axis on which admission turns and the basis on which a 'place in the world' is secured, here we see that it may exceptionally be the means of confining the individual to that place.

2. Humanity and emplacement: place and relationships

Let me now return to the question of admission and residence. Nationality may remain a privileged legal status for admission into the state of nationality, but it is clearly not the sole status by which admission may be secured. How might humanity as inflected in international human rights law constrain state discretion in the admission of non-nationals and support their right to reside within a state? In this section I first examine how distinctions between nationals and non-nationals can be attenuated on the basis of a person's family ties within a state and the protection of the right to family life. That is, I seek to explore the extent to which international

---

[71] HRC, General Comment No 27, para 16 and Concluding Observations on the Russian Federation, UN Doc ICCPR, A/50/40, Vol. I (1995), 65 (para 398).

[72] See UN Security Council resolution 1267 (1999) and related resolutions, <http://www.un.org/sc/committees/1267/information.shtml)> accessed 29 March 2011.

[73] See *Nabil Sayadi and Patricia Vinck v Belgium*, UN Doc CCPR/C/94/D/1472/2006 (views adopted 22 October 2008) paras 10.5–10.8. While the HRC has acknowledged that the obligation to comply with the Security Council decisions 'may constitute a "restriction" covered by article 12, paragraph 3, which is necessary to protect national security or public order' (para 10.7), the Committee has maintained that it is still under an obligation to determine whether the national measures implementing the SC resolutions conform with the Covenant. The circumstances of the case may be such that they do not disclose a need to restrict the right to leave on the grounds of national security or public order—for example where a criminal investigation has been dismissed and the relevant state party has requested that the names be deleted from the sanctions list.

law has recognized a more relational conception of 'place' such that it is a person's familial and social ties which form the basis of the right to enter and reside in the state and thus which emplace them in its territory. The relevant relationship in question is not limited to that of the bond of nationality. Secondly, I examine how a state's discretion in expelling non-nationals is constrained by the principle of *non-refoulement* which I examine in the context of the prohibition of expulsion to torture or ill-treatment.

2.1 The right to enter one's 'own country': a relational perspective

A more relational conception of place emerges from the dissenting opinions in the case of *Stewart v Canada* before the HRC discussed above. On the minority's approach, one's 'own country' in article 12(4) of the ICCPR is not limited to those who have 'formal links to that state';[74] rather the aim of the article is to protect 'the strong personal and emotional links an individual may have with the territory where he lives and with the social circumstances obtaining in it'.[75] That is, an individual is not to be deprived of 'the web of relationships that form his or her social environment'.[76] A similar opinion was recently expressed by Judge Cançado Trindade of the ICJ who asserted that article 12(4) 'extends an unrestricted protection against expulsion to aliens who...have developed such a close relationship with the State of residence that [it] has practically become his "home country" '.[77] It has therefore been argued that those who have been lawfully present for an extended period should be protected from expulsion on the basis of 'acquired rights' or 'legitimate expectations'.[78] On this approach, the expression, 'his own country', requires matters such as 'long standing residence, close personal and family ties and intentions to remain (as well as the absence of such ties elsewhere)' to be considered. In the case of a non-national, the connection would need to be strong to support a finding that the country was 'his own', however, it would be open to an 'alien' to show such ties.[79] Here we are reminded of Arendt's analysis that the first loss which the 'rightless suffered' was the loss of their 'homes' that is 'the loss of the entire social texture into which they were born and in which they established for themselves a distinct place in the world'.[80] Having a place in the world is not merely a matter of possessing the right to enter and reside in a state of nationality to which a person's ties are merely formal, but to reside where one's relational community is situated.

---

[74] *Stewart v Canada*, individual opinion of Elizabeth Evatt and Cecilia Quiroga (co-signed by Francisco Urbina), para 5.

[75] Ibid.

[76] Ibid. See also the separate concurring opinion of Judge Martens in *Beldjoudi v France* (1992) 14 EHRR 801, 840, para 2.

[77] *Diallo Case (Republic of Guinea v Democratic Republic of the Congo)* ICJ, 2010 (30 November 2010), separate opinion, para 156.

[78] G Goodwin-Gill, *International Law and the Movement of Persons Between States* (Oxford: Clarendon Press, 1978) 255–9.

[79] *Stewart v Canada*, individual opinion of Elizabeth Evatt et al, para 6. See also separate opinion of Martin Scheinin in *Canepa v Canada*. Although he agreed that there had not been a violation of art 12(4), he argued that the Committee had adopted too narrow an interpretation of 'own country'.

[80] Arendt, *Origins*, 293.

Comparing the majority and dissenting opinions of the HRC, how one conceives of 'place', and whether one has the right to live and remain in that place turns on the scale of analysis adopted: is the relevant relationship that which exists at the international level (in the sense that 'nationality' is the prized relationship) or is it at the more local level—that of the relational community a person has established within a state.[81] This brings to the fore the frequently limited scale of what counts as legal ties for the purposes of international law, a point which has also been raised in the context of the law of self-determination. As noted by one writer, in determining what counts as legal ties for the purposes of 'territorial self-determination', social ties of cultural and religious relationships may be irrelevant whereas those identified with the formal 'administrative functions of the nation-state—powers of taxation, powers of protection... and so on' signify the requisite attachment.[82]

2.2 Emplacement and the right to respect for family and private life

While the more relational perspective of place did not hold sway before the HRC in interpreting article 12(4) of the ICCPR, the right to respect for family and private life may be the means by which entry and residence are secured in the place where a person's key relationships and social ties are located. Several human rights instruments express the principle that states must respect the family life of those in their territory.[83] Indirectly, the right to family life may secure admission to, and residence within, a state. Reflecting this, an EU Council Directive on the right to family reunification requires member states to 'authorize the entry and residence' of certain family members of third country nationals residing lawfully in a member state.[84] The discussion below focuses on the most developed jurisprudence in this area, namely that of the ECtHR.

While the ECtHR acknowledges that the right of a non-national to enter or remain in a country is not 'as such' guaranteed by the European Convention, and that under international law, the entry of non-nationals into a state and their residence is a matter of state discretion, the court has maintained that immigration controls must be exercised consistently with Convention obligations, including protection of the right to respect for family and private life.[85] The purpose of article 8 is to protect an

---

[81] See H Osofsky, 'Panel: Law and Geography' (2007) 5(2) *Santa Clara J Int L* 507.

[82] Nesiah, 'Placing International Law', 6.

[83] UDHR, arts 12 and 16(3); ICCPR, arts 17 and 23(1); ICESCR, art 10(1); CRC, inter alia, arts 9, 10 and 16; ICRMW, art 44 (in relation to documented migrant workers); ECHR, art 8; ACHR, arts 11(2) and 17(1); and ACHPR, art 18(1). See also CERD, General Recommendation No 30, 'Discrimination against Non-Citizens', adopted 1 October 2004, 'Report of the Committee on the Elimination of Racial Discrimination', 64th and 65th sessions, UN Doc A/59/18 (Supp), 2004, 93, 96 (para 28).

[84] Council Directive 2003/86/E of 22 September 2003 on 'The Right to Family Reunification' [2003] OJ/L 251/12, art 4(1). See also Council of Europe, Committee of Ministers, 'Recommendation on the Legal Status of Persons admitted for Family Reunification', Rec (2002) 4 (26 March 2002), especially art II (residence status of family members) and art IV (effective protection against expulsion of family members).

[85] See, for example, *Abdulaziz Cabales and Balkandali v United Kingdom* (1994) 7 EHRR 471, paras 59–60.

'individual against arbitrary action by the public authorities'.[86] As discussed below, however, respect for family life may also impose positive obligations on a state party. Assuming the exclusion or expulsion is in accordance with the law,[87] an interference with family life will be justified within the terms of article 8(2) of the ECHR where the state has struck a fair balance between the applicant's right to respect for family life and the state's pursuit of such legitimate aims as immigration control[88] and the prevention of crime and disorder.[89] The strength of a person's family ties in the state, and the feasibility of transferring those ties to the state of origin or a third state, are weighed against the public interest. This is particularly difficult to prove in the case of admission.[90] In the case of expulsion, the public interest often has to do with the commission of a crime by the individual concerned. In those circumstances, relevant factors include the nature and severity of the offence committed, the length of stay in the state from which the person is to be expelled, his or her family situation, such as the length of a marriage and whether there are children, the 'seriousness of the difficulties' the spouse and children are likely to face in the country of origin,[91] and 'the solidity of social, cultural and family ties with the host country and with the country of destination'.[92]

Though the interpretation of this right by the ECtHR has been notoriously inconsistent, the court's more recent jurisprudence on article 8 has made significant inroads into the margin of appreciation enjoyed by states in the area of immigration control.[93] The court has been particularly open to applicants where they are nationals of the state of residence in all but name such as where they have been born and have lived all of their life in the state in question and have established their family life there.[94] While article 8 does not provide absolute protection against expulsion for any category of non-national, 'very serious reasons'[95] would be required to justify

---

[86] See *Konstatinov v Netherlands*, Application No 16351/03, judgment of ECtHR of 26 April 2007, para 46.

[87] See *Al-Nashif v Bulgaria* (2003) 36 EHRR 37, paras 117–128 for a case in which the interference was not 'in accordance with the law'.

[88] For example, *Gül v Switzerland* (1996) 22 EHRR 93, para 38; *Sen v Netherlands* (2003) 36 EHRR 7, paras 33–42; and *Konstatinov v Netherlands*, paras 46–53 (re exclusion).

[89] *Boultif v Switzerland* (2001) 33 EHRR 50, paras 47–56.   [90] See *Gül v Switzerland*.

[91] *Boultif v Switzerland*, para 48.

[92] *Üner v Netherlands* (2007) 45 EHRR 14, paras 57–8. This includes consideration of the best interests and welfare of the children (para 58). See also *Maslov v Austria*, Application No 1638/03, judgment of the ECtHR of 23 June 2008, para 82. See also Council of Europe, Committee of Ministers 'Recommendation concerning the Security of Residence of Long-term Migrants', Rec (2000) 15 (13 September 2000) and EU Council Directive 2003/109/EC of 25 November 2003 concerning 'The Status of Third-country Nationals who are Long-term Residents', art 12.

[93] For a discussion of this jurisprudence, see D Thym, 'Respect for Private and Family Life under Article 8 ECHR in Immigration Cases: A Human Right to Regularize Illegal Stay?' (2008) 57(1) *ICLQ* 87.

[94] See *Beldjoudi v France* (1992) 14 EHRR 801which concerned the deportation of an Algerian national who was born and had lived all of his life in France. To all intents and purposes the court found that he was a 'quasi national'. Indeed Judge Martens assimilated his position to that of a national such that he would have examined his expulsion under art 3(1) of the Fourth Protocol to the ECHR (the prohibition of the expulsion of nationals) (840 (para 2)). See also *Üner v Netherlands*, para 58.

[95] *Maslov v Austria*, para 75.

the expulsion of 'aliens who have spent most, if not all, their childhood in the host country, were brought up there and received their education there'.[96] The Grand Chamber of the ECtHR has also found that article 8 may impose a positive obligation on states to grant certain long-term residents a residence permit,[97] however, as the ECHR is subsidiary to national human rights protection, article 8 does not guarantee the right to a particular residence permit.[98] In some circumstances, the obligation may even extend to people 'residing illegally' within a state. Thus, in a case concerning an applicant who had negligently failed to take steps to regularize her stay, the court argued that the Netherlands had 'indulged in excessive formalism' in attaching 'paramount importance' to the applicant's illegal status,[99] and had failed to strike a fair balance between the state's interest in immigration control and the applicant's right to family life. However, the court did emphasize that this was a case in which lawful residence would have been possible if steps had been taken at the appropriate time.[100]

The court will also consider the deportation of long-term residents under the category of a violation of the right to respect for private life. The Grand Chamber has found that 'the totality of social ties between settled migrants and the community in which they are living constitutes part of the concept of "private life" within the meaning of article 8'.[101] Irrespective of whether 'family life' exists, expulsion of a 'settled migrant' will therefore 'constitut[e] an interference with his or her right to respect for private life'[102] and a violation of article 8 when the interference cannot be justified. Therefore well-established family and social ties may mitigate the

---

[96] Ibid, para 74 and *Üner v Netherlands*, para 58. The potential of the right to family life to cut across immigration law and states' regulation of admission and expulsion is also demonstrated by a decision of the HRC in which the majority of the Committee determined that the expulsion of a child's parents would constitute an arbitrary interference with the family (contrary to art 17(1) of the ICCPR in conjunction with art 23) as the child, an Australian citizen, had lived in Australia for thirteen years. In such circumstances, the state party needed to demonstrate additional factors justifying the removal of both parents over and above a simple enforcement of its immigration law in order to avoid a characterization of arbitrariness (*Winata v Australia*, UN Doc CCPR/C/72/D/930/2000 (views adopted 26 July 2001) paras 7.1–7.3). Several members of the Committee, however, dissented on the basis that the majority's interpretation encouraged 'queue-jumping' and ignored 'prevailing standards of international law' by which states may regulate the entry and residence of non-nationals in their territory. (See individual opinion of Committee Members Prafullachandra Natwarlal Bhagwati, Tawfik Khalil, David Kretzmer, and Max Yalden (dissenting), paras 4 and 6.)

[97] *Kurić & Ors v Slovenia*, Application No 26828/06, judgment of the ECtHR of 13 July 2010, paras 359–76, 407. (The case has been referred to the Grand Chamber.) (See further Chapter 2.) (In that case, the residence status of the applicants was stronger than that of long-term migrants for they had settled in Slovenia as citizens of the former Socialist Federal Republic of Yugoslavia and 'registered their permanent residence in the same way as citizens of the then Socialist Republic of Slovenia' (para 357).)

[98] *Sisojeva et al v Latvia* (2007) 45 EHRR 33, para 91.

[99] *Rodrigues da Silva & Hoogkamer v Netherlands* (2007) 44 EHRR 34, para 44.

[100] Ibid, para 43. The judgment has been criticized for paying insufficient regard to the sanctions of immigration law. See Thym, 'Respect for Private and Family Life', 102.

[101] *Maslov v Austria*, Application No 1638/03, judgment of the ECtHR of 23 June 2008, para 63

[102] Ibid. See also *Kurić v Slovenia*, paras 352 and 359–76. In *Slivenko v Latvia* (2004) 39 EHRR 24, the applicants were 'removed from the country where they had developed, uninterruptedly since birth, the network of personal, social and economic relations that make up the private life of every human being' (para 96) which constituted a clear interference with their private life.

effects of a person's status as a non-national and give rise to an intermediate cat-egory in which admission and the right to remain may be secured without the formal status of nationality being conferred. Here the law looks beyond formal status to the relationships existing between people and to the effects on those rela-tionships of the otherwise rigid distinctions drawn between nationals and non-nationals in terms of entry and residence. In this way, the right to respect for family and private life may prevent a person from being removed from the place in which his or her 'web of relationships' is located. Humanity, however, remains a tenuous status. Whether a non-national's exclusion or expulsion will be considered to vio-late the right to family and private life depends upon a delicate balance of factors and is particularly weak in admission cases. It is also noteworthy that it has been argued that state practice outside of the European context is more accepting of the expulsion of long-term residents.[103]

2.3 Non-refoulement

Finally, at least temporary admission and protection from expulsion may be granted, albeit often rather grudgingly, where the principle of *non-refoulement* applies. For those who meet the Convention definition of a refugee, article 33 of the Refugee Convention prohibits the return or expulsion of a refugee to 'the fron-tiers of territories where his life or freedom would be threatened on account of his race, religion, nationality, membership of a particular social group or political opinion'[104] subject to the exceptions in article 33(2).[105] Crucially, in treaty and customary international law, *non-refoulement* encompasses non-return and non-rejection at the border,[106] which 'implies at least temporary admission to deter-mine an individual's status'.[107] When we turn to international human rights law, it has been said that an expanded prohibition of return applies such that 'an indi-vidual is protected whenever there exists a real risk of violation of one of the indi-vidual's core fundamental rights in the country of destination'.[108] For the purpose

---

[103] Martin, 'The Authority and Responsibility of States', 36.   [104] Art 33(1).

[105] Eg. where there are reasonable grounds for regarding the refugee as a 'danger' to the host state's 'security'. The prohibition in art 33(1) is said to be recognized as customary international law. See E Lauterpacht and D Bethlehem, 'The Scope and Content of the Principle of Non-Refoulement: Opinion' in E Feller, V Türk and F Nicholson (eds), *Refugee Protection in International Law: UNHCR's Global Consultations on International Protection* (Cambridge: Cambridge University Press, 2003) 87, 149 (para 218). See further 149–64.

[106] *R (European Roma Rights Centre & Ors) v Immigration Officer at Prague Airport & Anor (UNHCR intervening)* [2004] UKHL 55; [2005] 2 AC 1, para 26 (in relation to customary interna-tional law). See also Lauterpacht and Bethlehem, 'The Scope and Content of the Principle of Non-Refoulement', 113 (para 76) (on art 33(1) of the Refugee Convention); 159 (para 242) (on customary international law), and *Declaration on Territorial Asylum* 1967, UN General Assembly Resolution A/RES/2312(XXII) (14 December 1967) art 3(1).

[107] G Goodwin-Gill and J McAdam, *The Refugee in International Law* (3rd edn) (Oxford: Oxford University Press, 2007) 215.

[108] V Vandova, 'Protection of Non-Citizens against Removal under International Human Rights Law' in A Edwards and C Ferstman (eds), *Human Security and Non-Citizens: Law, Policy and International Affairs* (Cambridge: Cambridge University Press, 2010) 495, 500. See further J McAdam, *Complementary Protection in International Refugee Law* (Oxford: Oxford University Press, 2007) chs 3–5.

of the discussion below, however, I will focus on the well-established prohibition of expulsion to a territory where there is a real risk of an individual's being subjected to torture or to cruel, inhuman, or degrading treatment or punishment.[109] Here the prohibition is absolute. The prohibition not only refers to the state to which non-nationals are expelled but also to any state to which they may subsequently be expelled.[110] Similarly in the asylum context, to deport an asylum seeker to an intermediary state without ensuring that that state's asylum procedure provides adequate protection against his being removed to the state of origin or to another territory where he faces a real risk of torture or ill-treatment would constitute a violation of the prohibition against torture or ill-treatment.[111] Although the principle of *non-refoulement* is not limited to non-return to the state of nationality, where return to the state of nationality is in question, international law looks beyond the formal status of nationality, and beyond the protection the legal status of nationality would otherwise afford, to the treatment to which the individual risks being exposed on return.

The absolute nature of the prohibition of return to torture or ill-treatment in international human rights law, however, has come under considerable pressure in the counter-terrorism context, with some states asserting that a state's national security concerns must be taken into account such that the obligation not to expel is to be weighed against the interests of the community as a whole.[112] The absolute nature of the prohibition has also been questioned on the basis of the immigration status of the expellee.[113] On this approach, the right not to be returned to torture is qualified by the acts and status of the person to be expelled—namely, by the national security risk he or she poses and the vulnerability of the non-national to expulsion. While courts and human rights bodies have repeatedly affirmed that the prohibition of expulsion to torture is absolute irrespective of the expellee's identity and of any security concerns relating to him or her,[114] their willingness to take

---

[109] See CAT, art 3; ICCPR, art 7; and ECHR, art 3. For a discussion of the prohibition in customary international law, see Lauterpacht and Bethlehem, 'The Scope and Content of the Principle of *Non-Refoulement*', 150–64

[110] See Committee against Torture, General Comment No 1, 'Implementation of Article 3 of the Convention in the Context of Article 22 (*Refoulement* and Communications)', adopted 21 November 1997, UN Doc A/53/44 (16 September 1998) Annex IX, para 2.

[111] *M S S v Belgium and Greece*, Application No 30696/09, judgment of the ECtHR of 21 January 2011(Grand Chamber) paras 341–61.

[112] *Saadi v Italy* (2009) 49 EHRR 30, paras 117–23. See also the decision of the Supreme Court of Canada in *Suresh v Canada*, in which the court, though concluding that 'deportation to torture will generally violate the principles of fundamental justice' protected by the Canadian Charter (para 76), '[did] not exclude the possibility that in exceptional circumstances, deportation to face torture might be justified' for example where this is the outcome of the process of balancing Canada's interest in combating terrorism and the individual's interest in not being deported to torture. *Suresh v Canada (Minister of Citizenship and Immigration)* (2002) 41 ILM 954, para 78.

[113] Ibid (*Saadi v Italy*), para 119. The UK noted that states may use immigration law to protect themselves from external security threats and that the ECHR did not guarantee the right to political asylum.

[114] Eg *Chahal v United Kingdom* (1997) 23 EHRR 413, paras 79–81; *Saadi v Italy*, paras 138–9; *Paez v Sweden*, UN Doc CAT/C/18/D/39/1996 (views adopted 28 April 1997) para 14.5; and *Mansour Ahani v Canada*, UN Doc CCPR/C/80/D/1051/2002 (views adopted 29 March 2004) para 10.10.

into account diplomatic assurances from the receiving state when assessing the risk of torture or ill-treatment jeopardizes the protection of the expellee and places the absolute nature of the prohibition in question.[115]

Even where a state is under an obligation not to expel a non-national to torture or ill-treatment under international human rights law, the non-national's plight remains precarious. There is no recognized legal status flowing to the non-national from the state's obligation not to expel, and consequently few substantive rights are in practice enjoyed.[116] Protection from expulsion does not equate to a right of residence. Developing the concept of complementary protection, Jane McAdam has therefore argued that individuals whose need of international protection is derived from the extended principle of *non-refoulement* in international law ought to be granted a legal status equivalent to that of refugees under the Refugee Convention (provided they are not expressly excluded from the Convention regime).[117] In the EU context, third country nationals or stateless persons who do not qualify as refugees but in respect of whom substantial grounds have been shown for believing that, if returned to their country of origin or of former habitual residence, they would face a real risk of suffering serious harm,[118] may qualify for 'subsidiary protection status'.[119] Such protection includes the grant of a residence permit valid for at least one year and renewable, 'unless compelling reasons of national security or public order otherwise require'.[120] For those lacking such protection statuses, bare humanity remains a precarious status.

The discussion above of the right to family life and of the principle of *non-refoulement* brings to the fore the advantage that physical presence within a state (and presentation at a state's border in the case of *non-refoulement*) can make—especially when the *non-refoulement* of those within a state is compared with the plight of the Roma in the *Roma Rights* case we shall discuss presently. However, the analysis also underscores the tenuous nature of the residence 'humanity' (inflected in the right to family life or in the principle of *non-refoulement*) may secure. Whether exclusion or expulsion will be found to constitute an unjustified interference with the

[115] The weight given to these assurances will depend on the facts of the case. *Saadi v Italy*, para 148; *Ismoilov v Russia* (2009) 49 EHRR 42, para 127; *Alzery v Sweden*, UN Doc CCPR/C/88/D/1416/2005 (views adopted 25 October 2006) paras 11.3–11.5; and *Agiza v Sweden*, UN Doc CAT/C/34/D/233/2003 (views adopted 20 May 2005) paras 13.4–13.5.
[116] See McAdam, *Complementary Protection in International Refugee Law*, esp 198–208.
[117] Those who are excluded from the Refugee Convention regime (for example under art 1F) and are not removable or prosecutable, as may be the case for suspected terrorists, are to be granted a minimum status under human rights law. Ibid, 234–45.
[118] Council Directive 2004/83/EC of 29 April 2004 on 'Minimum Standards for the Qualification and Status of Third Country Nationals or Stateless Persons as Refugees or as Persons who otherwise need International Protection and the Content of the Protection Granted' [2004] OJ L304/12, arts 2(e) and 15.
[119] Ibid, art 2(e) and (f).
[120] Ibid, art 24(2). Protection from *refoulement* is provided in art 21. See Chapter VII of the Qualification Directive for the content of international protection. As argued by McAdam, however, the rights accorded to beneficiaries of subsidiary protection under the Directive are 'diluted' and 'differentiated' in relation to the rights enjoyed by refugees and also in terms of the latitude states enjoy in implementing rights. See McAdam, *Complementary Protection in International Refugee Law*, ch 2 and 110.

right to family life rests on a delicate balance of factors and a court's perception of the strength of the family ties within the excluding state and the state of origin, while the legal status and rights to which the principle of *non-refoulement* gives rise remains unclear. Moreover, as will be discussed further in Chapter 5, the harm from which the non-national is to be protected remains disputed: at least on some accounts, it would not as a rule extend to the harm suffered when expulsion to the state of origin results in lack of access to life-saving medicine available in the expelling state.[121]

3. Non-nationals and exclusion: the 'non-place' of containment

In the analysis above, we saw that international law constructs the spaces of the world as states and emplaces individuals within them through the legal bond of nationality, and exceptionally through rights such as the right to family life. I also touched on the function of the border in structuring global space: in international law, the border distinguishes one sovereign territory from another. In the discussion below, my interest is not so much in borders as a means of delimiting territorial and legal space as in their policy dimensions and role in categorizing people. National state borders are not, of course, natural lines; rather they are contingent outcomes of historical processes.[122] All borders are artificial in the sense that their location, significance, and identity *as* borders are ultimately the product of a decision.[123] Acknowledging this, Étienne Balibar describes borders as 'institutions':[124] they institute policy decisions, primarily in relation to immigration control. At the border, distinctions are drawn not only between nationals and non-nationals, but between different groups of non-nationals as well. To further grasp what it means to have a place in the world and be 'in place' in the international system, at least in the context of the movement of people across borders, we shall need to probe what it means to be 'out of place' and the steps taken to prevent it. As stated elsewhere, what is deemed to be 'out of place' helps to reinforce what is conceived to be 'in place'.[125] Here we see that the movement of people across borders is not only indexed to legal status but also to social standing. It is not only the national who may be 'in place' and possess the right to enter and reside in a state, but the legal non-national of a certain social standing.

In this section, I am concerned with the darker side of emplacement—namely the mechanisms employed to 'contain' undesirable non-nationals within their state of nationality. Here emplacement may become containment in that nationals are

---

[121] *N v United Kingdom* (2008) 47 EHRR 39 (Grand Chamber) (discussed in Chapter 5).

[122] M Foucher, *Fronts et frontières: un tour du monde géopolitique* (Paris: Fayard, 1988) 13.

[123] D Newman, 'Boundaries' in J Agnew, K Mitchell, and G Toal (eds), *A Companion to Political Geography* (Oxford: Blackwell Publishing Ltd, 2003) 123, 126 and Foucher, ibid, 9. See, also D Bardonnet, 'Les frontières terrestres' (1976) 153 *Hag R* 9, 21–2.

[124] É Balibar, *We, the People of Europe?: Reflections on Transnational Citizenship*, J Swenson (trans) (Princeton: Princeton University Press, 2004) 109.

[125] P K Rajaram and C Grundy-Warr, 'Introduction' in P K Rajaram and C Grundy-Warr (eds), *Borderscapes: Hidden Geographies and Politics at Territory's Edge* (Minneapolis: University of Minnesota Press, 2007) ix, xxvii.

denied the right to leave their state of nationality by a third state. (The analysis thus stands in contrast to section 1.2 above where the focus was on the state of nationality restricting the right to leave on grounds such as national security). In this respect, place and emplacement can be viewed from two perspectives. First, the excluding state, the place of the putative sphere of rights to which entry is sought, is in part constituted through the exclusion of undesirable non-nationals. The border of a state does not just mark the limit of a state's territory but is imbued with social and collective meaning. As helpfully stated by Balibar, to draw a border is to establish an identity, and to establish an identity is to draw a border.[126] He argues that the 'external border' becomes the 'inner border'[127] shaping communal identity. The external border creates internal unity and relativizes differences between individuals and social groups within the territory by subordinating these differences to the overarching distinction between 'ourselves' and 'foreigners'. In this way, the external frontier is seen as a 'projection and protection of an internal collective personality'.[128] Extraterritorial border controls are one means by which this collective identity is produced and protected.[129] Such controls also facilitate the characterization of the state in question as a sphere of rights to which entry is sought.

Secondly, through extraterritorial immigration control the state of the excluded non-national becomes the place of containment. Here a person possesses a place in the world in the sense of a state to live and reside in, and is to be contained within it, regardless of whether it is a refuge or an abyss. This is not to deny the underlying assumption of international refugee law that the state of nationality may become a state of persecution such that the right to seek asylum is engaged. But coupled with this recognition are practices which contain those seeking refuge within their state of nationality or residence such that the right to leave to seek asylum is denied. The assumption is that a person has a place and is to be contained within it irrespective of the substance of the nationality in question, such that the place of residence becomes what might be termed the 'non-place'. This containment is in part achieved through the externalization of borders.

For certain non-nationals, the border is confronted not at the state's territorial frontier, but outside its territory. Balibar aptly refers to this as the practice of 'transporting the actual borders beyond the borderline'.[130] No longer is entry into a community solely negotiated at the state's territorial boundary. Rather, in this context, the border itself is exported. National borders are being exported today by

---

[126] É Balibar, *Politics and the Other Scene*, C Jones, J Swenson, and C Turner (trans) (London: Verso, 2002) 76.

[127] Here Balibar is citing Fichte's phrase 'innere Grenzen'. Ibid, 78.

[128] É Balibar, 'The Nation Form: History and Ideology' in É Balibar and I Wallerstein, *Race, Nation, Class: Ambiguous Identities* (London: Verso, 1991) 86, 94–5.

[129] In a similar move, Torpey maintains that states have come to monopolize the 'legitimate means of movement'; that is, they have expropriated the exclusive right to regulate the movement of people. Torpey argues that this monopolization is integral to the construction of the modern territorial state in that modern territorial states need to distinguish between nationals and non-nationals. Torpey, *The Invention of the Passport*.

[130] É Balibar, 'Europe as Borderland', The Alexander von Humboldt Lecture in Human Geography, University of Nijmegen, 10 November 2004, 16, <http://socgeo.ruhosting.nl/colloquium/Europe%20as%20Borderland.pdf> accessed 30 March 2011.

many governments and in many ways, such that entry into foreign states is negotiated from within would-be entrants' state of nationality. State security is clearly one factor at work here. It has been said that we all have 'data doubles'—that is, 'virtual identities located in networked databases'—which often travel across borders with greater ease than their physical counterparts.[131] For example with no-fly lists, passengers may only depart for the state in question if they are given a 'board' status by that government.[132]

International law plays a central role in this process. For example, it 'regulates' 'extraterritorial enforcement of immigration controls' through carrier sanctions.[133] Annex 9 to the 1944 Convention on International Civil Aviation requires air carriers to take precautions at the point of embarkation to ensure that passengers possess the travel documents required by the states of transit and disembarkation.[134] The significance of such measures has only increased as they not only serve to control irregular migration, but also act as security measures. This is also typified by the Smuggling[135] and Trafficking[136] Protocols supplementing the 2000 United Nations Convention against Transnational Organized Crime. The overarching aim of these Protocols is to prevent non-nationals from leaving, and hence to contain them within, their state of origin. For example, the Protocols require states to adopt cooperative measures to prevent trafficking or smuggling and 'illegal' entry into the territory of the state party. 'Without prejudice to international commitments in relation to the free movement of people', states parties are to 'strengthen' their border controls in order to prevent and detect trafficking in persons and migrant smuggling.[137] In each case, sanctions are to be imposed on commercial carriers that fail to ensure their passengers possess the travel documents required for entry into the receiving state.[138] Where a person is trafficked or smuggled into a third state, the state of that person's nationality or permanent residence is obliged to facilitate his or her return to its territory.[139] In light of the obligations imposed on

[131] D Lyon, 'Filtering Flows, Friends and Foes: Global Surveillance' in M B Salter (ed), *Politics at the Airport* (Minneapolis: University of Minnesota Press, 2008) 29, 30, 36.

[132] M B Salter, 'The Global Airport: Managing Space, Speed, and Security' in M B Salter (ed), *Politics at the Airport* (Minneapolis: University of Minnesota Press, 2008) 1, 9.

[133] See D Fisher, S Martin, and A Schoenholtz, 'Migration and Security in International Law' in T A Aleinikoff and V Chetail (eds), *Migration and International Legal Norms* (The Hague: TMC Asser Press, 2003) 87.

[134] See s 3.33 reprinted in International Civil Aviation Organization, *International Standards and Recommended Practices: Facilitation—Annex 9 to the Convention on International Civil Aviation* (12th edn, July 2005).

[135] *Protocol against the Smuggling of Migrants by Land, Sea and Air Supplementing the United Nations Convention against Transnational Crime*, New York, 15 November 2000, entered into force 28 January 2004, 2241 *UNTS* 507; UN Doc. A/55/383.

[136] *Protocol to Prevent, Suppress and Punish Trafficking in Persons, Especially Women and Children, supplementing the United Nations Convention against Transnational Organized Crime*, New York, 15 November 2000, entered into force 25 December 2003, 2237 *UNTS* 319; UN Doc. A/55/383.

[137] See art 11(1) of each Protocol and Council of Europe Convention on Action against Trafficking in Human Beings, Warsaw, 16 May 2005, entered into force 1 February 2008, CETS No: 197, art 7(1).

[138] Art 11(2)–(4). I draw here on A Kesby, 'International Law and the Right to have Rights' in *Select Proceedings of the European Society of International law*, Vol 2, 2008 (Oxford: Hart, 2010) 133, 135.

[139] Trafficking Protocol, art 8; Smuggling Protocol, art 18.

states by the Smuggling Protocol, international law is said to permit, if not require, states to prevent their nationals from departing their territory by unauthorized or irregular means.[140] By criminalizing trafficking and smuggling, international law facilitates state security measures in the migration context.[141]

A further context for this is the extraterritorial application of immigration laws. Non-nationals are physically absent (in the sense that they remain within their state of nationality or at least outside of the state to which entry is sought) and yet are embraced by the law of that state to the extent that its immigration law applies extraterritorially to them, which might be termed physical absence and legal presence—but presence only for the purposes of exclusion. One example of this practice is an agreement entered into in 2001 by the governments of the UK and the Czech Republic permitting British immigration officers to grant or refuse passengers at Prague Airport leave to enter the UK before they boarded planes destined for the UK. The acknowledged object of the procedure was to stem the flow of asylum seekers, especially Roma asylum seekers, from the Czech Republic to the UK. In 2004 the House of Lords considered a challenge to these pre-clearance procedures by a number of Czech Roma who had been refused permission to leave Prague.[142] Rejecting their claims under the Refugee Convention and the customary international law principle of *non-refoulement*, Lord Bingham did not consider that they had presented themselves at the frontier of the UK 'save in a highly metaphorical sense'.[143] Hence there could be no argument that they were being returned to a country in which they had a well-founded fear of persecution. From another perspective, however, the Roma were in reality confronted with the 'UK border' while still in Prague, and not only in a 'metaphorical sense'. There was a disjuncture between the location of the 'geographical' border and the place at which the border was experienced by the Roma applicants in this case. Immigration rules which otherwise would have operated at UK ports applied extraterritorially to them. Such external borders serve to emplace—but in the sense of containing—non-nationals within their state of nationality such that it becomes (or is reinforced in being) a 'non-place'. The border is exported to the 'non-places' of the world. Indeed Jonathan Yovel argues that movement is often perceived as being from 'territories' (or we could add from 'non-places') to 'places': 'within territory nothing much ever occurs: movement is *from* there, it becomes discernible, worthy of linguistic signification (and of legal attention) when it is *towards* place'.[144] A state externalizes its immigration law so as to prevent entry into its territorial and primary legal space. A person

---

[140] C Harvey and R Barnidge, 'Human Rights, Free Movement, and the Right to Leave in International Law' (2007) 19(1) *IJRL* 1, 14.

[141] See Fisher, Martin, and Schoenholtz, 'Migration and Security in International Law', 87.

[142] *R (European Roma Rights Centre & Ors) v Immigration Officer at Prague Airport & Anor (UNHCR intervening)* [2004] UKHL 55; [2005] 2 AC 1 (hereafter the '*Roma Rights* case'). Here I draw on A Kesby, 'The Shifting and Multiple Border and International Law' (2007) 27(1) *OJLS* 101 and to a lesser extent Kesby, 'International Law and the Right to have Rights', 135–6.

[143] Ibid (*Roma Rights* case), para 26.

[144] J Yovel, 'Imagining Territories: Space, Place, and the Anticity' (1 January 2010) 7–8. University of Haifa Faculty of Law Legal Studies Research Paper, <http://ssrn.com/abstract=950895> accessed 30 March 2011 (original emphasis). I acknowledge with thanks the OUP reviewer who drew my attention to this article.

may be outside the territory of the state but captured by its law so as to ensure they do not enter its territory.

While the state border is being externalized, international law retains the fiction that the place at which the border is experienced remains unified and reduced to the territorial frontier. On this approach, the distinction between where territorial frontiers are located and where the border is experienced is ignored. Though the law of state responsibility ensures that a state is internationally responsible for the acts of its authorities outside its territory which breach international law, the *Roma Rights* case raises the new challenge of the de facto shift in the border to prevent primary international obligations being triggered in the first place. On this approach, the failure to grasp the complexity of borders in the contemporary world results in the denial of the right to leave a state to seek asylum. The fiction is retained that the territorial and the relevant legal border coincide, whereas here the border is deterritorialized so as to prevent entry to the state's territory and primary site of jurisdiction and protection of rights. This takes the form of the externalization of a state's borders which international law in part facilitates, for instance through the Trafficking and Smuggling Protocols, or ignores in the case of the extraterritorial application of immigration law to deny the right to leave to seek asylum. Though in theory those 'contained' within their state of origin possess a 'place in the world' to reside, the whole thrust of Arendt's analysis is the importance of being able to flee a place of persecution and secure a 'home' elsewhere—to be neither contained within a state of persecution nor excluded from all states.

Not everyone, however, is contained within their state of nationality. A striking feature of the evidence presented in the *Roma Rights* case is the different manner in which Roma and non-Roma experienced the process of attempting to cross the border between the Czech Republic and the UK. Balibar terms this the 'polysemic' nature of borders: 'they do not have the same meaning for everyone'.[145] We are reminded here that law is not only spatial, but also social, and that the spatial may be manipulated vis-à-vis certain subjects. The evidence of the European Roma Rights Center indicated that a Roma passenger was 400 times more likely to be refused pre-entry to the UK than an individual non-Roma.[146] The Roma were subjected to longer questioning by immigration officials than the non-Roma, and 80 per cent of Roma were subjected to a second interview as compared with less than 1 per cent of non-Roma.[147] Arguably, non-discrimination norms may go some way in attenuating the racially discriminatory effects of the border and in protecting against the arbitrary application of immigration law. In the *Roma Rights* case, for example, the House of Lords held that the operation at Prague Airport was 'inherently and systematically discriminatory and unlawful',[148] in breach of domestic legislation[149] and the UK's international law obligations.[150] Norms such as the prohibition of racial discrimination, though useful in addressing particular discriminatory effects of the border, leave in place what might be termed their 'socially discriminatory' effect.

---

[145] Balibar, *Politics and the Other Scene*, 81.
[146] *Roma Rights* case, para 92.   [147] Ibid, para 93.
[148] Ibid, para 97.   [149] Race Relations Act 1976, s (1)(a).
[150] Refugee Convention, art 3; ICERD, art 2(1)(a); ICCPR, art 26; and the customary international law principle of non-discrimination. *Roma Rights* case, paras 98–103.

The border not only distinguishes on racial, but also on social lines. While for a 'rich person from a rich country', borders signify a mere formality and the point at which their 'surplus of rights' may be exercised, for 'a poor person from a poor country', borders operate as discriminator and filter.[151] Balibar writes:

Today's borders (though in reality this has long been the case) are, to some extent, designed to perform precisely this task: not merely to give individuals from different social classes different experiences of the law, the civil administration, the police and elementary rights, such as the freedom of circulation and freedom of enterprise, but actively to *differentiate* between individuals in terms of social class.[152]

It was because Roma were considered by the British immigration officers to have a greater incentive to claim asylum than others that their reasons for travel were treated with such scepticism and leave to enter frequently denied. Paradoxically, those with a greater incentive to apply for asylum are prevented from doing so.[153] A 'dual regime of the circulation of individuals' is thereby established.[154] The fact that the needy asylum seeker must be contained within the state of nationality or residence such that if they were to leave they would be 'out of place' reveals a further dimension of what it means to be 'in place' in the international system (in the context of the movement of people across borders). It is not just to be a national with a physical place to reside but to be a national who is of a certain social standing and who, on crossing the international border legally, is still considered to be in place (though to a lesser extent than in the state of nationality).

Noting this dual regime, Audrey Macklin maintains that freedom of movement is indexed to the 'heft' of the legal and social citizenship[155] a person enjoys. She argues that '[i]n general, the heft of citizenship negatively correlates to the incentives to migrate, and positively correlates to the legal capacity to migrate'.[156] Non-entry mechanisms, such as visa schemes, externalized borders and carrier sanctions, are designed to target 'spontaneous migration' of people whose 'citizenship falls below a certain substantive threshold in the countries of origin'.[157] With this is to be contrasted the heft of the global entrepreneur/highly skilled worker who can take advantage of points-based migration.[158] Low social class and minimal substantive citizenship coupled with practices such as the externalization of borders, in effect contain 'undesirable' non-nationals within the state of origin. It is when the 'place' has become the 'non-place' (the place of the absence of substantive citizenship for all or a section of the population) that containment practices surface—practices often facilitated by or articulated through international law. And citizenship—here

---

[151] Balibar, *Politics and the Other Scene*, 83.   [152] Ibid, 81–2 (original emphasis).

[153] Notably, the appellants maintained that 'the operation in Prague was introduced because it would have been too politically sensitive to introduce visa control in respect of the Czech Republic, and was an inappropriate way of achieving the same result [namely the stemming of the flow of asylum seekers] by stealth'. See first instance judgment of Burton J, [2002] EWHC 1989, para 45.

[154] Balibar, *Politics and the Other Scene*, 82.

[155] By 'social citizenship' Macklin means 'the more voluminous package of rights, responsibilities, entitlements, duties, practices and attachments that define membership in a polity, and situate individuals within that community'. Macklin, 'Who is the Citizen's Other?', 334.

[156] Ibid, 357.

[157] Ibid, 358.   [158] Ibid, 358–9.

social and thus substantive citizenship—serves as the indicator that containment is required. That is, the movement of those lacking in substantive citizenship and who live in the non-places of the world, to the 'place' of perceived affluence, is to be impeded. Strikingly, the lack of substantive citizenship forms the rationale for exclusion and the formal legal status of nationality as the instrument of containment.

The flipside of the analysis above is that, when we turn to non-nationals present within the territory of a third state, it is the undocumented and 'undesirable' non-national who is out of place. A correlation between international practices of containment and the status (or more accurately the lack of status) of the non-national within the territory of the third state is seen when we consider the Trafficking and Smuggling Protocols discussed above. Though often presented as human rights instruments, their rationale is clearly that of stemming 'illegal' migration in that victims of trafficking enjoy few remedies and are treated as 'migration law transgressors' to be sent home.[159] Their need to be contained within their state of nationality translates into their being out of place when they leave that state; the prevailing practice is not to grant a trafficked person refugee status—and thereby emplace them (physically and legally) within the receiving state—but to return trafficked people to their state of nationality. Again nationality serves as the instrument of emplacement. Here it is helpful to draw on the insights of Hans Lindahl. He argues that boundaries do not only exclude—that is divide one legal and political order from another—and thereby members from non-members, nationals from non-nationals, but in doing so locate the excluding legal order and that which is excluded within a common 'single legal space'.[160] 'Illegally' present non-nationals are 'deemed to have their own place' within this broader legal space such that 'legal immigrants are emplaced, and illegal immigrants misplaced'.[161] He writes: 'The claim to a common, encompassing legal space in which, in principle, everyone has her/his own place, is the indispensable presupposition of immigration policy, European or otherwise.'[162] This is reflected in the regulation of the expulsion of non-nationals in international law. It is striking, for example, that the human rights provision which expressly provides for procedural safeguards in the context of the expulsion of non-nationals is limited to those lawfully present in a state.[163] A notable exception to this of course is a state's tolerance of the presence of undocumented migrants where this is perceived to be in its economic interests. The assumption that each person by virtue of their nationality possesses a 'place' in the international legal system may exacerbate the vulnerability of those whose place is tenuous at best.

In this section I have shown how the vulnerability of groups such as those wishing to leave their state of nationality and seek asylum elsewhere is exacerbated by external border controls coupled with analyses which present the formal legal

---

[159] Dauvergne, *Making People Illegal*, 83.
[160] H Lindahl, 'In Between: Immigration, Distributive Justice and Political Dialogue' (2009) 8(4) *Contemporary Political Theory* 415, 425.
[161] Ibid, 426.
[162] Ibid.
[163] Eg ICCPR, art 13. But see *Union Inter Africaine des Droits de l'Homme & Ors v Angola*, Communication No 159/96, 'Eleventh Annual Activity Report of the African Commission on Human and Peoples' Rights 1997–1998', DOC/OS/43(XXIII), 38, 41 (para 20).

status of nationality as a means of containing those lacking the requisite social and substantive citizenship within their state of nationality—practices which in part are facilitated by international law. The right to leave one's country and enter another is denied to those lacking the requisite social standing.

4. Conclusion

In this chapter we have considered the right to have rights as the right to enter and reside in a state. Here a 'place in the world' is a place to live, a place of lawful residence. This is a territorial and legally constructed conception of place. For all the sophistication of the present 'globalized' world, of people flows and flux, an enduring presupposition of the international legal order is that each person possesses a 'place in the world' where she can live and reside as of right. Nationality remains a prized possession and the axis on which this conception of the right to have rights turns. At the international level it is primarily nationality which provides the individual with a place to reside and protects him or her from the no man's land of statelessness. A person without a settled place to reside cannot claim and contest rights, and thus becomes vulnerable to expulsion and arbitrary treatment. The national is in place and the stateless person out of place. The very privileging of the legal status of nationality in the international legal order accounts at least in part for the persistent vulnerability of stateless people.

This place of lawful residence and putative protection, however, may become the non-place of containment. Those lacking substantive citizenship are contained within their state of nationality with international law acting as the instrument of containment in the case of externalized controls such as carrier sanctions. Through an examination of these containment practices, and the corresponding treatment of certain non-nationals within a state's territory, a further dimension of being 'in place' was revealed: it is not only the national but the lawfully present non-national with the requisite social standing who is 'in place' within the international legal order. Being in place is indexed to legal status and social standing. As a result, those most needing to leave and seek asylum are denied the right to do so.

This is not to deny that, with the development of international human rights law, the significance of nationality for entry and residence in a state has been attenuated. International human rights law introduces a relational perspective which, in certain circumstances, looks beyond formal status and seeks to preserve the 'web of relationships' a person has developed in a state. Yet humanity enjoys a tenuous status: emplacement hangs in the balance as the right to family life is pitted against public order, or is temporary in the case of *non-refoulement*. If nationality remains the primary legal status on which admission to a state turns, then can the right to have rights be articulated as the right to a nationality, and if so, how is this right to be conceived?

2

The Right to have Rights as Nationality

Arendt articulated the right to have rights against the backdrop of the mass denationalizations and statelessness of the inter-war period and the Second World War.
Indeed, her own experience of statelessness revealed 'the infinitely complex red-
tape existence of [being a] stateless perso[n]'.[1] She was acutely aware of the vulnerability of stateless people evidenced most graphically during the Nazi period.
As Arendt documented in *Eichmann in Jerusalem*, it was stateless Jews who were
most vulnerable to deportation to the camps. At times nationality could serve as a
protection.[2] In the ensuing years, international legal scholars and advocates have
framed the right to have rights in terms of the right to a nationality—a conceptualization which gained impetus with the inclusion of the right to a nationality
in the UDHR.[3] Thus, as in Chapter 1, the present chapter examines the right to
have rights from the perspective of public international law. Four different conceptions of the right to a nationality are examined and critiqued—namely, what
I have termed the formal, human rights, democratic governance, and substantive
belonging approaches. Each presents a distinct take on how nationality stands in
relation to citizenship and humanity. If, in Chapter 1, a 'place in the world' was
used in its most tangible sense of a place of lawful residence, at issue in this chapter is a more qualitative notion of 'place' in the sense of the rights or protection
which the right to a nationality confers, along with the relevant site of right-bearing or protection. The aim of the analysis is to examine the emancipatory potential and the limits of the right to have rights conceived in relation to nationality.
Thus, I do not seek to specify the content of the right to a nationality for doc-
trinal purposes, nor is my purpose to survey the role or functions of nationality

---

[1] Letter from Arendt to Jaspers of 29 January 1946. H Arendt and K Jaspers, *Hannah Arendt, Karl
Jaspers: Correspondence, 1926–1969*, L Kohler and H Saner (eds), R Kimber and R Kimber (trans)
(New York: Harcourt Brace Jovanovich, 1992) 28.

[2] H Arendt, *Eichmann in Jerusalem: A Report on the Banality of Evil* (revised and enlarged edn)
(Harmondsworth: Penguin, 1976) 115, 162–80. Arendt writes: 'one could do as one pleased only
with the stateless people; the Jews had had to lose their nationality before they could be exterminated'
(240). See also H Arendt, *The Origins of Totalitarianism* (revised edn) (New York: Harcourt, [1973])
296, 447 and H G Adler, *Der verwaltete Mensch: Studien zur Deportation der Juden aus Deutschland*
(Tübingen: Mohr, 1974). According to Adler, the fate of Jewish people of foreign nationality in
Germany depended on Germany's relations with the country of nationality and the likelihood of
reprisals against Germany. He refers to a proposal that Jewish people of dual German and English or
American nationality be spared deportation to the camps and interned and exchanged for interned
German nationals (270–1).

[3] See art 15.

in international law or to provide a treatise on the regulation of nationality in international law.[4] Rather, I examine how different conceptions of the right to a nationality affect outcomes for marginalized groups, and in particular stateless people. More specifically, I explore the need or exclusion which the given articulation of the right to a nationality seeks to address. Whichever conception of the right to a nationality is adopted, however, I argue that a border of right-bearing is instituted exacerbating the vulnerability of those who do not fall within its grasp: the national becomes the subject of rights.

1. The formal or thin conception: the right to a nationality as a question of international public order

The 'formal' or 'thin' conception approaches nationality and the right to a nationality as a question of international public order. In question is how the regulation of nationality affects inter-state relations. Here nationality is an international legal status denoting membership of a state whose functions relate to the international sphere. The locus of nationality is the international sphere, with nationality constituting a formal legal status at the international level. How nationality is defined, and the consequences of nationality at the national level are considered to be beyond the purview of international law to the extent that they do not affect inter-state relations. On this conception of the right to a nationality, nationality as an international legal status stands apart from the (domestic) legal and political status of citizenship: the national need not be a citizen. Leaving to one side the distinction between nationals and non-nationals, on this approach the primary border of right-bearing lies along the national/citizen axis. A difficulty in describing this conception of the right to a nationality is that it spans the period prior and subsequent to the development of international human rights law. Some of the writers referred to below were writing prior to the development of international human rights law when nationality was considered a privileged status conferred at the discretion of a state, rather than a right of the individual. Thus, it might be argued that it is inappropriate to relate their conception of nationality to how the right to a nationality might be articulated today. While it is true that some aspects of this formal conception have been superseded by more contemporary developments in international law, most notably international human rights law,[5] significant elements of the formal, thin conception of nationality and of its regulation

---

[4] See P Weis, *Nationality and Statelessness in International Law* (2nd edn) (Alphen aan den Rijn: Sijthoff and Noordhoff, 1979); R Donner, *The Regulation of Nationality in International Law* (2nd edn) (Irvington-on-Hudson, New York: Transnational Publishers, 1994); Y Zilbershats, *The Human Right to Citizenship* (Ardsley: Transnational Publishers, 2002); A M Boll, *Multiple Nationality and International Law* (Leiden: Martinus Nijhoff Publishers, 2007); and L van Waas, *Nationality Matters: Statelessness under International Law* (Antwerp: Intersentia, 2008).

[5] See section 2 below.

persist, and sit alongside more contemporary approaches to nationality and international law. In particular, there is a tendency for analyses to focus on the external, inter-state aspects of nationality. Even when now conceived as a right, it is often a public order conception of the right that prevails in that the focus is on the international aspects of nationality, namely the importance of diplomatic protection and of the right to enter and reside in the state of nationality. The regulation and incidents of nationality at the national level are largely seen as the privileged domain of state sovereignty. In the words of the well-known dictum, questions of nationality are 'in principle within [the] reserved domain' of state jurisdiction.[6]

When conceived as a formal international legal status, the 'place in the world' conferred by nationality pertains to the international sphere: it is a legal status relevant to relations between states. More precisely, it denotes 'the allocation of individuals, termed nationals, to a specific State—the State of nationality—as members of that State, a relationship which confers upon the State of nationality' the right to protect its nationals in relation to other states, and the duty to admit and allow nationals to reside on its territory.[7] Nationality in international law is treated as dealing with the external aspects of state membership. It is an 'outward-looking'[8] status which 'stresses the international protections afforded by membership'.[9] Moreover, it is an objective legal status in that international law should not inquire into the 'quality of the relation' between the individual and the state. That nationality is to be conceived as a formal legal status denoting protection in the international sphere in part accounts for the severe criticism sustained by the ICJ's judgment in the *Nottebohm Case*[10] in which the conception of nationality as a purely formal, objective status was brought into question. As is well known, the majority in *Nottebohm* held that Liechtenstein could not assert diplomatic protection against Guatemala as the naturalization conferred on Nottebohm by Liechtenstein was not based on a 'genuine connection' with Liechtenstein. On the majority's reasoning, nationality is the legal expression of social attachment. It is a status conferred in recognition of the quality of the relationship and strength of the ties between an individual and a state. Nationality is said to be 'a legal bond having as its basis a social fact of attachment, a genuine connection of existence, interests and sentiments, together with the existence of reciprocal rights and duties'.[11] The seemingly objective legal bond between an individual and a state will only be recognized by a state against which it is being opposed if the legal bond of nationality accords with the 'factual situation'. The majority's application of the 'effective link' doctrine in the context of diplomatic protection, where dual or multiple nationality is not in question, has been subject

[6] *Nationality Decrees Issued in Tunis and Morocco* PCIJ Rep 1923, Ser B, No 4, 7, 24.
[7] Weis, *Nationality and Statelessness*, 59.
[8] R Y Jennings, *General Course on Principles of International Law* (1967) 121 *Recueil des Cours* 452.
[9] ILA, 'Final Report on Women's Equality and Nationality in International Law' (2000) 69 *Int'l L Ass'n Rep Conf* 248, 259.
[10] *Nottebohm Case* (*Liechtenstein v Guatemala*) (second phase) ICJ Rep 1955, 4.
[11] Ibid, 23.

to considerable criticism[12] and it has been argued that *Nottebohm* is to be confined to its facts.[13]

The thin or formal conception of nationality is primarily a public order approach to nationality: nationality serves an ordering function between states as the status by which individuals are ascribed to states and distinguished from 'aliens'.[14] This continues the narrative of the link between nationality and territorial emplacement or human geography[15] discussed in Chapter 1. In the international system, not only territory but also populations are attributed to states,[16] with nationality forming the link of attribution. The national is in place and the stateless person out of place. Interestingly, this emphasis on international order also arose in the debate on the inclusion of the right to a nationality in the UDHR. Given the structure of the international system as a system of sovereign states, it was imperative that an individual possess a nationality. To be without a nationality signified falling between the cracks of the international legal system.[17] In proposing the inclusion of a right to a nationality in the UDHR during the debates in the Third Committee, the French delegate argued that 'as the United Nations was itself based on the principle of nationality, it could not accept the existence of hundreds of thousands of stateless persons'.[18] In part, this public order approach to the right to a nationality flows from the view that nationality is, or to a significant extent remains, the principal link between the individual and international law. Thus Hersch Lauterpacht,

---

[12] See, ibid 46, 59–60, 63 (dissenting opinions). See further J M Jones, 'The Nottebohm Case' (1956) 5(2) *ICLQ* 230, 244; J L Kunz, 'The Nottebohm Judgment' (1960) 54(3) *AJIL* 536; Jennings, *General Course*, 459; and *Flegenheimer Claim* (1958–I) 25 ILR 91. According to the ILC, 'it is necessary to be mindful of the fact that if the genuine link requirement proposed by *Nottebohm* was strictly applied it would exclude millions of persons from the benefit of diplomatic protection as in today's world of economic globalization and migration there are millions of persons who have moved away from their State of nationality and made their lives in States whose nationality they never acquire or have acquired nationality by birth or descent from States with which they have a tenuous connection'. ILC, 'Commentary to the Draft Articles on Diplomatic Protection' in 'Report of the International Law Commission on the Work of its Fifty-eight Session (1 May–9 June and 3 July–11 August 2006)', UN Doc A/61/10 (2006), Chapter IV (Diplomatic Protection), 13, 33 (para 5) (hereafter 'Commentary to the ILC's Draft Articles on Diplomatic Protection').

[13] Ibid (ILC). Current state practice on multiple nationality has been said to weigh against nationality (as an international legal concept) connoting allegiance or social attachment. Boll, *Multiple Nationality*, 296–9. Cf Independent International Fact-Finding Mission on the Conflict in Georgia, Vol II, September 2009, 158–60, <http://www.ceiig.ch/Report.html> accessed 31 March 2011.

[14] See Jennings, *General Course*, 452.

[15] See also P J Spiro, 'Mandated Membership, Diluted Identity: Citizenship, Globalization, and International Law' in A Brysk and G Shafir (eds), *People Out of Place: Globalization, Human Rights, and the Citizenship Gap* (New York: Routledge, 2004) 87, 94.

[16] See I Brownlie, 'The Relations of Nationality in Public International Law' (1963) 39 *BYIL* 284, 290.

[17] The vulnerability of those without a nationality was expressed by an early international commission which pronounced that a state 'does not commit an international delinquency in inflicting an injury upon an individual lacking nationality, and consequently no State is empowered to intervene or complain on his behalf either before or after the injury'. *Dickson Car Wheel Company v United Mexican States* UN Reports, Vol IV, 688. See also R Jennings and A Watts (eds), *Oppenheim's International Law* (9th edn) (Harlow: Longman, 1992) 849 (para 376).

[18] United Nations Official Records of the Third Session of the General Assembly, Part I, Social, Humanitarian and Cultural Questions. Third Committee Summary Records of Meetings 21 September–8 December 1948, 122nd meeting, 4 November 1948, 348 (hereafter 'Third Committee Debate').

a firm advocate of international human rights law and of the individual as a subject of international law, maintained that 'the existence of sovereign States claiming to be the indispensable link between the individual and international law' necessitated the inclusion of the right to a nationality in the international bill of rights.[19] In the post-1945 international legal system, it is argued that '[t]o the extent that individuals are not subjects of international law [that is, are not "directly endowed with international rights and duties"], nationality is the link between individuals and international law'.[20]

1.1 Nationality and citizenship

What then of the relationship between nationality and citizenship in international law on this account of the right to a nationality? Arguably on this approach, citizenship (as a legal and political status at the domestic level) does not figure as a concept of relevance to international law.[21] Nationality remains a purely formal status denoting membership of a state for the purposes of international law with the content and substance of that membership at the national level remaining a matter for municipal law. In Paul Weis's oft-cited formulation, nationality pertains to the external aspect of state membership and citizenship to the internal relationship between the individual and the state, which under the law of most states connotes 'full membership' (including political rights).[22] Nationality is to be understood and examined in terms of the rights and duties between an individual and a state which are 'international' in 'character'.[23] More precisely, international law is concerned with the 'status' of nationality (the rights and duties of the state of nationality in relation to other states) as opposed to the municipal 'relationship' between a national and the state of nationality (which confers 'mutual rights and duties on both').[24] According to this approach, nationality as a formal legal status will be effective when it serves the purposes of inter-state relations, namely diplomatic protection and the state of nationality's obligation to permit the entry and residence of its nationals. The 'effectiveness' of nationality—and of the right to a nationality—relates to the international sphere only. It is nationality and not citizenship which is said to be internationally relevant. Nationality governs inter-state relations and citizenship individual-state relations. Nationality is a passive, formal status to be contrasted with the political and civil rights which might attach to 'citizenship'. It is salient to note the historical roots of this distinction (at least in states which historically adopted a feudal conception of nationality such as in Anglo-Saxon law).[25] Whereas nationality in international law evolved from the

---

[19] H Lauterpacht, *International Law and Human Rights* (London: Steven & Sons Ltd, 1950) 347.
[20] K Parlett, *The Individual in the International Legal System: Continuity and Change in International Law* (Cambridge: Cambridge University Press, 2011) 28.
[21] See, for example, Boll, *Multiple Nationality*, 58–9.
[22] Weis, *Nationality and Statelessness*, 4–5.   [23] Ibid, 32.   [24] Ibid, 59.
[25] According to Weis, in states which derive their law from Roman law, 'nationality is not determined by a territorial link but is a purely personal relationship' and denotes political status. Weis, *Nationality and Statelessness*, 4.

medieval European concept of a 'subject' tied to a territory and to a sovereign to whom allegiance was owed, citizenship has its roots in the Greek and Roman idea of membership of the *polis* with its attendant rights and duties.[26] In the case of the former, politics took place between sovereigns and in the latter between citizens within the community.[27] The 'subject' was passive—lacking a political voice— whereas the citizen constituted the subject of politics.

Hans Kelsen perhaps most clearly expressed the logical consequences of separating nationality from citizenship. He stated that '[f]rom the point of view of international law', it was of 'no importance' that pursuant to the German law of 15 September 1934, only persons of 'German or cognate blood' enjoyed full political rights and were called 'citizens' (*Staatsbürger*) and that the others were designated as 'nationals' (*Staatsangehörige*).[28] Of course, drawing such distinctions on the grounds of 'race' would now clearly violate the prohibition of racial discrimination. Leaving to one side such extreme examples, contemporary commentators have reiterated that nationality and citizenship need not coincide: a person can be a national without being a citizen with full political and civil rights.[29] On this approach, the international legal concept of nationality is a passive status distinct from the active persona and rights of citizenship. Nationality stands apart from citizenship: political rights, though perhaps desirable, are not integral to being a national.[30] A strict ' "legal-realistic" definition of citizenship [used here as a synonym for nationality]'[31] is to be maintained. Nils Butenschøn, for example, argues that, whereas international human rights law stands on the building block of the UDHR and is part of a 'normative legal order', 'the universal institution of citizenship has no such common normative denominator'.[32] It does not necessarily entail equal rights and political participation.[33] Indeed, it is the formal nature of nationality to which some writers point in support of the possibility of dual and multiple nationality. Multiple nationality is said to have 'reinforce[d] the significance and consequences of nationality on the international plane, diplomatic protection, admission, and not imposing certain obligations on aliens'.[34] According to Alfred Boll, while the consequences of nation-

---

[26] See further Boll, *Multiple Nationality*, 61–9.   [27] Ibid, 66.

[28] H Kelsen, *General Theory of Law & State* (New Brunswick: Transaction Publishers, 2006), 235–6. Weis, however, qualifies this and argues that 'if provisions of municipal law concerning nationality amount to an infringement of essential elements of the conception of nationality in international law, they do become relevant for international law' as was the case with Staatsangehörige who on Weis's approach were not German nationals under international law (Weis, *Nationality and Statelessness*, 6, 60). See also J W Garner 'Recent German Nationality Legislation' (1936) 30(1) *AJIL* 96, 99.

[29] Jennings and Watts, *Oppenheim's International Law*, 856–7 (para 378); Boll, *Multiple Nationality*, 71–2; Weis, *Nationality and Statelessness*, 5–7; C Tiburcio, *The Human Rights of Aliens under International and Comparative Law* (Hague: Martinus Nijhoff Publishers, 2001) 2–3; ILA, 'Final Report on Women's Equality and Nationality in International Law', 259; and R Bauböck, 'Citizenship and Migration—Concepts and Controversies' in R Bauböck (ed), *Migration and Citizenship: Legal Status, Rights and Political Participation* (Amsterdam: Amsterdam University Press, 2006) 15, 16–17.

[30] I return to this question in Chapter 3.

[31] N A Butenschøn, 'Citizenship and Human Rights: Some Thoughts on a Complex Relationship' in M Bergsmo (ed), *Human Rights and Criminal Justice for the Downtrodden: Essays in Honour of Asbjørn Eide* (Leiden: Brill, 2003) 555, 559.

[32] Ibid.

[33] Ibid, 559–60.   [34] Boll, *Multiple Nationality*, 292.

ality and citizenship may have merged in some states' municipal law, they have not done so for the purposes of international law.[35]

Unlike citizenship, nationality is said to be a 'unified whole' and a constant status: it cannot be lost in part.[36] Whereas citizenship rights may be denied in part, for example on the basis of minority or mental capacity, nationality status remains constant.[37] Writers have argued that the distinction between the two terms needs to be maintained in order to protect individuals against an arbitrary deprivation of nationality on political grounds. It has been said that when states denationalize they are in fact often seeking to deny the rights of citizenship—rights which it is asserted pertain to a person's legal position within a state. This internal legal position is fundamentally different from the legal bond of an individual to a state in international law.[38] Ian Brownlie similarly argues that exclusion from the internal status of citizenship is to be 'distinguished from acts of deprivation of nationality which are intended to have international effect'.[39]

Thus, on the formal conception of the right to a nationality, nationality relates to legal membership of a state for inter-state purposes. The rights of nationals within the state thus become a question of citizenship and beyond the scope of international law or a matter for international human rights law to the extent that the state is bound by its norms. On this approach, nationality stands apart from both citizenship and humanity. A right to a nationality becomes a right to be attributed to a state for the purposes of international order. The national has the right to enter and reside in the state and may benefit from diplomatic protection when the state decides to act on his or her behalf.[40] As seen in Chapter 1, the right to enter and remain in a state may be of considerable value to an individual. A salient feature of this formal conception of the right to a nationality therefore is the recognition of this public order element of nationality. However, this thin conception of nationality also supports what could be termed a politics of formal membership. Dissociating nationality from citizenship sustains inequality between nationals because not all nationals are necessarily citizens. Protection from statelessness is achieved, but only at the expense of the creation of distinctions between nationals within the state and the reduction of nationality to a purely formal international legal status. There is a disjunction between the 'international' and the 'national' significance of the status. As will be discussed further below, on Arendt's articulation of the right to have rights, the two were interrelated. Right-bearing and protection at the national and international levels are connected. Arendt highlighted the link between participatory political communities founded on plurality on the one

[35] Ibid.
[36] H Lessing, *Das Recht der Staatsangehörigkeit und die Aberkennung der Staatsangehörigkeit zu Straf- und Sicherungszwecken* (Lvgdvni Batavorvm: E J Brill, 1937) 149.
[37] Ibid, 149–52. See also Boll, *Multiple Nationality*, 81.
[38] Lessing, *Das Recht der Staatsangehörigkeit*, 157–8.
[39] Brownlie, 'The Relations of Nationality', 319. Donner also argues that deprivation of nationality without expulsion may not be prohibited by international law 'as being a matter of domestic concern, unless the State has earlier bound itself by treaty, as under the European Convention of Human Rights'. Donner, *The Regulation of Nationality*, 245.
[40] See further section 2.3 below.

hand, and protection against arbitrary deprivation of nationality and statelessness on the other. The right to have rights was not merely the right to an international legal status—to protection at the international level—but 'the right to belong to a political community'[41] with such belonging denoting active as opposed to formal membership. Arendt argued that without the equality of status conferred by membership of a political community, the individual quickly becomes superfluous and the state prone to 'dissolv[e] into an anarchic mass of over- and underprivileged individuals'.[42] Legal status is a necessary though not sufficient element in this equality of status. Nationality as a purely formal legal status which stands apart from the rights of citizenship may exacerbate the very conditions which 'the right to have rights' as conceived by Arendt was to alleviate.

The thin conception of nationality may also support a politics of formal membership in the second sense of a posited formal equality of nationalities across states. In cases such as *Nottebohm*, the inequity of looking beyond formal nationality is evident. Yet beyond such a scenario, a formal conception which is oriented to ensuring that each person has the right to some nationality—irrespective of the quality or substance of that nationality—may conceal the inequalities between nationalities behind principles such as the formal equality of states. Ayelet Shachar, for example, argues that international law, in focusing on statelessness and the need for an individual to be attached to a polity, posits a 'formal equality of status. It says nothing about rectifying inequalities that correlate with the birthright assignment of membership in "this or that" country'.[43] The quality of the particular nationality remains unexamined and inequalities between states are sidelined. To address some such inequities, Shachar proposes the imposition of a 'birthright privilege levy' on those who have a windfall in the 'birthright lottery' in order to improve the 'life prospects' of those 'allotted less'.[44] Leaving to one side the possible merits and demerits of the proposal, Shachar's analysis points to the innovative strategies which may emerge from looking beyond nationality as a formal international legal status. In sum, the formal conception of nationality may exclude from its scope those denied the rights of citizenship within a state such that the right to have rights is the right to nationality but not to citizenship.

Finally, before turning from this formal conception of nationality let me briefly address the claim that the rise in multiple nationality means that the significance of nationality as a legal status is diminishing. Some scholars assert that states' increasing tolerance (and even embrace)[45] of dual or multiple nationality points to 'postnational'

---

[41] H Arendt, ' "The Rights of Man" What are They?' (1949) 3(1) *Modern Review* (New York) 24, 37.

[42] Arendt, *Origins*, 290.

[43] A Shachar, *The Birthright Lottery: Citizenship and Global Inequality* (Cambridge, Massachusetts: Harvard University Press, 2009), 9.

[44] Ibid, 15. She conceives of birthright nationality as a form of 'inherited property' as it is the means by which intergenerational transfers in wealth occur.

[45] For example, some countries of emigration have encouraged dual nationality as a means of retaining links with emigrants living abroad. See T Faist, 'The Fixed and Porous Boundaries of Dual Citizenship' in T Faist (ed), *Dual Citizenship in Europe: From Nationhood to Societal Integration* (Aldershot: Ashgate, 2007) 1, 5; and C Dauvergne, *Making People Illegal: What Globalization Means for Migration and Law* (New York: Cambridge University Press, 2008) 133–5.

conceptions of nationality and citizenship.[46] While no single meaning is attributed to the term 'postnationality', common issues are the decline of state sovereignty and the rise of the 'transnational subject'.[47] Multiple nationality is posited as a stage in the trajectory towards an international political framework in which states no longer dominate.[48] As the state's role in international governance diminishes, so too—it is argued—will the value and significance of the international legal status of nationality.[49] As noted by Linda Bosniak, while the precise causal relationship between multiple nationality and claims as to the decline of sovereignty is unclear, analysts assume the existence of a strong nexus between the two.[50] The same can be said of the claim that multiple nationality is linked to the rise of the 'transnational subject'. An evident aspect of the latter claim is that multiple nationality fosters and facilitates 'overlapping loyalties'[51] and 'layered community identifications'[52] as opposed to allegiance to the one state. Notwithstanding these assertions, it is perhaps more accurate to speak of a 'pluralization of memberships' and of 'divided' as opposed to 'displaced' state sovereignty.[53] Moreover, from the perspective of those at the margins such as undocumented migrants—those, indeed, who are the focus of this book—nationality as a formal legal status is not decreasing in significance or becoming denationalized or deterritorialized, but rather '[n]arrow, formal, legal citizenship... is undergoing a resurgence of importance in globalizing times'[54] as states reassert their 'embattled sovereignty'[55] through nationality laws.[56]

2. The human rights orientation: nationality as an instrument for the protection of rights

What then might be the contribution of a human rights approach to the right to a nationality? In this section I argue that on a human rights approach, nationality is not only an element of international public order but equally a powerful tool of potential exclusion at the domestic level. Crucially, a human rights approach shifts the analysis from nationality as a status concerning international public order to nationality as a status integral to the protection and rights of the individual at

---

[46] P Spiro, 'Dual Citizenship: A Postnational View' in T Faist and P Kivisto (eds), *Dual Citizenship in Global Perspective: From Unitary to Multiple Citizenship* (Basingstoke: Palgrave Macmillan, 2007) 189.

[47] L Bosniak, 'Multiple Nationality and the Postnational Transformation of Citizenship' (2001) 42(4) *Va J Int'l L* 979, 984. See also Faist, 'The Fixed and Porous Boundaries of Dual Citizenship', 15–16.

[48] K Rubenstein and D Adler, 'International Citizenship: The Future of Nationality in a Globalized World' (1999) 7(2) *Ind J Global Legal Stud* 519, 533.

[49] Ibid.

[50] Bosniak, 'Multiple Nationality', 993.

[51] T Faist, 'Introduction: The Shifting Boundaries of the Political' in T Faist and P Kivisto (eds), *Dual Citizenship in Global Perspective: From Unitary to Multiple Citizenship* (Basingstoke: Palgrave Macmillan, 2007) 1, 20.

[52] P Spiro 'Dual Nationality and the Meaning of Citizenship' (1997) 46(4) *Emory L J* 1411, 1453.

[53] Bosniak, Multiple Nationality', 998.   [54] Dauvergne, *Making People Illegal*, 121.

[55] Ibid, 138.

[56] For example, Dauvergne argues that this is directly linked to the worldwide crackdown on illegal migration. Ibid, 119.

the international and national levels. Whereas on the public order conception of nationality, nationality stands apart from both citizenship and humanity, on the human rights approach nationality and humanity stand in a complex series of relationships. 'Humanity', as asserted in international human rights law, facilitates the conferral of nationality through articulating nationality as a right and constraining state discretion in its conferral. Moreover, the articulation of nationality as a right reflects the significance of nationality for the protection of human rights. Nationality does indeed facilitate the protection of human rights, but as will be seen, it does so only at the risk of positing the national as *the* subject of rights.

2.1 The right to a nationality: curtailing state discretion in the regulation of nationality

Before turning to the significance of nationality for the protection of rights, let me briefly examine the changes a human rights orientation has brought to state discretion in the regulation of nationality. Article 15 of the UDHR provides that 'everyone has the right to a nationality'[57] and that no one is to be arbitrarily deprived of his nationality nor denied the right to change his nationality.[58] The idea that nationality is a human right to be included in the UDHR was not without controversy. The US and UK delegates, though not opposing the proposal, argued that it was unrealistic to assert that the right was inalienable.[59] Due to the 'complexity' of the issues involved, the right to a nationality was omitted from the ICCPR.[60] Instead, the Covenant provides for the circumscribed right of children to a nationality, which has been articulated in terms of a state's duty to avoid rendering a child stateless.[61] Several human rights treaties, however, recognize the right to a nationality.[62]

---

[57] Art 15(1).   [58] Art 15(2).   [59] Third Committee Debate, 352 (US) and 354 (UK).
[60] See debates in the Third Committee in 1962 and 1963 referred to in M Bossuyt, *Guide to the 'Travaux Préparatoires' of the International Covenant on Civil and Political Rights* (Dordrecht: Martinus Nijhoff Publishers, 1987) 463–7.
[61] ICCPR, art 24(3); *Gorji-Dinka v Cameroon*, UN Doc CCPR/C/83/D/1134/2002 (views adopted 17 March 2005) para 4.10; *Rajan v New Zealand*, UN Doc CCPR/C/78/D/820/1998 (views adopted 6 August 2003) para 7.5; and HRC, General Comment No 17, 'Article 24 (Rights of the Child)', adopted 7 April 1989, *Compilation of General Comments and General Recommendations adopted by Human Rights Treaty Bodies*, UN Doc HRI/GEN/1/Rev.7 (12 May 2004) 146 (para 8).
[62] In relation to a general right to a nationality see also the Convention on the Reduction of Statelessness, New York, 30 August 1961, entered into force 13 December 1975, 989 *UNTS* 175, especially arts 1–4, 8, 9; the Convention Relating to the Status of Stateless Persons, New York, 28 September 1954, entered into force 6 June 1960, 360 *UNTS* 117, art 32; ACHR, art 20; ArabCHR, art 29; European Convention on Nationality, Strasbourg, 6 November 1997, entered into force 1 March 2000, 2135 *UNTS* 213, arts 4–9; and ILC, 'Draft Articles on Nationality of Natural Persons in Relation to the Succession of States (with commentaries)', 'Report of the International Law Commission on the Work of its Fifty-first Session', A/CN.4/SER.A/1999/Add.1 (Vol II, Part 2), 23, especially arts 1 and 4 (hereafter 'Draft Articles on Nationality of Natural Persons in Relation to the Succession of States'). In relation to the non-discriminatory conferral of the right see ICERD, art 5(d)(iii); Convention on the Nationality of Married Women, New York, 20 February 1967, entered into force 11 August 1958, 309 *UNTS* 65, arts 1–3; CEDAW, art 9; Convention on the Rights of Persons with Disabilities, New York, 13 December 2006, entered into force 3 May 2008, UN General Assembly Resolution A/RES/61/106, art 18(1)(a); and ACHPR, art 5. The African Commission on Human and Peoples' Rights has found that an arbitrary deprivation of nationality may violate art 5 and the right to equal protection before the law—art 3(2). See *John K Modise v Botswana*, Communication No 97/93, 'Fourteenth Annual Activity Report

From the early drafting debates on article 15 of the UDHR onwards, it has been unclear which state is to guarantee the right to a nationality. As originally conceived, article 15 did not even contain a general right to a nationality, with the draft only protecting the right to retain and change one's nationality.[63] In terms of human rights instruments, only the ACHR imposes a duty on a state to grant its nationality on the basis of birth on the state's territory in the absence of a right to any other nationality.[64] Attempts to give content to the right to a nationality have largely taken the form of Conventions and Declarations, the most significant of which is the 1961 Convention on the Reduction of Statelessness.[65] The Convention is significant for imposing positive obligations on states to grant nationality.[66] It seeks to reduce statelessness by attributing nationality on the basis of either the *jus soli*[67] or *jus sanguinis*[68] principle—that is, nationality is to be conferred by reference to a pre-existing link between the stateless person and the state in question. Causes of statelessness, such as a change in personal status on marriage or deprivation of nationality, are also addressed.[69] Crucially, states parties are prohibited from depriving a person of nationality if such deprivation would render him or her stateless.[70] Although this prohibition is subject to exceptions,[71] due process rights with which states are obliged to accord[72] may go some way in preventing the arbitrary deprivation of nationality. At present, however, few states have ratified or acceded to the Convention.[73]

Insofar as it is recognized, the 'right to a nationality' represents a considerable shift in international law on the regulation of nationality. As noted above, nationality has generally been conceived to be a status or relationship granted at a state's discretion: questions of nationality are 'in principle' within the 'reserved domain' of state jurisdiction,[74] with the state's right to use its discretion being restricted

---

of the African Commission on Human and Peoples' Rights 2000–2001', AHG/229(XXXVII) 28, 41 (para 88). In relation to the right of children to a nationality see CRC, arts 7 and 8; ICCPR, art 24(3); and ICRMW, art 29 (re children of migrant workers). The UN General Assembly and the Human Rights Council have adopted several resolutions on statelessness and human rights and the arbitrary deprivation of nationality reaffirming that the right to a nationality is a human right which is not to be denied on discriminatory grounds. See, for example, General Assembly Resolution, 'Office of the United Nations High Commissioner for Human Rights', UN Doc A/RES/50/152 (21 December 1995) para 16; UN Human Rights Council, 'Human Rights and Arbitrary Deprivation of Nationality', UN Doc A/HRC/RES/7/10 (27 March 2008) paras 1–3; UN Doc A/HRC/RES/10/13 (26 March 2009) especially paras 1–3, and UN Doc A/HRC/RES/13/2 (24 March 2010) paras 1–3.

[63] See J M Chan, 'The Right to a Nationality as a Human Right' (1991) 12(1) *Human Rights Law Journal* 1, 3.

[64] ACHR, art 20(2).

[65] Contrary to the recommendation of the ILC Special Rapporteur, what was adopted was a Convention on the reduction, rather than on the elimination, of statelessness. ILC, 'Report on the Elimination or Reduction of Statelessness' (Special Rapporteur R Córdova) (30 March 1953) in *Yearbook of the International Law Commission*, 1953, Vol II, 167, 169 (para 19).

[66] See P Weis, 'The United Nations Convention on the Reduction of Statelessness, 1961' (1962) 11(4) *ICLQ* 1073, 1074, 1080–2.

[67] Art 1.

[68] Art 4(1).   [69] Art 5(1).   [70] Art 8(1).   [71] See especially art 8(3).

[72] Art 8(4).   [73] As of 16 June 2011 there were thirty-eight state parties to the Convention.

[74] *Nationality Decrees Issued in Tunis and Morocco* PCIJ Rep 1923, Ser B, No 4, 7, 24.

by the obligations it has undertaken towards other states.[75] When posited as an inherent right of all human beings, nationality is no longer within the exclusive jurisdiction of states;[76] rather, the regulation of nationality is said to have 'evolved' so as to embrace 'human rights issues'.[77] In particular, states' jurisdiction is constrained 'by their obligation to provide individuals with the equal and effective protection of the law' and by their duty to prevent and reduce statelessness.[78]

From a human rights perspective, it is argued that the international regulation of nationality has come to focus more on issues of 'exclusion' than on 'interstate stability'.[79] At stake in the arbitrary loss of nationality is not simply lack of protection at the international level but exclusion from full membership of the national community. Such exclusion often takes the form of racial discrimination, making the prohibition of the arbitrary deprivation of nationality a key instrument in combating exclusion when it is read together with the norm of non-discrimination and equality before the law.[80] The discriminatory denial of nationality arises in a range of contexts, from state succession[81] to the treatment of resident minorities.[82] In relation to the latter, the IACtHR has found that the principles of non-discrimination and equality before the law require that states' nationality laws must not be 'discriminatory or have discriminatory effects on certain groups of [the] population when exercising their rights'.[83] Where nationality is conferred on the basis of the *jus soli* principle, to refuse to confer the state's nationality on children who are born in a state's territory of migrant parents constitutes an arbitrary deprivation of their right to a nationality.[84]

---

[75] Ibid, 24. The case demonstrated that whether a matter is within a state's domestic jurisdiction is a question of international law. See also *Acquisition of Polish Nationality*, Advisory Opinion, PCIJ Rep 1923, Ser B, No 7, 6, 16.

[76] *Proposed Amendments to the Naturalization Provisions of the Constitution of Costa Rica*, Advisory Opinion of the IACtHR of 19 January 1984, OC–4/84, Ser A, No 4, para 32 (hereafter '*Proposed Amendments*').

[77] Ibid, paras 32 and 33. See also Draft Articles on Nationality of Natural Persons in Relation to the Succession of States, preambular paras 2 and 3, and commentary thereto, 24 (paras 4–5).

[78] *Case of the Yean and Bosico Children v The Dominican Republic*, judgment of the IACtHR of 8 September 2005, Ser C, No 130, para 140 (hereafter '*Case of the Yean and Bosico Children*'). See also Convention on the Reduction of Statelessness, art 8(1) subject to the exclusions in art 8(2) and (3).

[79] Spiro, 'Mandated Membership', 88.

[80] For example, ICCPR, art 26; Convention on the Reduction of Statelessness, art 9; ICERD, art 5(d)(iii); CERD, General Recommendation No 30, 'Discrimination against Non-Citizens', adopted 1 October 2004, 'Report of the Committee on the Elimination of Racial Discrimination', 64th and 65th sessions, UN Doc A/59/18 (Supp) (2004) 93, 95 (para 14); and European Convention on Nationality, art 5.

[81] See ILC, Draft Articles on Nationality of Natural Persons in Relation to the Succession of States, art 15.

[82] In the African context, see B Manby, *Struggles for Citizenship in Africa* (London: Zed Books, 2009).

[83] *Case of the Yean and Bosico Children*, para 141.

[84] *Case of the Yean and Bosico Children*. The discriminatory treatment here was based not only on migratory status but also on the children's membership of a vulnerable minority namely 'the Haitian population and Dominicans of Haitian origin in the Dominican Republic' (para 168). Likewise in addressing denationalizations by Ethiopia in the wake of the war with Eritrea, the Eritrea–Ethiopia Claims Commission found that it was arbitrary to denationalize those Ethiopians of Eritrean origin who remained in Ethiopia and did not pose a security threat and to force them to register as aliens and obtain a residence permit. Eritrea–Ethiopia Claims Commission, *The State of Eritrea v The*

2.2 Nationality and the protection of human rights

Crucially, it is the importance of the legal status of nationality for the protection of human rights which animates the articulation of the right to a nationality on the human rights approach. As stated by Hersch Lauterpacht, nationality 'is now increasingly regarded as an instrument for securing the rights of the individual in the national and international spheres'.[85] As the 'right to have rights', nationality is 'amongst the most important rights a state can assign to individuals'.[86] By including the right to a nationality among the 'universal human rights' of the UDHR, the drafters were affirming that, notwithstanding their character as rights belonging to all humanity, nationality was of enduring significance for their protection, thereby necessitating that a right to a nationality be included in the charter of rights.[87]

According to the IACtHR, nationality as an 'inherent right of all human beings'[88] has an external and internal aspect. Unlike the thin conception of nationality, the 'rights' of citizenship are not delinked from the rights of nationality, rather the court maintains that:

[t]he right to a nationality...provides the individual with a minimal measure of legal protection in international relations through the link his nationality establishes between him and the state in question; and, second, the protection therein accorded the individual against the arbitrary deprivation of his nationality, without which he would be deprived for all practical purposes of all of his political rights as well as of those civil rights that are tied to the nationality of the individual.[89]

On this analysis, nationality is the basis on which protection is achieved at the international level and key rights are conferred at the domestic level. In *Case of the Yean and Bosico Children*, the court affirmed that nationality is 'a requirement for the exercise of specific rights': 'as the political and legal bond that connects a person to a specific state, it allows the individual to acquire and exercise rights and obligations inherent in membership in a political community'.[90] The case concerned two children of Haitian origin[91] born in the Dominican Republic who had been denied birth certificates and Dominican nationality, notwithstanding the state's practice of granting nationality to all children born in its territory.[92] As a result of

Federal Democratic Republic of Ethiopia, Partial Award, Civilian Claims, Eritrea's Claims 15, 16, 23 and 27–32, 17 December 2004, paras 74–5.

[85] H Lauterpacht, 'Foreword to the First Edition' in P Weis, *Nationality and Statelessness in International Law* (2nd edn) (Alphen aan den Rijn: Sijthoff & Noordhoff, 1979) xi.

[86] ILA, 'Final Report on Women's Equality and Nationality', 257. See also D Weissbrodt, *The Human Rights of Non-Citizens* (New York: Oxford University Press, 2008) 81–2 and *Trop v Dulles* (1958) 356 US 86, 101. Denationalization was said to constitute 'the total destruction of the individual's status in organized society'. It 'strips the citizen of his status in the national and international political community' such that he has lost 'the right to have rights' (101–2).

[87] H Lauterpacht, *International Law and Human Rights* (London: Steven & Sons Ltd, 1950) 347–8.

[88] *Proposed Amendments*, para 32.

[89] Ibid, para 34.   [90] *Case of the Yean and Bosico Children*, para 137.

[91] Their respective mothers were of Dominican nationality, however their fathers were Haitian (ibid, paras 109(6) and(7)).

[92] Limited exceptions applied such as to the children of foreign diplomats resident in the country or of 'foreigners who are in transit' (ibid, para 148).

this practice, Dominican children of Haitian origin have 'difficulty in obtaining an identity card or a Dominican passport, attending public schools, and having access to healthcare and social assistance services'.[93] For example, Violeta Bosico was unable to enrol in a day school for the fourth grade because she did not have a birth certificate, and was compelled to enrol in an evening school for adults which provided a compressed education in which two grades were taught in one year.[94] Moreover, without identity and nationality documents the children were constantly exposed to the threat of expulsion. In the words of the court, in being kept stateless they were placed 'in a situation of extreme vulnerability, as regards the exercise and enjoyment of their rights'.[95]

The facts of the case demonstrate that nationality is not simply a necessary legal status for the exercise of a limited range of national rights, but in practice often for the full range of human rights, from rights of freedom of movement to the right to education and health care.[96] Nationality does not merely connect a person with a state, and thereby with the international system, rather it may be a status essential for political participation and for the enjoyment of a range of civil, political, economic, and social rights that—international human rights norms notwithstanding—are often tied to nationality at the domestic level. Indeed, it is the very link between nationality and these rights at the domestic level that at times prompts states to resort to denationalization as a tool to deprive their opponents of fundamental rights and remove them from their territory.[97] An arbitrary deprivation of nationality may be the indirect means of seeking to silence criticism, to stymie freedom of expression, and to exclude opponents from political office.[98]

---

[93] Ibid, para 109(11).

[94] Ibid, para 109(35) and (36).   [95] Ibid, para 166.

[96] For example, in affirming the right to a nationality, the Human Rights Council has noted that 'the full enjoyment of all human rights and fundamental freedoms of an individual might be impeded as a result of arbitrary deprivation of nationality' and has expressed its concern 'that persons arbitrarily deprived of nationality may be affected by poverty, social exclusion and legal incapacity which have an adverse impact on their enjoyment of relevant civil, political, economic, social and cultural rights, in particular in the areas of education, housing, employment and health'. Human Rights Council, 'Human Rights and Arbitrary Deprivation of Nationality', UN Doc A/HRC/RES/13/2 (24 March 2010) paras 6–7. See further UNHCR, Executive Committee, 'Conclusion on Identification, Prevention and Reduction of Statelessness and Protection of Stateless Persons', 6 October 2006, No 106 (LVII)—2006 in 'Report of the Fifty-seventh Session of the Executive Committee of the High Commissioner's Programme', A/AC.96/1035 (10 October 2006) 13. The Committee 'express[ed] concern at the serious and precarious conditions faced by many stateless persons, which can include the absence of a legal identity and non-enjoyment of civil, political, economic, social and cultural rights as a result of non-access to education; limited freedom of movement; situations of prolonged detention; inability to seek employment; non-access to property ownership; non-access to basic health care' (preambular para 3). See also M Adjami and J Harrington, 'The Scope and Content of Article 15 of the Universal Declaration of Human Rights' (2008) 27(3) *Refugee Survey Quarterly* 93, 94 and Manby, *Struggles for Citizenship in Africa*, esp 22, 119–26.

[97] See *Case 9855 (Haiti)*, Resolution No 20/88 of IACHR, 24 March 1988 in 'Annual Report of the Inter-American Commission on Human Rights 1987–1988', OEA/Ser.L/V/II.74 doc. 10 rev.1 (16 September 1988), <http://www.cidh.oas.org/annualrep/87.88eng/Haiti9855.htm> accessed 6 April 2011.

[98] See *Baruch Ivcher Bronstein v Peru*, Petition No 11,762/97, judgment of the IACtHR of 6 February 2001, Ser C, No 74. See also Manby, *Struggles for Citizenship in Africa*, 127–40.

Finally, the significance of nationality for the enjoyment of human rights is seen when we consider that an arbitrary deprivation of nationality may unjustifiably interfere with a person's right to respect for family and private life.[99] Of potential benefit to a stateless or excluded person here is the ECtHR's broad interpretation of the right to private life so as to embrace 'the totality of social ties between settled migrants and the community in which they are living'.[100] Nationality is the securest means of protecting those ties. While the right to acquire or retain a particular nationality is not included in the ECHR, an arbitrary denial of nationality may raise an issue under article 8 for its impact on the private life of the individual.[101] A recent case before the court concerned nationality and residence laws enacted following Slovenia's independence from the former Socialist Federal Republic of Yugoslavia (SFRY) according to which permanent residents of Slovenia who were former nationals of SFRY, and of one of its constituent republics other than Slovenia, were given six months to apply for Slovenian nationality. Those permanent residents who did not apply for Slovenian nationality were 'erased' without notice from the register of permanent residents and became unlawfully resident foreigners, a situation which resulted in significant personal hardship. In holding that a refusal of permanent residency to individuals who had spent the substantial portion of their lives on the state's territory violated their right to private and/or family life,[102] the court was particularly mindful of the effect of the denial on the stateless applicants given the requirement of lawful residence for naturalization and of 'international law standards aimed at the avoidance of statelessness, especially in situations of State succession'.[103]

2.3 Diplomatic protection

Nationality as an instrument for the protection of human rights can also be seen in the context of the law on diplomatic protection according to which the state of nationality invokes the responsibility of a third state for an internationally wrongful act inflicted on its national.[104] In the opinion of the ILC's Special Rapporteur on Diplomatic Protection, the development of international human rights law has not rendered diplomatic protection 'obsolete'.[105] Rather, he contends that diplomatic

---

[99] *Kurić & Ors v Slovenia*, Application No 26828/06, judgment of the ECtHR of 13 July 2010, para 353. (The case has been referred to the Grand Chamber.) See also *Karassev v Finland*, Application No 31414/96, decision as to admissibility of the ECtHR of 12 January 1999 and E Ersbøll, 'The Right to a Nationality and the European Convention on Human Rights' in S Lagoutte, H Sano, and P Scharff Smith (eds), *Human Rights in Turmoil: Facing Threats, Consolidating Achievements* (Leiden: Martinus Nijhoff Publishers, 2006) 249, 266–7.

[100] *Kurić v Slovenia*, para 352.

[101] Ibid, para 353.   [102] See ibid, paras 359–61.

[103] Ibid, para 376. However, the court did not address the question whether the conferral of nationality itself was required under art 8. (Also the applicants' claim that they lacked the opportunity to acquire Slovenian citizenship in 1991 had previously been declared inadmissible. See para 355.)

[104] I discuss the position of stateless people and refugees below.

[105] ILC, 'First Report on Diplomatic Protection' (Special Rapporteur J Dugard), UN Doc A/CN.4/506 (7 March 2000) 7 (para 17), 7–10 (paras 22–32).

protection is the most effective remedy for human rights violations.[106] Indeed, the purpose of diplomatic protection is now said to lie in the protection of the rights of the individual rather than those of the state of nationality asserting protection.[107] According to the Special Rapporteur, as remedies for human rights violations continue to be weak under international conventions, diplomatic protection, as a remedy recognized in customary international law, 'remains an important weapon in the arsenal of human rights protection'.[108] While individuals may hold rights under customary international law and international conventions, their capacity to enforce those rights is limited. Arguably, for some detainees at Guantánamo Bay, diplomatic protection proved more efficacious in securing their release than assertions of their human rights.[109] The remedial safeguards afforded by diplomatic protection, however, should not be overstated. As traditionally conceived, whether a state chooses to exercise diplomatic protection is a matter of state discretion,[110] although there is said to be support for the principle that there is some obligation on states to protect their nationals when they suffer a serious violation of their human rights abroad.[111] Saliently, in an international system the efficacy of diplomatic protection will often depend upon the power differentials and the national interest of the states in question.

---

[106] Ibid, para 32. For a recent example of a state asserting diplomatic protection in relation to the violation of its national's human rights, see *Diallo Case (Republic of Guinea v Democratic Republic of the Congo)* ICJ, 2010 (30 November 2010). Contrast Judge Cançado Trindade who asserts that diplomatic protection should not be resuscitated as a means of protecting human rights rather the individual must be 'rescued' as the subject of rights (*Diallo Case*, separate opinion, para 215).

[107] Under traditional international law, an internationally wrongful act suffered by an individual at the hands of a third state is taken to be an injury to the state of nationality itself, such that in exercising diplomatic protection, the state of nationality is seeking reparation and a remedy for the wrong on its own behalf. In the famous statement of the PCIJ, by exercising diplomatic protection, 'a State is in reality asserting its own rights—its right to ensure, in the person of its subjects, respect for the rules of international law'. *Mavrommatis Palestine Concessions (Greece v UK)* PCIJ Rep 1924, Ser A, No 2, 6, 12. As to the claims of some writers that this is a fiction and a state acts as an agent of the injured individual and enforces the right of the individual see ILC, 'First Report on Diplomatic Protection', 22–7 (paras 61–74). See also C F Amerasinghe, *Diplomatic Protection* (Oxford: Oxford University Press, 2008) 76 and Judge Cançado Trindade, *Diallo Case*, separate opinion. He emphasized that the case was to be construed as 'an *inter-State contentious case before the ICJ*, pertaining entirely to *the rights of the individual concerned*' (para 5) (original emphasis).

[108] ILC, 'First Report on Diplomatic Protection', 10 (para 32).

[109] Dauvergne notes that 'British citizenship has proven more valuable than Canadian and Australian citizenships for Guantánamo detainees'. Dauvergne, *Making People Illegal*, 120 (fn 6). For a critique of diplomatic protection in the context of Guantánamo see L McGregor, 'Legal Routes to Restoring Individual Rights at Guantánamo Bay: The Effectiveness of *habeas corpus* Applications and Efforts to Obtain Diplomatic Protection' in A Edwards and C Ferstman (eds), *Human Security and Non-Citizens: Law, Policy and International Affairs* (Cambridge: Cambridge University Press, 2010) 560, 569–85.

[110] See, for example, *Barcelona Traction Light and Power Co Ltd (Belgium v Spain)* (Second Phase) 1970 ICJ Rep 3, 44 (para 79).

[111] See ILC, 'Commentary to the ILC's Draft Articles on Diplomatic Protection', 29–30 (subpara (3)) and art 19(a) and Amerasinghe, *Diplomatic Protection*, 79–90. In *Boumediene v Bosnia and Herzegovina* (2009) 48 EHRR SE10 the ECtHR left open the question whether Bosnia and Herzegovina was obliged under the ECHR to bring a claim vis-à-vis the US in relation to applicants detained in Guantánamo Bay (para 62). (The ILA has also advocated that a state's failure to exercise diplomatic protection be subject to judicial review at the national level. ILA, 'Final Report on Diplomatic Protection of Persons and Property' (2006) 72 *Int'l L Ass'n Rep Conf* 353, 398 (Summary of Committee's Conclusions, 'Nationality of Claims', para 2). On the question of judicial review, see also *R (on the application of Abbasi) v Secretary of State for Foreign and Commonwealth Affairs* [2002] EWCA Civ 1598.)

In underlining the importance of diplomatic protection as a remedy for human rights violations, we again see the privileging of the legal status of nationality and thus of the significance of the right to a nationality for the protection of human rights.

2.4 Nationality as eclipsing humanity?

From the above discussion it can be seen that articulating nationality as a human right brought nationality and humanity into a complex relationship. In positing the right to a nationality, human rights law points to the significance of the legal status of nationality for the protection of the individual at the international and domestic levels and facilitates the conferral of this status. Yet this interplay of nationality and humanity risks turning on itself such that nationality cannibalizes humanity. Humanity is eclipsed by nationality.[112] The subject of rights becomes the national.

Haro van Panhuys argues that, in characterizing the right to a nationality as a human right, the Universal Declaration declares 'a right...to something which in view of the very context of [the rules of international law] tends to be outdated'.[113] Such a right is a '*testimonium paupertatis*' in that it concedes that nationality provides a protection which international law by itself cannot confer on a person.[114] At the moment of the declaration of universal rights, membership of a national community is asserted as the site of the realization of human rights. In so doing, international human rights law points to the state as the community in which human rights are enjoyed and protected. Humans exist in community and this community is the national community. At least in part the human is defined as the national, humanity as nationality. We are reminded here of Arendt's critique of the rights of man in the context of the French Revolution. At the moment of the liberation of man and his rights, man collapsed back into the citizen. She argues that since the time of the French Declaration, the 'rights of man' have been equated with those of a 'people' and thus have become dependent upon, rather than independent of, governments.[115] Similarly, the plight of stateless people in the inter-war period and during the Second World War revealed that human rights could not be guaranteed for those who had lost nationally guaranteed rights.[116]

An example of 'man' (the human) collapsing into, or being erased by the national, is found in sections of the IACtHR's judgment in *Case of the Yean and Bosico Children*, where the court argues that the conferral of nationality is a precondition for being a subject of rights—what the court terms juridical personality. Nationality may not only be a 'requirement for the exercise of specific rights' but also a precondition for being a subject of rights per se. It is 'a prerequisite for recognition of juridical personality'.[117] On the court's reasoning therefore, a stateless person in lacking 'a

---

[112] See also Equal Rights Trust, *Unravelling Anomaly: Detention, Discrimination and the Protection Needs of Stateless Persons* (London: Prontaprint Bayswater, 2010), xiv.

[113] H F van Panhuys, *The Rôle of Nationality in International Law: An Outline* (Leiden: Sijthoff, 1959) 220–1.

[114] Ibid.

[115] Arendt, *Origins*, 291–3.   [116] Ibid, 269.

[117] *Case of the Yean and Bosico Children*, para 178.

juridical and political connection with any state' is deprived of a 'recognized juridical personality'.[118] This, it argues, denies 'absolutely an individual's condition of being a subject of rights and renders him vulnerable to non-observance of his rights by the state or other individuals'.[119] On the court's approach, the right to have rights is the right to a nationality in the sense of conferring juridical personality which allows a person to be the holder of rights. Such an approach cannot but exacerbate the vulnerability of stateless people as it affirms that to be denied the legal status of nationality is to be denied human rights—to be denied all legal rights. Humanity alone is insufficient for being a subject of rights.[120] Indeed, the court's approach would seem to confirm Arendt's analysis that to be stateless is to be 'depriv[ed] of legality'.[121] In Arendt's words, the stateless 'no longer [have] a place within humanity'.[122]

Similarly, positing diplomatic protection as a key instrument for the protection of human rights may exacerbate the vulnerability of stateless people. According to the generally accepted position, when a third state injures an individual, it is the state of nationality which may assert diplomatic protection. The rule of the nationality of claims provides that states have the right to exercise diplomatic protection when their nationals are injured by an internationally wrongful act of another state.[123] The vulnerability of refugees and stateless people in this regard is demonstrated by the facts of a case before the English courts.[124] The case concerned non-British nationals who were long-term residents of the UK detained in Guantánamo Bay, two of whom had also been granted asylum in the UK. They asserted a legitimate expectation that the British government would make a formal request for their return to the UK. The court, however, agreed with the Secretary of State that a state only has standing to make claims in international law on behalf of its own nationals.[125] This is not to deny that there is support for the extension of diplomatic protection to stateless people and refugees. For example, article 8 of the ILC's Draft Articles on Diplomatic Protection provides that a state may exercise diplomatic protection in respect of a stateless person and in respect of a person who is recognized as a refugee by that state, and who at the date of injury, and at the date of the official presentation of the claim, is lawfully and habitually resident in that state.[126] At present however, the ILC

---

[118] Ibid.   [119] Ibid, para 179.

[120] As argued by Gerald Neuman, this is a 'deeply conservative' approach for a human rights court and a return to Arendt's idea of nationality as 'the right to have rights'. G L Neuman, 'The Resilience of Nationality' (2007) 101 *Am Soc'y Int'l L Proc* 97, 98.   [121] Arendt, *Origins*, 295.

[122] H Arendt, 'Statelessness' lecture, 1955, Hannah Arendt Papers, The Library of Congress, (Series: Speeches and Writings File, 1923–1975, nd) para 14.

[123] See ILC's Draft Articles on Diplomatic Protection 2006, arts 1 and 3 subject to the exception in arts 3(2) and 8 discussed below.

[124] *R (Al Rawi & Ors) v Secretary of State for Foreign and Commonwealth Affairs & Anor (UNHCR intervening)* [2006] EWHC 972 (Admin) and [2006] EWCA Civ 1279.

[125] The Court of Appeal focused more on the Secretary of State's contention that any formal representations would be 'ineffective and counterproductive' ([2006] EWCA Civ 1279, para 122), however, in doing so the court stated that art 8 of the ILC's Draft Articles on Diplomatic Protection 2006 concerning diplomatic protection in relation to stateless persons and refugees (discussed below) is *lex ferenda* and not *lex lata* (para 118).

[126] See also ILA, 'Final Report on Diplomatic Protection of Persons', 398 (Nationality of claims, para 6). The ILA considers that diplomatic protection will develop such that any state may assert diplomatic protection 'in respect of an injured individual whose injury results from a violation of a

has acknowledged that this constitutes a 'progressive development of the law'.[127] Moreover, that it was considered necessary to find a means of extending diplomatic protection to stateless people and refugees affirms the importance of the functions of nationality for the protection of rights. Thus, articulating the right to have rights as the right to a nationality may emasculate humanity and perpetuate the vulnerability of the inevitable remainder denied the right to a nationality.

3. The democratic governance orientation: the right to a nationality as essential for democratic governance

Having examined the right to a nationality from the perspective of the relation of nationality to humanity, I shall now return to the question of nationality's relationship to citizenship. In section 1 we saw that, on its formal or thin conception, nationality is dissociated from citizenship such that it is largely irrelevant from an international legal perspective whether the national also possesses the rights of citizenship. Nationality as an international legal concept stands apart from citizenship at the domestic level. In this section I examine the inverse proposition, namely that international law may limit states' discretion in determining criteria for the conferral of nationality, and require that these criteria be shaped by democratic principles relating to citizenship as a political concept. Democratic principles may now necessitate that the status of nationality be conferred on the habitual residents of a state. It is argued that ensuring a government reflects the plurality of voices of the governed requires that habitual residents possess the right to vote, a right which is often (though not always) contingent on holding the status of nationality. While this approach is clearly related to the human rights approach discussed above, the emphasis here lies more on democratic inclusion than on overcoming discriminatory exclusion. On this approach, the relevant sphere of belonging and inclusion is the national political community with nationality as the status which provides the individual with a voice within it. As will be seen, however, on one articulation democratic governance and political participation are framed in terms of the right to vote and stand for election rather than a more substantive conception of political participation and public action.

It has been argued that if large numbers of habitual residents are denied the right to become nationals this could impede democratic representation in the state in question. An example of this, noted by Diane Orentlicher, is found in international criticism of restrictive nationality laws in certain Baltic states in the 1990s which excluded resident minorities from automatically being considered nationals. A Council of Europe report on Estonia, for example, stated:

[I]f substantial parts of the population of a country are denied the right to become citizens, and thereby are also denied for instance the right to vote in parliamentary elections,

---

fundamental international obligation where no effective remedy is available from either the defendant state or the state of nationality', 395 (para 170).

[127] Commentary to the ILC's Draft Articles on Diplomatic Protection, 48 (para 2).

this could affect the character of the democratic system in that country. As regards the European Convention on Human Rights, the question could be raised whether in such a situation the elections to the legislature would sufficiently ensure the free expression of the opinion of the people, as required by Article 3 of the First Protocol to the Convention.[128]

On this approach, democratic principles form the justificatory basis for the conferral of the legal status of nationality. Nationality serves as the bridge for political participation within the state of residence. In contrast to nationality conceived as an international protection norm, this conception of the right to a nationality 'recognizes...democratic self-governance values; the point now is to guarantee political participation in a person's place of residence'.[129] Here we see the interrelation between nationality as a legal status and citizenship as a political concept (a relationship also noted in the context of dual nationality):[130] the democratic dimension of citizenship—namely the requirement of 'congruence between the permanently resident population and those who determine government, the demos'[131]—forms the basis of the conferral of the legal status of nationality.[132] As argued by Orentlicher this points to an emerging right to nationality (or rather to citizenship in Orentlicher's terminology) for long-term residents which builds on human rights norms premised on the state of residence as the guarantor of fundamental rights—the 'effective realization' of which often 'turns on full citizenship'.[133]

On this approach, nationality as a legal status (at the national and international levels) does not stand apart from citizenship as a political concept, rather conceptions of citizenship and of democratic governance within the state are to shape international legal approaches to the regulation of nationality. A key concern is that the regulation of nationality be in accord with the flourishing of democracy and with the government representing the plurality of views of the governed. Although not concerning the right to a nationality as such, a case before the ECtHR illustrates this dynamic.[134] The case concerns a law prohibiting multiple nationals from taking up office as members of parliament. Of particular relevance is the court's focus of analysis. Multiple nationality is not treated as a matter of state discretion and as raising complex issues of conflicting loyalties implicating the international order,[135] rather, the court's focus lies on how exclusion of multiple nationals from parliamentary office will affect the plurality of views within the state, in particular the existence of opposition parties necessary for robust democracy to flourish given that all of those affected by the prohibition were members of the opposition. On the

---

[128] R Pekkanen and H Danelius, *Human Rights in the Republic of Estonia*, Report to the Parliamentary Assembly of the Council of Europe, Doc AS/Ad hoc-Bur-EE (43) 2, 17 December 1991, para 36 (reprinted in (1992) 13 *Hum Rts LJ* 236) and cited in D F Orentlicher, 'Citizenship and National Identity' in D Wippman (ed), *International Law and Ethnic Conflict* (Ithaca: Cornell University Press, 1998) 296, 305.
[129] Spiro, 'Mandated Membership', 99.
[130] See Faist, 'Fixed and Porous Boundaries of Dual Citizenship', 9–10.   [131] Ibid, 10.
[132] Ibid, 13.   [133] Orentlicher, 'Citizenship and National Identity', 323.
[134] *Tănase v Moldova*, Application No 7/08, judgment of the ECtHR of 27 April 2010 (Grand Chamber).
[135] See Boll, *Multiple Nationality*, 191–203.

facts of the case,[136] this exclusion constituted a disproportionate interference with article 3 of the First Protocol to the ECHR which requires states parties to hold free elections 'under conditions which will ensure the free expression of the opinion of the people in the choice of the legislature'. The court stated that in order to promote '[p]luralism and democracy...based on dialogue and a spirit of compromise...it is important to ensure access to the political arena for opposition parties on terms which allow them to represent their electorate, draw attention to their preoccupations and defend their interests'.[137] Building on the court's reasoning, a further link could be drawn between participatory political communities founded on plurality on the one hand, and protection against arbitrary deprivation of nationality and statelessness on the other. A political community based on plurality may not only serve as the foundation for a flourishing democracy but also as a bulwark against arbitrary deprivation of nationality and statelessness.

There are hints here of the active status Arendt envisaged when articulating the right to have rights. As articulated by Arendt, the right to have rights expresses the need to guarantee to each individual 'a place in the world which makes opinions significant and actions effective'[138]—where he or she can live, act, and contribute to public life as of right and not out of charity. It connotes membership of the political community.[139] To be denied a political voice in the community and the rights of citizenship, and yet to possess a formal legal status of nationality, is to have lost the right to have rights in the fullest sense of having the right to shape the world we hold in common with others—what Arendt terms 'the right to action'.[140] Richard Bernstein, for example, argues that Arendt's experience of statelessness revealed to her the meaning and importance of politics.[141] The agency and the subjectivity Arendt had in mind cannot be reduced to nationality as a formal legal status as per section 1 above, nor can it be reduced to human rights. Her approach points to an agency and subjectivity lacking both in the conception of nationality as a formal legal status and in approaches which reduce citizenship to rights.[142] However, Arendt's 'right to action' also exceeds the conception of 'democratic legitimacy' underlying the democratically oriented conception of the right to a nationality discussed above. Orentlicher, for example, argues that a country's democratic nature would be fundamentally subverted by denying full citizenship to long-time residents as the legitimacy of governmental power depends upon the consent of the governed.[143] The right to action, however, cannot be reduced to the right to vote and stand for election. Arguably,

---

[136] The court noted that the legislative amendments in question had been introduced seventeen years after independence and as part of a package in which all measures were detrimental to the opposition. *Tänase v Moldova*, paras 174 and 179.

[137] Ibid, para 178.

[138] Arendt, *Origins*, 296.

[139] See also M-C Caloz-Tschopp, *Les sans-Etat dans la philosophie d'Hannah Arendt: Les humains superflus, le droit d'avoir des droits et la citoyenneté* (Lausanne: Payot Lausanne 2000), 224, 252–3.

[140] Arendt, *Origins*, 296.

[141] R J Bernstein, 'Hannah Arendt on the Stateless' (2005) 11(1) *parallax* 46, 54.

[142] For a critique of approaches which privilege human rights over citizenship and reduce democratic politics to human rights, see P Tambakaki, *Human Rights, or Citizenship?* (Abingdon: Birkbeck Law Press, 2010).

[143] Orentlicher, 'Citizenship and National Identity', 323.

the democratic governance approach to the right to a nationality is open to a similar critique to that which Susan Marks gives of the democratic norm thesis. It limits democracy to 'legitimating government by others' rather than 'popular self-rule on a footing of equality among citizens'.[144] This legitimation of the rule of others falls short of the agency to which Arendt's work points.

Undeniably, Arendt's articulation of the right to have rights is shaped by her republican conception of politics and her construction of humanity as constituted in political community.[145] We need not, however, adopt her theoretical framework in its entirety to note the challenge her work poses for international law—the challenge of drawing the link between protection against arbitrary deprivation of nationality, statelessness, and political agency. Arendt draws our attention to the limits of positing the formal legal status of nationality as the answer to statelessness or to the exclusion of other marginalized groups from the national community, and to the danger of dissociating the international from the national, and the legal from the political. The legal status denoting membership must be accompanied by a voice in shaping the political community.[146]

4. The substantive belonging orientation: the right to a nationality and substantive membership

In a further and final conception of the right to a nationality, the exclusion or 'need' to be addressed by the articulation of the right is far more encompassing than that of the denial of the legal status of nationality or of political participation. What is at stake is substantive belonging. The place denied the stateless embraces nationality as an international legal status (the international functions of nationality such as diplomatic protection and the right to reside) as well as legal, political, and social citizenship within the state of nationality. It is a question of legal, political, and social inclusion. This articulation brings to the fore the exclusions and limits of the conceptions discussed above, though in still articulating the right to have rights in relation to the national it clearly also privileges the national as the subject of rights.

In exploring a more substantive conception of the right to a nationality, the work of Audrey Macklin is instructive. Drawing on Arendt's analysis of statelessness

---

[144] S Marks, *The Riddle of all Constitutions: International Law, Democracy, and the Critique of Ideology* (Oxford: Oxford University Press, 2000) 2.

[145] See further Chapter 3.

[146] This is not, however, to imply that the national community is the sole political community of relevance today or that democracy is primarily territorial (see Marks, *The Riddle of all Constitutions*, ch 5). An issue beyond the scope of the present chapter is the effect of globalizing processes upon national political communities. Cosmopolitan democracy theorists such as David Held argue that globalizing processes tend to turn national communities into 'decision takers' for others and thereby weaken the value of national citizenship to those disadvantaged by such processes (D Held, 'Democracy and Globalization' in D Archibugi, D Held, and M Köhler (eds), *Re-imagining Political Community* (Cambridge: Polity Press, 1998) 11, 12). In order for democracy to encompass a plurality of voices and be founded on equality and participation, it is argued that the sphere in which politics takes place needs to be reconceived such that democracy is engendered at all levels of the political community, from local and national polities to regional and global networks.

Macklin presents statelessness as the citizen's other.[147] Citizenship on Macklin's approach denotes full presence (legal, political, social, and substantive inclusion) in a state, and statelessness denotes its absence. Her notion of citizenship embraces 'legal citizenship' (nationality in international law), 'the formal status of membership in a state',[148] and 'social citizenship'. By 'social citizenship' Macklin means 'the more voluminous package of rights, responsibilities, entitlements, duties, practices and attachments that define membership in a polity, and situate individuals within that community'.[149] The national/citizen is not only 'in place' in the public order sense of being allocated to a state as its member, but also enjoys substantive membership within the state of nationality. It needs to be noted at this point, however, that Macklin was not writing in the context of 'the right to a nationality'. Her depiction of statelessness as the citizen's other is an analytical tool aimed at bridging discourses on legal and social citizenship and at illuminating a matrix of subject positions with the citizen at one end and the stateless at the other. I draw on her work here not to reify 'citizenship', nor doctrinally to specify the content of the 'right to a nationality', but rather to help us gain a fuller appreciation of the 'lack' or need in the world to which the right to have rights—examined here as the right to a nationality—may point, and thus to how the right to a nationality or other attempts to address the condition of statelessness may be shaped and oriented. As in Chapter 1, probing who is considered to be 'out of place' in the international system sheds light on what it is to be 'in place'. Macklin's approach challenges us to reconceive statelessness and nationality ('citizenship' in Macklin's terminology) in international law. We need to think with and beyond Arendt's republican conception of citizenship, for the reason that while Arendt's analysis of statelessness is insightful, her work arguably privileges political over social inclusion and substantive equality.[150]

Arendt's analysis of statelessness forms the starting point for Macklin's examination of the meaning of citizenship. From Arendt, we learn that statelessness is 'an existential condition of rightlessness'.[151] Macklin recalls Arendt's depiction of stateless people as 'the most symptomatic group in contemporary politics'.[152] The mass denationalizations and expulsions of the inter-war period and the Nazi era made clear to Arendt that 'the core of statelessness ... is identical with the refugee question'—both lacked substantive protection.[153] In being deprived of their citizenship and expelled, the refugee and the stateless were 'rightless'. Yet, as argued by Macklin, in the ensuing years, international law has only recognized the refugee as 'intrinsically abject'.[154] In part, this can be traced to the early misconception that the de facto stateless would be refugees and qualify for protection under the Refugee Convention.[155] Macklin argues that statelessness has come to be treated

[147] A Macklin, 'Who is the Citizen's Other? Considering the Heft of Citizenship' (2007) 8(2) *Theoretical Inq L* 333.
[148] Ibid, 334.
[149] Ibid.   [150] See further Chapter 3.
[151] Macklin, 'Who is the Citizen's Other?', 345.
[152] Arendt, *Origins*, 277 and Macklin, ibid, 339.
[153] Arendt, ibid, 279 and Macklin, ibid, 339.   [154] Ibid (Macklin) 340.
[155] See C Batchelor, 'Statelessness and the Problem of Resolving Nationality Status' (1998) 10(1/2) *IJRL* 156, 172.

as 'an administrative anomaly in the global filing system that assigns every human being to at least one state'.[156] The Statelessness Conventions, for example are solely concerned with statelessness de jure.[157] According to the 1954 Statelessness Convention, a person is stateless if he or she is 'not considered as a national by any State under the operation of its law'.[158] As for the de facto stateless, the delegates of the Conference on the Status of Stateless Persons recommended that states 'consider sympathetically' conferring the benefits of the Convention when it considers that a person has valid reasons for having renounced the protection of the state of which he or she is a national.[159] The contemporary assumption is that the rights of de facto stateless people are to be protected by human rights law.[160] Humanity is to serve as the default or safety net in the absence of the legal status of nationality.[161] Notwithstanding the development of international human rights norms, the vulnerability of stateless people persists. Macklin saliently notes that 'the existential rightlessness of the *apatride* remains an awkward concession for the international human rights regime to recognize in law'.[162] This is reflected in approaches to statelessness in international human rights law. While an arbitrary denial or deprivation of nationality on the grounds of race or ethnicity may constitute degrading treatment (under article 3 of the ECHR),[163] statelessness itself is rarely examined in terms of inhuman or degrading treatment.[164] To designate statelessness in this way (whether de jure or de facto), however, may more fully capture the abject

---

[156] Macklin, 'Who is the Citizen's Other?', 340.

[157] This is said to account for a 'minority of the world's stateless population'. M Manly and L van Waas, 'The Value of the Human Security Framework in Addressing Statelessness' in A Edwards and C Ferstman (eds), *Human Security and Non-Citizens: Law, Policy and International Affairs* (Cambridge: Cambridge University Press, 2010) 49, 56.

[158] Art 1(1).

[159] See recommendation in the Final Act of the United Nations Conference on the Status of Stateless Persons done at New York on 28 September 1954.

[160] In terms of the protection of stateless people under the 1954 Stateless Convention, while states are to 'accord to stateless persons within their territories treatment at least as favourable as that accorded to their nationals' in areas such as religion (art 4), access to courts (art 16(2)), and elementary public education (art 22(1)), in relation to other more controversial though essential rights, such as 'wage-earning employment' (art 17(1)), housing (art 21), and freedom of movement (art 26), stateless people are only to be treated as favourably as 'aliens generally in the same circumstances'. Crucially, a number of rights are limited to stateless people lawfully present in a state's territory (eg housing (art 21)). Moreover, the Convention does not stipulate the procedures for determining whether a person is stateless.

[161] Eg van Waas, *Nationality Matters*, 24–5. (Cf D Weissbrodt and C Collins, 'The Human Rights of Stateless People' (2006) 28(1) *Hum Rts Q* 245 who define statelessness as 'the condition of having no legal or effective [nationality]' (245–6).)

[162] Macklin, 'Who is the Citizen's Other?', 340.

[163] See *Zeibek v Greece*, Application No 34372/97, Decision on admissibility (European Commission of Human Rights (First Chamber), 21 May 1997 and Ersbøll, 'The Right to a Nationality and the European Convention on Human Rights', 259–62.

[164] In *Modise v Botswana*, constant expulsion as a consequence of the state of nationality's failure to recognize the applicant's nationality was found to constitute inhuman or degrading treatment (para 91). In *Case of the Yean and Bosico Children*, the IACtHR 'acknowledge[d] the situation of vulnerability' in which the children had been placed when they failed to obtain Dominican nationality, but did not make a finding in relation to art 5 of the ACHR. Instead, it took these circumstances into account when establishing reparations (para 204). However, it found that the threat of expulsion to which the authorities had exposed the children placed their mothers and sister in a situation of 'uncertainty and insecurity' (para 205) in violation of their right to humane treatment in art 5 (para 206).

nature of the condition than an examination of the particular rights infringed by an arbitrary deprivation of nationality resulting in statelessness such as the right to enter one's own country. Recognizing this, some early commentators on the right to a nationality asserted that denationalization as a punishment is 'neither necessary nor proportionate for the purpose of criminal sanction' and may constitute 'a cruel, inhuman treatment or punishment'.[165]

Even where de facto statelessness is recognized in international law, the de facto loss of nationality largely pertains to the international functions of nationality such as diplomatic protection when the national is abroad. Macklin contrasts this approach to statelessness to the refugee regime which examines the quality of citizenship: it 'addresses the nature of the relationship between state and citizen' and takes persecution to include, at a minimum, serious violations of fundamental civil and political rights.[166] Having said this, shifts towards the protection of the de facto stateless and the articulation of the right to an 'effective nationality' can be identified. It has been argued that de facto statelessness may be minimized and an 'effective nationality' achieved where nationality is conferred on the basis of the 'genuine links' existing between the individual and a state. This has been referred to as a *jus connectionis*: a 'right of attachment' such that a person has 'the nationality of the State to which he has proved to be most closely attached in his conditions of life'.[167] This might embrace links which a person may be able to establish over time, such as residence, as found in the 1997 European Convention on Nationality.[168] In the context of the attribution of nationality, the *Nottebohm* concept of an effective link may serve to enhance protection of the individual through facilitating conferral of the legal status of nationality by the state with which he or she has the closest ties. It is assumed that nationality will be, or at least is more likely to be, 'effective', that is, embrace 'the functions which are inherent in its concept'[169] where close ties exist between the national and the state of nationality. The aim is to move beyond formal solutions to statelessness, and to reduce the number of people who are not just 'stateless' but 'unprotected'.[170] Undeniably, the conferral of a nationality on the basis of a genuine link represents a significant step towards translating the right to a nationality into the right to a given nationality. It may also go some way towards minimizing the inequity of 'birthright citizenship'.[171] In privileging

---

[165] M McDougal, H D Lasswell, and L Chen, 'Nationality and Human Rights: The Protection of the Individual in External Arenas' (1973) 83(5) *Yale LJ* 900, 959.

[166] Macklin, 'Who is the Citizen's Other?', 341.

[167] ILC, 'Nationality, including Statelessness' (Special Rapporteur M O Hudson), UN Doc A/CN.4/50 (21 February 1952) in *Yearbook of the International Law Commission 1952*, Vol II, 3, 20 and Batchelor, 'Statelessness and the Problem of Resolving Nationality Status', 179–81. As was discussed in Chapter 1 in the context of the right to family life, the idea of an 'effective nationality' also surfaces in international human rights law. In this context, however, it is a question of the law protecting 'social ties' in the absence of the legal status of nationality. (See R Sloane, 'Breaking the Genuine Link: The Contemporary International Legal Regulation of Nationality' (2009) 50(1) *Harv Int'l LJ* 1, 56–7.) The genuine links between a person and a state point to the existence of nationality 'as a social fact' as opposed to nationality as a legal status.

[168] See, for example, art 6(3).

[169] ILC, 'Nationality, including Statelessness', 20.   [170] Ibid.

[171] See Shachar, *Birthright Lottery*, 164–90.

residence, however, it once again highlights the significance of lawful residence in a state; that is of the right to have rights as the right to enter and reside discussed in Chapter 1.[172] Moreover, an 'effective' nationality conceived as the 'functions which are inherent' in the concept of nationality as traditionally understood in international law need not translate into substantive membership.

In order more fully to grasp what is meant by 'substantive membership', let me now return to Macklin's analysis of examining statelessness as the citizen's 'other'; that is of identifying the void citizenship is to fill. The substantive protection stateless people have lost is perhaps best understood in light of Macklin's extension of statelessness to 'nominal citizenship in a failed state'.[173] She argues that this conception of statelessness 'addresses the denial of state protection in forms associated with both legal citizenship (access to territory, diplomatic protection), and social citizenship (fundamental rights, entitlements, equality, human security,[174] etc)'.[175] In turn, this corresponds to a conception of citizenship which 'encompasses the functional elements of legal and social citizenship'.[176] On this analysis, citizenship and statelessness are 'idealized representations of presence and absence'.[177] If citizenship represents full legal, political, and social presence within a state, statelessness represents their absence. The citizen enjoys a multifaceted 'place' within the state while still enjoying international protection via the external functions of nationality. Macklin's analysis points to a rich understanding of statelessness and thus to the need for any posited solution or rights addressing the condition to be correspondingly multifaceted. At one level the analysis reveals the inadequacy of presenting any one right as the answer to such a condition. At another, it poses the challenge of the right to a nationality being oriented towards full membership within a state embracing prevailing conceptions of the legal concept of nationality, but extending beyond these to include political and substantive membership. In this way, the right to a nationality may become part of what has been termed citizenship's 'progressive project'[178] in that the posited 'inclusion' is one of substantive belonging and of 'political equality' in its more emancipatory articulations of embracing respect for civil and political rights, but also for social, economic, and cultural rights.[179] Indeed so formulated, the 'right to a nationality' is perhaps best articulated as the 'right to citizenship'. Such a conception not only questions

[172] See, Dauvergne, *Making People Illegal*, 123, 137–8.

[173] Macklin, 'Who is the Citizen's Other?', 353.

[174] See also C Sokoloff, 'Denial of Citizenship: A Challenge to Human Security', prepared for Advisory Board on Human Security, February 2005, which conceives of citizenship as an 'an instrument of empowerment rather than merely a set of passive rights', 5.

[175] Macklin, 'Who is the Citizen's Other?', 353.

[176] Ibid. See also J Bhabha, 'Arendt's Children: Do Today's Migrant Children have a Right to have Rights?' (2009) 31(2) *Hum Rts Q* 410 in relation to 'functionally stateless' child migrants.

[177] Macklin, 'Who is the Citizen's Other?', 354.

[178] Rubenstein and Adler, 'International Citizenship: The Future of Nationality in a Globalized World', 547. Unlike Rubenstein and Adler, however, the progressive projective I envisage here is not that of an international political framework in which states no longer dominate (533).

[179] See Marks, *The Riddle of all Constitutions*, 59, 71–2, 110.

prevailing understandings of statelessness, but also raises the pointed issue of the substance of the nationality enjoyed by many de jure nationals today.[180]

As with any conception, the emancipatory potential of this approach is far from guaranteed. It may equally be captured for a regressive politics[181] or, as noted in section 2 above, may exacerbate the vulnerability of non-nationals such that the national becomes *the* subject of rights. This being said, a right to nationality oriented toward substantive belonging moves us beyond the conundrum identified in Chapter 1, namely that nationality is a formal legal status when allocating individuals as nationals to states, but expands to a substantive concept (the quality of their legal and social citizenship) when forming the basis of containment and external border control.

5. Conclusion

This chapter has explored the right to have rights in terms of the right to a nationality. The key question posed by the chapter concerned the scope of the protection afforded by the right to a nationality: what is the 'place in the world' nationality confers? I explored four conceptualizations of the right, namely the formal, human rights, democratic governance, and substantive membership approaches. Each presents a divergent articulation of the locus of nationality (whether in the international and/or the national sphere) and of the need or exclusion which the right to a nationality is to address—from the conferral of the formal international legal status to legal, political, and social citizenship. Each conceptualization also gives rise to a unique configuration of the relation of nationality to humanity and citizenship respectively. I have argued that it is when the right to a nationality is oriented towards substantive membership—the fourth conception—that international law may inch towards fostering the substantive protection of the individual. Clearly, this is an idealized conception. It points to the individual holding a rich, multifaceted place in the world which embraces nationality as an international and domestic legal status as traditionally conceived, but which also connotes political agency and substantive inclusion at the domestic level. Nationality does not stand apart from citizenship, and the link has been made between, on the one hand, membership in a political community founded on plurality and substantive inclusion, and on the other hand, protection against arbitrary deprivation of nationality and statelessness. It posits a politics of substantive rather than formal membership, of protection in fact and not just in law, and a politics of addressing inequality within and between states.

---

[180] As noted by Butenschøn, if a 'normative model of citizenship' is adopted, 'we would easily have to conclude that the majority of the people in the world do not hold (legitimate) citizenship': Butenschøn, 'Citizenship and Human Rights', 559–60.

[181] For the potential of a regressive politics in the context of 'mandated membership', see Spiro, 'Mandated Membership', 103 and P J Spiro, *Beyond Citizenship: American Identity After Globalization* (New York: Oxford University Press, 2008).

Yet any articulation of the right to have rights as the right to a nationality clearly presents a bind. To elevate the status of nationality in international law—to privilege nationality to the detriment of humanity—may be to exacerbate the vulnerability of those denied the legal status of nationality. Humanity and nationality may oscillate in their interrelation from being mutually affirming, where international human rights law facilitates the conferral of a nationality with nationality forming the instrument of human rights protection, to cannibalistic. The national subsumes the human such that to cease to be a national is to cease to hold human rights: the national is *the* subject of rights. A further conundrum presents itself. If the national is also the citizen, if inclusion in a political community is an element of the right to have rights, then how are we to account for enduring exclusions from full membership of the political community? With this in mind, in Chapter 3 I turn to a third conception of the right to have rights only touched on in this chapter, namely membership of the political community. Holding a 'place in the world' and being 'in place' are now examined in relation to membership of the political community.

3

The Right to have Rights as Citizenship

If, for public international lawyers, the right to have rights is founded on the international legal status of nationality, for political theorists such as Arendt it brings into focus the political status of citizenship. Having a 'place in the world' is articulated in terms of membership of the political community. In exploring this articulation of the right to have rights in the present chapter, Arendt's conception of citizenship forms the starting point of the analysis. For Arendt, the fully human life is lived within a political community, for it is within such a community that individuals can disclose their unique singularity through public action. Arendt writes: '[i]n acting and speaking, men show who they are, reveal actively their unique personal identities and thus make their appearance in the human world'.[1] Crucially, it is the legal and political status of citizenship[2] which confers the equality necessary for political speech and action and for the mutual recognition of rights. In instituting equality, citizenship overcomes all 'natural' differences.[3] While the private and social spheres are spheres of differentiation, Arendt maintained that the political sphere is the sphere of equality in which individuals are judged by their actions and opinions and not by irrelevant personal characteristics. Equality, Arendt provocatively asserted, is the product of 'human organization': 'we become equal as members of a group on the strength of our decision to guarantee ourselves mutually equal rights'.[4] On Arendt's account, rights are what members of the political community reciprocally grant one another as they come together in their plurality and construct a common world.[5] If this is so then it is essential that each person be a member of a political community. Such membership is a prerequisite for the enjoyment of all rights. In Arendt's words, '[o]nly the loss of a polity itself expels [a person] from

---

[1] H Arendt, *The Human Condition* (2nd edn) (Chicago: University of Chicago Press, 1998) 179.

[2] As noted by Mark Antaki, in articulating the right to have rights, Arendt emphasized the importance of not only belonging to a legal order, but also to a political community. M Antaki, 'The Critical Modernism of Hannah Arendt' (2007) 8(1) *Theoretical Inq L* 251, 256.

[3] See also H Arendt, *The Origins of Totalitarianism* (revised edn) (New York: Harcourt, [1973]) 301. Arendt writes: 'The human being who has lost his place in a community, his political status in the struggle of his time, and the legal personality which makes his actions and part of his destiny a consistent whole, is left with those qualities which usually can become articulate only in the sphere of private life and must remain unqualified, mere existence in all matters of public concern.'

[4] Arendt, *Origins*, 301.

[5] H Arendt, 'Introduction *into* Politics' in *The Promise of Politics* (New York: Schocken Books, 2005) 93, 93–6, 106–7 and Arendt's 'Concluding Remarks' in H Arendt, *The Burden of Our Time* (London: Secker and Warburg, 1951) 429, 437, 439. See also É Balibar, '(De)Constructing the Human as Human Institution: A Reflection on the Coherence of Hannah Arendt's Practical Philosophy' (2007) 74(3) *Social Research* 727, 733.

humanity'.[6] As noted by Étienne Balibar, for Arendt, rights are still associated with the human but the human is defined as the individual existing in political community.[7] Humans and their attendant rights are embedded within political communities. On its most extreme formulation, the human is the citizen—a person holds rights by virtue of their membership of a political community. The citizen is the subject of rights. Richard Bernstein calls this Arendt's 'situated, humanistic orientation':[8] rights are to be 'concertedly embodied in, and protected by, political institutions'.[9] Arendt's experiences of totalitarianism had impressed upon her the importance of the laws and institutions of the public sphere, the de-legitimation of which was one of the elements which crystallized into totalitarianism.[10] This is not to deny that there is a more performative side to Arendt's work—namely, a politics of praxis which precedes the instituted political community. The emphasis in this chapter, however, is on the institutional side of her work,[11] namely that equality is the product of political organization. I discuss a more performative interpretation of the right to have rights in Chapter 5.

Clearly this is an idealized, theoretical account of the right to have rights as citizenship. In practice, internal exclusions from citizenship persist. Not every citizen is in place: exclusions permeate the body of citizens. The question explored in this chapter is the protection accorded by international human rights law to the internally excluded. What is the role of international human rights law in facilitating full membership of the political community? The lens through which I explore this issue is the denial of the right to vote to convicted prisoners. After the progressive enfranchisement of excluded groups such as women, in a number of states serving convicted prisoners remain disenfranchised.[12] Such disenfranchisement has been traced to the Ancient Greek city state. Criminals who were deemed to be 'infamous' 'were prohibited from appearing in court, voting, making speeches, attending assemblies, and serving in the army'.[13] In later periods, those convicted of serious crimes were

---

[6] Arendt, *Origins*, 297.

[7] Balibar, '(De)Constructing the Human as Human Institution', 733–4.

[8] R J Bernstein, 'Hannah Arendt on the Stateless' (2005) 11(1) *parallax* 46, 56.   [9] Ibid, 57.

[10] D R Villa, 'Introduction: The Development of Arendt's Political Thought' in D Villa (ed), *The Cambridge Companion to Hannah Arendt* (Cambridge: Cambridge University Press, 2002) 1, 4–5 and M Canovan, *Hannah Arendt: A Reinterpretation of Her Political Thought* (Cambridge: Cambridge University Press, 1994) 201.

[11] For a discussion of how Arendt's work embraces both institutionalism and praxis, see Balibar, '(De)Constructing the Human as Human Institution'.

[12] See L Ispahani, 'Voting Rights and Human Rights: A Comparative Analysis of Criminal Disenfranchisement Laws' in A C Ewald and B Rottinghaus (eds), *Criminal Disenfranchisement in an International Perspective* (New York: Cambridge University Press, 2009) 25 and the further contributions in that volume. According to Chris Uggen, Mischelle Van Brakle, and Heather McLaughlin, voting rights for prisoners 'fall along a continuum. Some nations such as Canada, Denmark, and South Africa, allow inmates to vote while in prison. Other countries, such as Egypt and the UK, ban all prisoners from voting. [Note, however, that the absolute ban in the UK is under review.] In between those extremes are countries that allow prisoners to vote under certain conditions, such as Australia, Belgium, and Japan'. See C Uggen, M Van Brakle, and H McLaughlin, 'Punishment and Social Exclusion: National Differences in Prisoner Disenfranchisement' in Ewald and Rottinghaus, *Criminal Disenfranchisement in an International Perspective*, 59, 60.

[13] J A Pickens, 'Special Project—The Collateral Consequences of a Criminal Conviction' (1969) 23(5) *Vand L Rev* 929, 941.

deemed to be 'civilly dead' and therefore lacking in all civil and proprietary rights.[14] Of course, civil disabilities attending criminal conviction today are not necessarily limited to disenfranchisement or to the period of imprisonment. Notoriously, in the United States some ex-offenders are excluded from key political, social, and economic rights, which has been said to render them 'internal exiles'[15] and 'society's outcasts'.[16]

Voting in periodic elections by no means exhausts the meaning of citizenship or of the right to have rights as membership of the political community.[17] Even taking the issue of political participation, Arendt herself favoured direct forms of such participation. She was critical of the party system and advocated citizens' participation in local councils situated within a broader federated structure.[18] Notwithstanding these limitations, the right to vote serves as a useful point of departure for it remains a powerful signifier of full membership of the political community[19] as evidenced by historic and ongoing struggles to extend the franchise to all citizens. What then is the place that international human rights law, and select constitutional courts, accord to these internally excluded citizens within the political community? How, in this context, is citizenship conceived in international human rights law? I argue that the political equality of prisoners posited by international law remains tenuous. International law embraces two arguably conflicting conceptions of citizenship— namely citizenship as a privilege and citizenship as a status of equality conferred on all without differentiation. In the final sections of the chapter, I discuss prisoner disenfranchisement as an issue situated at the interstices of (at least) three overlapping borders of exclusion—deviancy, 'race', and poverty (or more broadly 'social exclusion'), and I call into question legal and Arendtian analyses which privilege political membership and inclusion for the protection and recognition of rights.

1. The right to vote in international human rights instruments

Political participation, as expressed in human rights treaties, has been characterized as a 'keystone right' and an essential prerequisite to the enjoyment of all other rights[20] in that the welfare of citizens will only be advanced where they have a voice

---

[14] Ibid, 941–50. See further A C Ewald, ' "Civil Death": The Ideological Paradox of Criminal Disenfranchisement Law in the United States' (2002) *Wis L Rev* 1045, 1059–61.

[15] N D Demleitner, 'Preventing Internal Exile: The Need for Restrictions on Collateral Sentencing Consequences' (1999) 11(1) *Stan L & Pol'y Rev* 153, 157.

[16] Ibid, 154.

[17] See further the discussion of the democratic governance approach to the right to a nationality in Chapter 2, section 3, and of substantive membership in Chapter 2, section 4.

[18] See H Arendt, *On Revolution* (London: Penguin Books, 1990) 267–8 and H Arendt, *The Jewish Writings* (New York: Schocken Books, 2007) 196–7, 400 (re Palestine).

[19] Richard Lippke, for example, argues that the right to political participation signifies that individuals have 'equal status in society'. R L Lippke, 'The Disenfranchisement of Felons' (2001) 20(6) *Law and Philosophy* 553, 556.

[20] G H Fox, 'The Right to Political Participation in International Law' (1992) 17(2) *Yale J Int'l L* 539, 595.

in the decisions of government.[21] Indeed, political rights are widely acknowledged as being integral to (though by no means exhaustive of) democracy conceived as popular control by citizens and political equality.[22] When we examine human rights instruments, however, it is evident that the right to vote is a qualified rather than an absolute right to be enjoyed by every citizen. In the case of the ICCPR, citizens' political rights are not to be subject to discriminatory and 'unreasonable restrictions'.[23] During the drafting of the ICCPR, there was general consensus that while the right to vote could not be restricted on an impermissible ground of discrimination (those provided in article 2(1) such as 'race, colour, sex'), it could be subject to 'reasonable' non-discriminatory limitations. From the comments of certain delegates, and from state practice at the time, the exclusion of convicted prisoners appears to have been considered a reasonable restriction. Thus, a proposal by the French delegate that rights could be enjoyed 'without any discrimination whatsoever' was changed to 'without arbitrary restrictions' (and later to 'without unreasonable restrictions') in order—in the delegates' words—to take into account exceptions such as 'lunatics or convicts'.[24]

It was said that the meaning of 'universal suffrage' was imprecise and could not be taken literally in light of the numerous exceptions to the right to vote. The issue was to ensure that no citizen would be the 'victim of a fundamental inequality'.[25] Indeed it was (at least in part) due to the numerous limitations on the right to vote in state practice that certain states opposed the inclusion of an article on the right to vote in the UDHR and the ICCPR. The inclusion of the right to vote in the UDHR was said to have given rise to more differences of opinion than any other.[26] Clearly, Western states were also concerned about the implications of universal suffrage for their colonies. Yet there were some delegates who viewed political participation to be the guarantor of all other rights. Noting that the first action of a dictator is to destroy

[21] See further J Waldron, 'Participation: The Right of Rights' in *Law and Disagreement* (Oxford: Clarendon Press, 1999) 232. While not claiming that the right to participate has moral priority over other rights, Jeremy Waldron argues that the 'right of rights' (that is, William Cobbett's 'right of having a share in the making of the laws, to which the good of the whole makes it his duty to submit') is 'the right to participate'. Participation, Waldron contends, is the answer to the problem of authority and disagreement about rights. He writes: 'right-bearers have the right to resolve disagreements about what rights they have among themselves and on roughly equal terms' (254). Thus participation he argues is fundamental to a 'theory of rights'.
[22] See D Beetham, 'Human Rights and Democracy: A Multifaceted Relationship' in D Beetham, *Democracy and Human Rights* (Cambridge: Polity, 1999) 89.
[23] Art 25.
[24] Commission on Human Rights, 9th Session, 'Summary Record of the 364th Meeting held at the Palais des Nations, Geneva, on 28 April 1953', UN Doc E/CN.4/SR.364 (30 September 1953) 7–8.
[25] Commission on Human Rights, 9th Session, 'Summary Record of the 363rd Meeting held at Palais des Nations, Geneva, 27 April 1953', UN Doc E/CN.4/SR.363 (28 September 1953) 10 (France).
[26] *Official Records of the United Nations General Assembly*, Third Committee, 21 September–8 December 1948, 133rd meeting (12 November 1948) 459 (Cuba). In the early drafting stages of the ICCPR, the UK's delegate asserted that the qualifications which may be imposed upon political rights were so varied that it was impossible to include them in the Covenant. Disagreement also arose as to whether political rights were individual or collective in nature. Further, a split emerged between the Western and Eastern blocs as to inclusion of the phrase 'universal and equal' suffrage (proposed by the then USSR and opposed by countries such as the UK and France) and whether the right to vote and stand for elections implied a multiparty system.

representative institutions, the Indian delegate stated that '[c]ivil liberties and fundamental freedoms [can] exist only where people [are] able to participate in government by means of periodic elections on the basis of universal and equal suffrage'.[27] Writing in 1945 Hersch Lauterpacht expressed a similar view. He argued that government by consent is 'the direct corollary of the principle of equality'. In tyrannical government where political participation has been erased, there is no room for other fundamental rights of man.[28]

In examining the *travaux préparatoires* of the UDHR and the ICCPR it is noteworthy that the delegates failed to consider the possible discriminatory effect of so-called 'non-discriminatory' exceptions, such as the disenfranchisement of convicted prisoners. The debates do not raise the potentially disproportionate impact of prisoner disenfranchisement upon certain social groups (that is, that it may be an indirect form of discrimination). In the case of regional instruments, the ACHR explicitly provides for the limitation of the right to participate in government, inter alia, on the basis of 'civil and mental capacity' or 'sentencing by a competent court in criminal proceedings'.[29] The main text of the ECHR does not even include the right to vote. Instead, a decidedly weak article (article 3) is included in the First Protocol to the Convention. As adopted, article 3 is framed in terms of an institutional guarantee to free elections, that is, in terms of a state party's obligation to hold free elections. However, it has been interpreted by the ECtHR as impliedly recognizing the principle of universal suffrage[30] and the rights of the individual to vote and to stand for election—rights which are said to be neither absolute nor unlimited.[31]

Insofar as is revealed by the drafting history of the respective international and regional human rights instruments, the right to vote does not then extend to the convicted prisoner. For several governments, even to include the right to vote in a human rights instrument was controversial. The convicted prisoner could be placed outside the political community.

2. Citizenship and deviancy

Does international human rights law affirm then that deviant citizens forfeit their political status within the community—their right to belong to the political community? Is citizenship a privilege to be denied those who are deviant and undeserving? Notwithstanding the drafting history discussed above, in the jurisprudence of human rights bodies and certain constitutional courts there has been a trend towards questioning the disenfranchisement of convicted prisoners, or at least to questioning their automatic disenfranchisement and restricting disenfranchisement

---

[27] *Official Records of the United Nations General Assembly*, Third Committee, 5th Session, 291st Meeting, A/AC.3/SR.291 (20 October 1950), 129 (para 50) (in relation to the ICCPR).
[28] H Lauterpacht, *An International Bill of the Rights of Man* (New York: Columbia University Press, 1945) 135, 143.
[29] Art 23(2). Art XX of the American Declaration of the Rights and Duties of Man 1948 limits such rights to those having 'legal capacity'.
[30] *Mathieu-Mohin v Belgium* (1988) 10 EHRR 1, para 51.   [31] Ibid, para 52.

to the narrowest confines possible. Though expressed in different ways, and within different legal frameworks, the thrust of the criticism of prisoner disenfranchisement is to question exclusion from political participation on the basis of deviancy alone. Citizenship is construed as being independent of perceived moral worth. A recent theme in one line of cases is the importance of democratic inclusion and equality. Deviancy does not automatically deny the convicted prisoner the right to membership in the political community. Notably, however, it is absolute bans on prisoner voting which are questioned. As will be discussed below, where disenfranchisement is considered a proportionate measure, it may be permissible.

In *Hirst v United Kingdom (No 2)*, a leading case concerning the automatic disenfranchisement of convicted prisoners, the ECtHR affirmed that deviancy does not automatically bar the prisoner from membership of the political community.[32] According to the Grand Chamber, the right to vote is not a privilege: '[i]n the twenty-first century, the presumption in a democratic state must be in favour of inclusion'.[33] No longer is the right to vote confined to an 'elite' but instead embraces universal suffrage.[34] The rights guaranteed in article 3 of the First Protocol of the ECHR are said to be 'crucial to establishing and maintaining the foundations of an effective and meaningful democracy governed by the rule of law'.[35] Whereas the former European Commission of Human Rights accepted that disenfranchisement may flow from the dishonour of certain crimes,[36] the Grand Chamber maintained that automatic disenfranchisement based 'purely on what might offend public opinion' cannot be reconciled with the Convention system.[37] The status of a convicted prisoner remains that of a bearer of human rights. Prisoners continue to enjoy all of their Convention rights except insofar as the right to liberty is justifiably restricted. The court affirmed that historical notions of the civic death of the convicted prisoner are incompatible with the Convention system. Thus, on the court's approach, exclusions from universal suffrage undermine 'democratic validity'.[38] Similarly, the HRC maintains that 'Article 25 lies at the core of democratic government based on the consent of the people'.[39]

Constitutional cases have also linked the right to vote to democratic inclusion. Strikingly, some of these cases have drawn a more explicit connection between the right to vote and respect for human dignity and equality than that employed by the international human rights bodies. According to Sachs J of the Constitutional Court of South Africa '[t]he vote of each and every citizen is a badge of dignity

---

[32] *Hirst v United Kingdom (No 2)* (2006) 42 EHRR 41 (Grand Chamber) (hereafter '*Hirst (No 2)* (Grand Chamber)').

[33] Ibid, para 59.

[34] Ibid. See also *Agiz v Cyprus* (2005) 41 EHRR 11, para 28.

[35] *Hirst (No 2)* (Grand Chamber), para 58.

[36] For example, *H v Netherlands*, Application No 9914/82, DR 33, decision of the European Commission of Human Rights of 4 July 1983, 242, 246.

[37] *Hirst (No 2)* (Grand Chamber), para 70. See also *Hirst v United Kingdom (No 2)* (2004) 38 EHRR 40 (Chamber), para 41 (hereafter '*Hirst (No 2)* (Chamber)').

[38] Ibid (Grand Chamber), para 62.

[39] HRC, General Comment No 25, 'The Right to Participate in Public Affairs, Voting Rights and the Right of Equal Access to Public Service (art 25)', adopted 12 July 1996, UN Doc CCPR/C/21/Rev.1/Add.7 (27 August 1996) para 1.

and of personhood. Quite literally, it says that everybody counts'.[40] In the same vein, McLachlin CJ of the Supreme Court of Canada (delivering the opinion of the majority in *Sauvé v Attorney-General of Canada (No 2)*, a prisoner disenfranchisement case) reasoned that to deny the right to vote to a particular group would violate the principles of equal rights and equal membership embodied in and protected by the Canadian Charter of Rights and Freedoms.[41] Like the ECtHR, the majority opinion of the Supreme Court of Canada dismisses as 'ancient' and 'obsolete' the notion that certain classes of people are not 'morally worthy to vote'.[42] By disenfranchising prisoners, the government of Canada was making this precise statement. It was asserting that certain people do not 'deserve' to be considered members of the community and therefore may be deprived of their basic constitutional rights.[43] Disenfranchisement implies that those denied the vote are 'no longer valued as members of the community' but rather are 'temporary outcasts from [the] system of rights and democracy'.[44] It is to be contrasted with the denial of the franchise to youths which rests on their lack of experience, rather than on their 'worth'. The majority emphasized that voting is a right and not a privilege and does not depend upon assumptions or perceptions of 'decent and responsible citizenry'.[45]

Human rights principles of democratic inclusion, human dignity, and equality may therefore require that the right to vote be conferred on each citizen. In principle, 'deviants' retain their political voice in the community. The importance of such human rights principles to retaining the universality of membership is seen when the majority approaches above are contrasted with certain dissenting opinions which maintain that deviancy severs the nexus or social contract between the individual and the community. Imprisonment acts as a temporary banishment imposed to protect the community from the deleterious effects of the offender's views and behaviour (a view akin to retaining the 'purity of the ballot box'). Gonthier J, delivering the opinion of the minority in *Sauvé (No 2)*, asserted that a convicted prisoner is not being excluded from political rights on the basis of an 'irrelevant personal characteristic' which is discriminatory and bears no relation to responsible citizenship, such as race, but on the grounds of his own criminal acts.[46] He argues that the disenfranchisement of convicted prisoners reflects that prisoners have 'assaulted'

---

[40] *August v Electoral Commission & Ors* 1999 (3) SALR 1, para 17. Note that s 10 of the Constitution of the Republic of South Africa 1996 provides for the right to human dignity. Sachs J's view was reaffirmed by the court in *Minister of Home Affairs v National Institute for Crime Prevention and the Re-integration of Offenders (NICRO)* 2004 (5) BCLR 445 (CC) (hereafter '*NICRO* case') in which the majority of the court declared invalid legislation which deprived convicted prisoners serving sentences without the option of a fine of the right to vote for the period of their imprisonment. The majority emphasized the importance of the right to vote as a marker of the value and dignity of the individual and of his or her full membership of society and affirmed the reasoning of Sachs J that universal suffrage is a 'badge of dignity and of personhood' (para 28).

[41] *Sauvé v Attorney-General of Canada (No 2)* [2002] 3 SCR 519, 2002 SCC 68 (hereafter '*Sauvé (No 2)*'), para 35.

[42] Ibid, para 43.

[43] Ibid, para 37.   [44] Ibid, para 40.

[45] Ibid, para 33 citing the decision of Arbour JA in *Sauvé v Attorney-General of Canada* (1992) 7 OR (3d) 481 (CA), 487.

[46] *Sauvé (No 2)*, paras 69–70.

the special relationship of rights and duties which exists between a community and its citizens.[47] By attacking the 'stability' and 'order' of society,[48] prisoners convicted of serious offences have abrogated the social contract such that the 'nexus' between the individual and the community is temporarily suspended.[49]

Notwithstanding these overarching principles of democratic inclusion and equality extolled by human rights bodies and by some constitutional courts, the trend in prisoner disenfranchisement cases is towards restricting rather than abolishing the practice.[50] Convicted prisoners' membership of the political community remains tenuous. While the blanket exclusion of all serving prisoners from the political community is questionable, certain subclasses of prisoners may legitimately be denied the right to vote. As was seen above, the right to vote is not articulated as an absolute right in international human rights instruments. Reasonable restrictions are permitted. It is a question of whether restrictions on the right pursue a legitimate aim and the means employed are proportionate to that aim.[51] Moreover, the right must not be curtailed to such an extent as to impair its very essence and deprive it of effectiveness.[52] The HRC has stated that in only prohibiting 'unreasonable restrictions', article 25 recognizes that a number of states deprive criminal offenders of certain political rights.[53] Whether a restriction is reasonable is determined 'on a case-by-case basis, having regard in particular to the purpose of such restrictions and the principle of proportionality'.[54] The Committee acknowledges that conviction for an offence may be a basis for suspending the right to vote provided the period of suspension is proportionate to the offence and the sentence.[55] Prisoners who have been deprived of their liberty, but who have not been convicted, are not to be excluded from exercising the right to vote.[56]

Most human rights bodies and constitutional courts have accepted that prisoner disenfranchisement may pursue legitimate government aims. Although the Chamber of the ECtHR expressed doubts as to the validity 'in the modern day'[57]

---

[47] Ibid, para 117.   [48] Ibid, para 116.

[49] Ibid, para 119. In the *NICRO* case, the minority focused on the threat which crime poses to the nation. Notwithstanding the significance of the right to vote for South African democracy, the minority argued that in a country 'notoriously plagued by the scourge of crime', criminal conduct and irresponsibility should not be rewarded with the right to vote (para 117 (Madala J) and paras 139–45 (Ngcobo J)).

[50] It has been argued that 'the right to universal and equal suffrage' without disproportionate limitation has emerged as a customary norm in international law. R J Wilson 'The Right to Universal, Equal, and Non-Discriminatory Suffrage as a Norm of Customary International Law: Protecting the Prisoner's Right to Vote' in Ewald and Rottinghaus, *Criminal Disenfranchisement in an International Perspective*, 109, 112.

[51] See, for example, *Mathieu-Mohin v Belgium* (1988) 10 EHRR 1, para 52 and HRC, General Comment No 25, para 14.

[52] Ibid (*Mathieu-Mohin v Belgium*).

[53] *Weinberger v Uruguay*, UN Doc CCPR/C/11/D/28/1978 (views adopted 29 October 1980) para 15.

[54] *Gillot et al v France*, UN Doc CCPR/C/75/D/932/2000 (views adopted 15 July 2002) para 13.2.

[55] HRC, General Comment No 25, para 14.

[56] Ibid. *Fongum Gorji-Dinka v Cameroon*, UN Doc CCPR/C/83/D/1134/2002 (views adopted 17 March 2005) para 5.6.

[57] *Hirst (No 2)* (Chamber), para 47. See also the HRC's 2001 Concluding Observations for the UK in which the Committee stated that it 'fail[ed] to discern the justification for such a practice in

of the UK government's purported objectives for a blanket ban—objectives such as preventing crime, punishing offenders, and enhancing civic responsibility and respect for the rule of law—the Grand Chamber found that such objectives are not 'untenable or *per se* incompatible with' article 3 of the First Protocol,[58] as the article does not specify the aims which a measure must pursue.[59] Government objectives in disenfranchising convicted serving prisoners have been most rigorously questioned by the Supreme Court of Canada. In the opinion of the majority in *Sauvé (No 2)*, the 'broad, symbolic'[60] nature of the government's objectives, namely, 'to enhance civic responsibility and respect for the rule of law' and 'to provide additional punishment'[61] made it questionable whether they served a constitutionally valid purpose and were capable of justifying limitations on the right to vote.[62]

It is in relation to the question of proportionality that human rights bodies and constitutional courts have exposed disenfranchisement laws to the greatest scrutiny, with several courts holding that absolute bans disenfranchising all serving prisoners are disproportionate measures. In *Hirst (No 2)*, the Grand Chamber of the ECtHR found that a blanket disenfranchisement of all convicted prisoners was a disproportionate and arbitrary measure in applying automatically to all serving prisoners irrespective of the length of their sentence, the nature or gravity of their offence, and their individual circumstances.[63] The Grand Chamber noted that the criminal courts make no reference to disenfranchisement in sentencing; thus apart from the imposition of a sentence of imprisonment there was no 'direct link between the facts of any individual case and the removal of the right to vote'.[64] While a wide margin of appreciation was to be accorded state parties, parliament had also failed to engage in substantive debate as to the 'continued justification in light of modern day penal policy and of current human rights standards for maintaining...a general restriction on the right of prisoners to vote'.[65] On this analysis, automatic prisoner disenfranchisement laws are clearly disproportionate, but prisoners may be disenfranchised when parliament has identified the legitimate aims of disenfranchisement and national courts have assessed the proportionality of the measure.[66]

modern times' and considered that it constitutes an additional punishment and hence does not contribute towards the prisoner's reformation and social rehabilitation, contrary to art 10(3), in conjunction with art 25 of the Covenant. (UN Doc CCPR/CO/73/UK; CCPR/CO/73/UKOT (adopted 6 December 2001), para 10).

[58] *Hirst (No 2)* (Grand Chamber), para 75.
[59] Ibid, paras 74–5. See also *Frodl v Austria* (2011) 52 EHRR 5, para 30.
[60] *Sauvé (No 2)*, para 16.   [61] Ibid, para 21.
[62] Ibid, paras 22–6. Notwithstanding this doubt, the majority proceeded to analyse the proportionality of the government's stated objects concluding that indeed the limits could not be justified.
[63] *Hirst (No 2)* (Grand Chamber), para 82. Exceptions included those imprisoned for contempt of court or for defaulting on fines. As of April 2011, the UK had failed to revoke the absolute ban. See further *Greens and M T v United Kingdom*, Application Nos 60041/08 and 60054/08, judgment of the ECtHR of 23 November 2010, and S Easton, *Prisoners' Rights: Principles and Practice* (Abingdon: Routledge, 2011) 214–19.
[64] *Hirst (No 2)* (Grand Chamber), para 77. See also *Frodl v Austria*, para 34.
[65] *Hirst (No 2)* (Grand Chamber), para 79.
[66] See N V Demleitner, 'US Felon Disenfranchisement: Parting Ways with Western Europe' in Ewald and Rottinghaus, *Criminal Disenfranchisement in an International Perspective*, 79, 98. Having said this, there is some uncertainty as to how the *Hirst* criteria will be applied in the future. A subsequent case

When we turn to constitutional courts, blanket bans have been held to be disproportionate but those limited to a subsection of prisoners (such as those serving three years or more) have been held to be constitutionally valid.[67] The Supreme Court of Canada is one of the few courts or bodies which has held that the disenfranchisement of prisoners serving sentences of two years or more[68] is unconstitutional, arguing that the measure did not promote—that is, was not rationally connected to—the government's asserted objectives of enhancing respect for the rule of law and imposing legitimate punishment.[69] The court stated that disenfranchisement does not send an 'educative message' of the importance of respect for law and democracy, but rather misrepresents and undermines both, for the legitimacy and force of the law derives from the law being made by, and on behalf of, citizens. In a democracy, the power of the lawmakers and the legitimacy of the law are derived from citizens' right to vote and the government cannot use that power to disenfranchise those from whom its power is derived. According to the majority, having a voice in making the law is integrally related to being obliged to obey it:[70] '[d]enying a citizen the right to vote denies the basis of democratic legitimacy'.[71] So it is that a government which disenfranchises a section of the citizenry 'jeopardizes its claim to representative democracy, and erodes the basis of its right to convict and punish law-breakers'.[72] Indeed, the history of democracy has been that

has emphasized that disenfranchisement is to be 'an exception' (*Frodl v Austria*, para 35) and suggested that there must not only be a link between the disenfranchisement and the individual's circumstances but 'a link between the offence committed and issues relating to elections and democratic institutions' (paras 34–5).

[67] See *Roach v Electoral Commissioner* [2007] HCA 43; (2007) 233 CLR 162 (hereafter '*Roach* case'). A majority of the High Court of Australia upheld a challenge to the constitutional validity of a law disenfranchising all serving prisoners. However, the entire court held that a previous law which disenfranchised prisoners serving sentences of three years or longer was valid. See also *August v Electoral Commission* (above). In that case the Constitutional Court of South Africa held that in the absence of a statutory limitation on the right to vote, the Independent Electoral Commission could not take administrative decisions which had the effect of disenfranchising prisoners by refusing to allow them to register and vote. Notably, the court left open the question whether parliament could have disqualified all or any prisoners (paras 20, 31). In the *NICRO* case the court held that legislation depriving convicted prisoners, serving sentences without the option of a fine, of the right to vote was unconstitutional and invalid. The majority held that clear policy reasons were needed to justify the blanket exclusion from so fundamental a right as the right to vote, whereas here the government had relied on 'logistical and cost issues' (para 66). Moreover, there was insufficient information even to begin to examine whether the measures accorded with the criteria for limiting rights under the constitution. How the court would respond to more robust government justifications for disenfranchisement remains undecided.

[68] Section 51(e) of the Canada Elections Act denied the right to vote in federal elections to prisoners serving sentences of two years or more.

[69] *Sauvé (No 2)*. As it was conceded that the voting restriction violated the right to vote guaranteed by s 3 of the Charter, the question was whether the infringement could be justified under s 1 of the Charter. This required the government to show that the infringement achieved a constitutionally valid purpose or objective and that the violation was warranted 'that is, that it is rationally connected, causes minimal impairment, and is proportionate to the benefit achieved' (para 7). Having found that there was no rational connection between the denial of the right to vote and the objectives of enhancing respect for the law and ensuring appropriate punishment, the majority went on to argue that the law clearly also failed to meet the requirements of minimal impairment and proportionality.

[70] Ibid, para 31.

[71] Ibid, para 32.

[72] Ibid, para 34.

of 'progressive enfranchisement'[73] such that the disenfranchisement of convicted prisoners is inimical to a 'democracy built upon principles of inclusiveness, equality, and citizen participation'.[74] In the opinion of the court, disenfranchisement is likely to exacerbate prisoners' disconnection from society and not rehabilitate.[75]

3. Looking beyond prisoner disenfranchisement: an Arendtian perspective?

What then is the quality of the membership accorded convicted prisoners in the political community which arises from the approaches of international human rights bodies and constitutional courts? While international human rights law has been efficacious in questioning the automatic exclusion of convicted prisoners from the right to vote, its victory has only been partial: international human rights law and domestic human rights principles serve as a break but not a bar on exclusion from the rights of citizenship on the grounds of deviancy. The 'political equality' of some prisoners remains tenuous, their membership of the political community uncertain. Imprisonment may no longer automatically signify exclusion from the political community, and yet exclusion persists, resurfacing within the body of serving prisoners. Even when challenges to prisoner disenfranchisement have been most vociferous as in *Sauvé (No 2)*, the slim margin of the majority (5 to 4) is sobering. It has been argued that as 'a policy at the nexus of punishment, democracy, and citizenship', the enfranchisement of prisoners 'hangs in the balance'.[76] What might be the contribution of an Arendtian approach to prisoner disenfranchisement? How might Arendt's work shift the analysis from one of proportionality to questioning the legitimacy of the pursued government objectives themselves? In the following discussion, I draw on the egalitarian as opposed to the elitist strands of Arendt's thought.[77]

Arendt famously and provocatively argued that we are not born equal but become so through political organization.[78] The laws and institutions of the polity create the equality we do not otherwise possess. According to Arendt, equality is not a 'universally valid principle',[79] or a product of nature, but instead a 'political concept',[80] the product of membership in the *polis*. To overcome the inequality between people, an 'outside' 'equalizing factor' is needed, which is the role political equality serves.[81] It is through membership of a political community, denoted by citizenship, that we recognize one another as equals.[82] Arendt argued that the 'mask' of legal personality, and the political status granted and guaranteed by the political community, hide

---

[73] Ibid, para 33.　　　[74] Ibid, para 41.　　　[75] Ibid, para 38.

[76] A Ewald and B Rottinghaus, 'Introduction' in Ewald and Rottinghaus, *Criminal Disenfranchisement in an International Perspective*, 1, 3.

[77] Arguably, her conception of politics as the sphere of freedom is consonant with prisoner disenfranchisement. See also J Klabbers, 'Possible Islands of Predictability: The Legal Thought of Hannah Arendt' (2007) 20(1) *LJIL* 1,18.

[78] Arendt, *Origins*, 301.

[79] Arendt, *On Revolution*, 275.　　　[80] See Bernstein, 'Hannah Arendt on the Stateless', 57–8.

[81] Arendt, *The Human Condition*, 215. See also Arendt, *On Revolution*, 30–1.

[82] See M R Somers, *Genealogies of Citizenship: Markets, Statelessness, and the Right to have Rights* (New York: Cambridge University Press, 2008) 126.

differences between people and thereby equalize.[83] Only with the mask of citizenship in place can a person act politically. Once the mask is affixed and civic and political equality[84] thereby conferred, can the 'voice' of the individual sound through.[85] It is the equality of status conferred by membership of the community—citizenship—which enables individuals to act politically and recognize one another's rights. Those without a recognized status are thrown back onto those characteristics which differentiate them from others.

In sum, Arendt reverses most constitutional formulae which found the rights of the citizen on the rights of man, citizenship on humanity. For her, citizenship must shape humanity and not humanity citizenship.[86] Humanity is constituted by citizenship: human rights can only be protected within the institutions of the political community. 'Abstract humanity' or, more precisely, what Arendt terms the condition of being 'a human being in general' without identifiers such as citizenship,[87] cannot be the basis of rights because, as conceived by Arendt, it is the sphere of differentiation, of natural difference, and inequality. Controversially, Arendt maintained that equality is limited to the public sphere of political participation. Citizens' equal political status is to be contrasted with the inequalities of the private sphere.[88] While the private and social spheres are spheres of differentiation, politics is the sphere of equality. In politics, citizens bring their uniqueness to bear in a productive manner through their speech and action. Speech and action enable citizens to step out of the private world (of difference and inequality) and assert their agency in the common world of public affairs. It was therefore crucial for Arendt that democratic political institutions protected the public sphere of equality from the inequality of the social and private sphere.

In light of Arendt's analysis, a striking feature of the prisoner disenfranchisement cases is the inconsistency of the recognition of the status of citizenship. On the one hand, prisoners are acknowledged as bearers of human rights and equal citizens. Citizenship is a status which does not depend upon 'moral worthiness'. Yet, if a prisoner is particularly morally unworthy, as evidenced by the gravity of the offence and length of sentence, then the mask of citizenship is stripped revealing

---

[83] Arendt, *On Revolution*, 106–9. See also Arendt, *Origins*, 301.

[84] See S Benhabib, *The Reluctant Modernism of Hannah Arendt* (Oxford: Rowman & Littlefield Publishers, 2000) 56.

[85] Arendt, *On Revolution*, 106. Therefore, for Arendt, the French Revolution in declaring the rights a man holds by virtue of being born rather than as a member of the body politic, could not inaugurate true equality; rather it 'equalized because it left all inhabitants equally without the protecting mask of a legal personality' (108).

[86] See also É Balibar, 'Is a Philosophy of Human Civic Rights Possible? New Reflections on Equaliberty' (2004) 103(2/3) *South Atlantic Quarterly* 311, 321. However, Balibar does not limit citizenship to the instituted political community. See Chapter 5.

[87] Arendt, *Origins*, 302.

[88] See H Arendt, 'Reflections on Little Rock' (1959) 6(1) *Dissent* 45. In this controversial essay, Arendt, while supporting the abolition of discriminatory laws, opposes the state's enforcement of desegregation in the private and social spheres. According to Arendt, in the social realm, differences persist and equality cannot be imposed. While the guiding principle of the body politic is equality, that of society is discrimination. On Arendt's analysis, discrimination is 'legitimate' when confined to the social sphere and 'destructive' when it encroaches on politics (51). Equality is said to have its 'origin in the body politic' alone and its sphere of influence is limited to that realm (50).

the 'natural man' beneath, and the denial of the right to vote is considered a proportionate measure. By lifting the veil of the formal equality of citizenship, distinctions between citizens (in particular between deviant and law-abiding citizens) come to the fore. The disenfranchised prisoner, like the slave of the ancient *polis*, is then considered to be 'without words' because their situation (here their moral unworthiness and imprisonment) has made them incapable of speech.[89] We need not accept Arendt's assertion that equality is only ever produced through institutions, and that there is no inherent equality between people, to acknowledge the consistency of the 'artificial' equality she posits and the inconsistency of that which surfaces in the disenfranchisement cases discussed above. An Arendtian approach to prisoner disenfranchisement might involve insisting further on the equality of citizenship, on the equality bestowed by the conferral of the status, which is a constant status divorced from moral worth. If, it might be argued, we take the equality of the status of citizenship seriously—a formal status of equality which is divorced from individual traits and perceived worth and desert—then any attempt to justify prisoner disenfranchisement may become questionable.

Indeed, Arendt's work poses the challenge to intensify the democratic inclusion posited by human rights and constitutional courts, and to take hold of the importance of all citizens belonging to what she terms the 'common world' of the public sphere. Her work brings into focus possible links between exclusion from the public sphere and total exclusion from the community—that is of rendering people superfluous and what she terms 'rightless', which was touched on in Chapter 2. Politics, she argued, is based on 'human plurality',[90] the equality and distinctiveness of each human being, and embraces a diversity of opinion. Each is human, yet none identical. Politics recognizes human plurality in that it takes place in the encounter between distinct individuals; the 'unique distinctness' of each person is revealed as they come together and speak and act.[91] Politics and democracy is to be founded on a plurality of perspectives and not merely on those which are congenial to the majority. On this analysis, deviancy is not a legitimate basis on which to deny political participation; rather, inclusion of convicted prisoners in the political community is necessary for plurality and democratic legitimacy and equality of membership. Prisoners are a part of the plurality on which politics is based. Convicted prisoners are recognized as belonging to the common sphere of existence with their fellow citizens. Without speech and action, and engagement in public affairs, Arendt asserted that the citizen is 'dead to the world' and 'worldless'. Arendt even goes so far as to assert that such a 'worldless' life cannot be a 'human life'.[92] She frequently linked 'worldlessness', being alienated from the political sphere, to superfluity. Those who do not belong to a world in common with others, who do not have a sphere in which they can act and express their opinions, are quickly rendered superfluous and reduced to objects of oppression. Given Arendt's approach, it was not surprising that she identified 'the right to action' and the right

---

[89] Arendt, *The Promise of Politics*, 118.
[90] See ibid, 93–6 and Arendt, *The Human Condition*, 7–8, 175–6, 220.
[91] Ibid (*The Human Condition*), 176.   [92] Ibid.

to opinion as the right to have rights. To withdraw from this common world, to be alienated from the world, was a perilous position.[93]

Yet need humanity be mediated by citizenship in the manner asserted by Arendt? Can humanity shape citizenship and not just citizenship humanity? Using Arendt against herself, her conception of the artificial equality of citizenship can serve as a tool which not only illuminates the inconsistencies in equality as posited by human rights bodies (noted above), but also serves as an inverted call to deepen the equality and non-discrimination norms posited by international human rights law, such that not only automatic disenfranchisement of prisoners but all disenfranchisement becomes contrary to the 'humanity' posited by international human rights law. Indeed, the non-discrimination norm has been instrumental in overcoming other exclusions from the right to vote such as on the grounds of gender. As discussed above, international legal analyses rightly underline the importance of the right to vote for democracy, but such analyses may instrumentalize the right by making the posited equality primarily significant in its relation to democracy. In addition to being integral to democracy, the right to vote (as has been helpfully emphasized by constitutional cases in South Africa and Canada), is a badge of dignity. It says that each person counts. It is a marker of inclusion and equality irrespective of whether that person in fact votes.

4. Citizenship, deviancy, and 'race'

If deviancy is one barrier to political participation, then ethnicity is a connected and perhaps more entrenched limitation. What is the place international human rights law accords the ethnically marginalized convicted prisoner within the political community? In societies divided along 'ethnoracial' lines,[94] the symbolic value of the right to vote as a marker of inclusion is intensified. As stated by the Constitutional Court of South Africa, in the South African context where the 'denial of the right to vote was used to entrench white supremacy and to marginalise the great majority of the people of [the]country', it is 'a precious right which must be vigilantly respected and protected'.[95]

The denial of the right to vote on the grounds of 'race' is recognized in international law as an egregious form of discrimination. As expressed by the ECtHR, combating racism is essential for 'reinforcing democracy's vision of a society in which diversity is not perceived as a threat but as a source of enrichment'.[96] In many states

---

[93] See Villa, 'The Development of Arendt's Political Thought', 6 and Arendt, *Origins*, 295–7.

[94] Loïc Wacquant argues that 'race' is a 'denegated form of ethnicity' and thus uses the term 'ethnoracial' in his work. See L Wacquant, *Punishing the Poor: The Neoliberal Government of Social Insecurity* (Durham: Duke University Press, 2009) 195. I nevertheless refer to the term 'race' as it is named as a proscribed ground of discrimination in international human rights instruments.

[95] *NICRO* case, para 47. Thus in the absence of clear policy reasons, legislation excluding convicted prisoners serving sentences without the option of a fine from so fundamental a right as the right to vote was unconstitutional and invalid.

[96] For a recent example in the complex historical and constitutional context of Bosnia and Herzegovina see *Sejdić & Anor v Bosnia and Herzegovina*, Application Nos 27996/06 and 34836/06, judgment of the ECtHR (Grand Chamber) of 22 December 2009, para 43.

today, the question raised by prisoner disenfranchisement is not direct discrimination, but indirect discrimination flowing from the disproportionate effect of the measure on ethnic minorities. It has been estimated, for example, that prisoner disenfranchisement laws have had the effect of disenfranchising at least one in seven African Americans in the US.[97] The vote is denied to prisoners in all but two of the US states,[98] and in several states, ex-felons are disenfranchised for life.[99] The sociologist Loïc Wacquant argues that such laws, coupled with the trends towards penalizing poverty (discussed below), and towards linking deviancy with 'race', are reversing the effects of the civil rights movement.[100] 'Race' serves as the means of identifying and extracting the deviant from the body of citizens and of denying him or her the full benefits of citizenship. To be 'black' or a member of the prevailing stigmatized ethnicity is to be deviant. Only thirty-five years after civil rights were granted to African Americans, the right to vote, Wacquant argues, is 'being taken back by the penal system'.[101] Of course the disproportionate impact of prisoner disenfranchisement laws on ethnic minorities is not limited to the US. In Australia where prisoners serving sentences of three years or more are disenfranchised, indigenous Australians have been recognized as being 'markedly over-represented in the prison population'.[102]

Recognizing the historic link between race and disenfranchisement, the United Nations Declaration on the Elimination of all Forms of Racial Discrimination prohibits discrimination 'by reason of race, colour or ethnic origin . . . in the enjoyment by any person of political and citizenship rights in his country, in particular the right to participate in elections through universal and equal suffrage and to take part in the government'.[103] ICERD reiterated this prohibition.[104] In the *travaux préparatoires* of the Convention, however, there is little discussion of racial discrimination in the exercise of political rights. In particular, there is no mention of the more subtle form of discrimination arising from disenfranchisement due to conviction for an offence.[105] However, there are signs of an emerging recognition that the disenfranchisement of prisoners may constitute indirect discrimination on the grounds of race.

---

[97] J Manza and C Uggen, *Locked Out: Felon Disenfranchisement and American Democracy* (Oxford: Oxford University Press, 2006) 80.

[98] E A Hull, 'Our "Crooked Timber": Why is American Punishment so Harsh?' in Ewald and Rottinghaus, *Criminal Disenfranchisement in an International Perspective*, 136.

[99] Ibid.

[100] See L Wacquant, 'From Slavery to Mass Incarceration' (Jan/Feb 2002) (13) *New Left Review* 41, 43 and Wacquant, *Punishing the Poor*, esp 195–208.

[101] Ibid ('From Slavery to Mass Incarceration'), 43 and ibid (*Punishing the Poor*), 198.

[102] *Roach* case, para 173. See also para 36: '[o]n 30 June 2006 there were 20,209 prisoners in Australian prisons who were serving a sentence; 24 per cent of the prison population was indigenous and the percentage varied across Australia, from 82 per cent in the Northern Territory to six per cent in Victoria. Some 35 per cent of prisoners were serving a term of two years or less'.

[103] UN Doc A/RES/1904 (XVIII), adopted 20 November 1963 (without vote), art 6.

[104] Art 5(c). See also ICCPR, art 25 which provides that the right to vote (art 25(b)) is to be enjoyed 'without any of the distinctions mentioned in article 2 and without unreasonable restrictions'. (See also ICCPR, art 26.)

[105] See, for example 'Summary Records of 20th Session of the Commission on Human Rights (1964)', 796th–800th meeting of the Commission, UN Docs E/CN.4/SR.796–E/CN.4/SR.800; 'Summary Records of the Third Committee (1965)', 1305th–1309th meetings, UN Doc A/C.3/SR.1305–A/C.3/SR.1309.

Disenfranchisement legislation which is couched in 'neutral' terms may still have a discriminatory effect and therefore come within the definition of 'racial discrimination' in article 1(1) of ICERD. In interpreting this article, CERD has stated that '[a] distinction is contrary to the Convention if it has either the purpose or the effect of impairing particular rights and freedoms. This is confirmed by the obligation placed upon States parties by article 2, paragraph 1 (c), to nullify any law or practice which has the effect of creating or perpetuating racial discrimination'.[106] In determining whether an action has an effect contrary to the Convention, it examines 'whether that action has an unjustifiable disparate impact upon a group distinguished by race, colour, descent, or national or ethnic origin'.[107] In line with this analysis, CERD's Concluding Observations for the US have expressed concern at the disproportionate impact of prisoner disenfranchisement laws on ethnic minorities,[108] in particular on African Americans who are 'disproportionately represented at every stage of the criminal justice system',[109] and has reiterated that the right of everyone to vote on a non-discriminatory basis is protected by article 5(c) of the Convention.[110]

The ECtHR has also accepted that article 14 of the ECHR extends to 'indirect discrimination'.[111] A general policy or measure which is not specifically aimed at a group may be discriminatory if it has 'disproportionately prejudicial effects' on that group.[112] Discrimination contrary to the Convention may result from 'a de facto situation'.[113] Such discrimination, however, is notoriously difficult to establish. Crucially therefore, the court has accepted that reliable statistical evidence of the differential impact of a neutral measure on a particular group may establish a rebuttable presumption of indirect discrimination and shift the burden to the state to show that the difference in treatment was objectively and reasonably justified.[114] In *DH v Czech Republic*, for example, the court accepted statistical evidence that the number of Roma children at special schools was disproportionately high giving rise to a strong presumption of indirect discrimination.[115] The difference in treatment did not stem from the wording of the statute relating to special schools, but from the manner in which the statute was applied in practice—a practice which resulted

---

[106] CERD, General Recommendation No 14, 'Definition of Discrimination (art 1, par1)', adopted 22 March 1993, UN Doc A/48/18 (15 September 1993) 115, para 1.

[107] Ibid, para 2 and *L R et al v Slovak Republic*, UN Doc CERD/C/66/D/31/2003 (opinion adopted 7 March 2005) para 10.4. See also HRC, General Comment No 18, 'Non-Discrimination', adopted 10 November 1989, UN Doc HRI/GEN/1/Rev.7 (12 May 2004) 146, paras 6, 7, 9.

[108] UN Doc A/56/18(SUPP) (2001), 66 (para 397) and UN Doc CERD/C/USA/CO/6 (adopted 5 March 2008) para 27.

[109] Ibid (2008).

[110] UN Doc A/56/18(SUPP) (2001) 66 (para 397). Similarly, the HRC has asserted that the disenfranchisement of citizens with a felony conviction 'has significant racial implications'. See Concluding Observations for the US, UN Doc CCPR/C/USA/CO/3/Rev.1 (adopted 27 July 2006) para 35. For the HRC's recognition of indirect discrimination, see, for example, *Althammer et al v Austria*, UN Doc CCPR/C/78/D/998/2001 (views adopted 8 August 2003) para 10.2

[111] See *DH v Czech Republic* (2008) 47 EHRR 3, para 175.   [112] Ibid.

[113] Ibid, para 175.

[114] Ibid, paras 188–9. Although it is unclear, the majority's reasoning suggests that discriminatory intent on the part of the authorities may need to be proved in some 'spheres' (but not in relation to 'cases concerning employment[,] the provision of services... [or] in the educational sphere' (para 194)).

[115] Ibid, paras 185–95.

in a disproportionate number of Roma children being placed in special schools. The state was then unable to establish that the difference in treatment between Roma and non-Roma children was objectively and reasonably justified and that there was a reasonable relationship of proportionality between the means used and the aim pursued.[116] Applying the court's reasoning to the context of prisoner disenfranchisement, in the case that applicants could provide statistical evidence of the discriminatory effect of the legislation, the question would then be whether the government could show that 'the difference in the impact of the [disenfranchisement] legislation was the result of objective factors unrelated to ethnic origin'.[117]

Clearly, the disproportionate representation of marginalized ethnic minorities within prisons is a complex issue, but it cannot but raise the question of institutional racism in the criminal justice system. Institutional racism is increasingly being recognized by international human rights bodies and instruments. The Durban Declaration of the World Conference Against Racism, Racial Discrimination, Xenophobia and Related Intolerance, for example, recognizes that racial discrimination in penal systems has led to the overrepresentation of certain groups among detained persons[118] and CERD has drawn attention to the endemic problem of racial discrimination in states' criminal justice systems.[119] In a similar vein, the HRC has expressed concern that the substantially higher representation of an ethnic group amongst persons accused of a crime than their representation within the general population 'points to underlying social causes and raises concerns regarding the possibility of discrimination in the administration of justice'.[120]

There has been some recognition in state jurisprudence that the overrepresentation of ethnic minorities in prisons is linked to institutional racism. As stated above, in *Sauvé (No 2)* McLachlin CJ noted the disproportionate effect of disenfranchisement on Canada's Aboriginal population, whose overrepresentation in the criminal justice system had already been denounced by the Supreme Court of Canada

---

[116] Ibid, paras 196–210.

[117] Ibid, para 195. The state must be able to establish that the difference in treatment pursues a 'legitimate aim' and that there is a 'reasonable relationship of proportionality' between the means used and the aim sought to be realised (para 196).

[118] Declaration of the World Conference against Racism, Racial Discrimination, Xenophobia and Related Intolerance held from 31 August–8 September 2001, Durban, South Africa. See United Nations, *World Conference Against Racism, Racial Discrimination, Xenophobia and Related Intolerance: Declaration and Programme of Action* (New York: United Nations Department of Public Information, 2002) 19 (para 25 of the Declaration).

[119] CERD, General Recommendation No 31, 'The Prevention of Racial Discrimination in the Administration and Functioning of the Criminal Justice System', adopted 17 August 2005, A/60/18 (SUPP)(2005), 98.

[120] Concluding Observations of the Human Rights Committee for New Zealand, UN Doc CCPR/C/NZL/CO/5 (adopted 25 March 2010) para 12. In terms of the Inter-American Commission on Human Rights, several NGOs have submitted a request for a 'Thematic Hearing on the Discriminatory Effects of Felony Disenfranchisement Laws, Policies and Practices in the Americas'. See submission by Lawyers Committee for Civil Rights Under Law, The Sentencing Project, and American Civil Liberties Union, dated 8 September 2009, <http://www.aclu.org/files/pdfs/humanrights/iachr_request_thematic_hrg_disenfranchisement.pdf> accessed 29 October 2010.

as a 'crisis'.[121] In the US, it is well established that state constitutional provisions which, though neutral on their face, have a disproportionate impact upon African Americans, and which are enacted with that intent, violate the equal protection provision of the Fourteenth Amendment.[122] An issue which has been the subject of some debate, however, is whether blanket prisoner disenfranchisement laws, when combined with historic racial discrimination in the criminal justice system, result in the denial of the right to vote to African American prisoners 'on account of race or color' contrary to section 2 of the Voting Rights Act (VRA). At present, the prevailing view is that the VRA does not apply to prisoner disenfranchisement laws.[123] It is argued that the broad language of section 2, which on its face could apply to felon disenfranchisement, must be read in the context of a historic policy of felon disenfranchisement and of the legislative history of the VRA.[124] An earlier line of cases, however, recognized that the right to vote is denied 'on account of race or color' where the discriminatory effect of the disenfranchisement is 'attributable to racial discrimination in the surrounding social and historical circumstances' which includes the criminal justice system.[125] Evidence established that 'criminal justice practices disproportionately affect minorities beyond what can be explained by non-racial means'.[126] In one case the plaintiffs presented statistical evidence of disparities in arrest, bail, pre-trial release rates, charging decisions, and sentencing outcomes in aspects of Washington's criminal justice system.[127] Expert evidence demonstrated that these disparities could be explained as having a racial bias.

Finally, there is the question of the proportionality of a measure which may exacerbate pre-existing marginalization. In *DH v Czech Republic*, the ECtHR noted that the differential treatment of the Roma compounded the isolation of a 'disadvantaged class' from the 'wider population'.[128] Similarly, in *Sauvé (No 2)* the majority found that disenfranchisement exacerbates the institutional and societal alienation of Aboriginal people. In the words of the majority, imprisoned Aboriginal people have

---

[121] *Sauvé (No 2)*, para 60. Unfortunately, similar arguments as to the disproportionate effect of prisoner disenfranchisement laws on Aboriginal Australians were not raised before the High Court of Australia in the *Roach* case—a case brought by an Australian citizen of indigenous descent who was serving a sentence of six years imprisonment (para 33). See also R Redman, D Brown, and B Mercurio, 'The Politics and Legality of Prisoner Disenfranchisement in Australian Federal Elections' in A C Ewald and B Rottinghaus (eds), *Criminal Disenfranchisement in an International Perspective* (New York: Cambridge University Press, 2009) 167, 202–3 (fn 139). It has been argued, however, that the Australian law disenfranchising prisoners serving sentences of three years or more has a disproportionate effect on Aboriginal Australians and constitutes indirect discrimination in violation of Australia's obligations under ICERD. See M A Winder, 'Disproportionate Disenfranchisement of Aboriginal Prisoners: A Conflict of Law that Australia should Address' (2010) 19(2) *Pac Rim L & Pol'y J* 387.

[122] *Hunter v Underwood* (1985) 471 US 222.

[123] See, for example, *Johnson v Bush* (11th Cir 2005) 405 F 3d 1214, 1234 and *Hayden v Pataki* (2nd Cir 2006) 449 F 3d 305, 322–3. In *Farrakhan v Gregoire* (9th Cir 2010) 623 F 3d 990, the 9th Circuit stated it would be necessary to at least show that 'the criminal justice system is infected by *intentional* discrimination or that the felon disenfranchisement law was enacted with such intent' (993) (original emphasis).

[124] See, for example, *Johnson v Bush* (11th Cir 2005) 405 F 3d 1214, 1227–8.

[125] *Farrakhan v State of Washington* (9th Cir 2003) 338 F 3d 1009, 1019–20 (hereafter '*Farrakhan I*').

[126] *Farrakhan v Gregoire* (9th Cir 2010) 590 F 3d 989, 1009.

[127] *Farrakhan I*, 1013.

[128] *DH v Czech Republic*, para 207.

'unique perspectives and needs'.[129] Therefore they must be included in the plurality of voices and needs which constitute society. The issue is not, as was asserted by Gonthier J in dissent, that the proportion of Aboriginal people affected is small, but the particularity of the voice which is silenced.[130] Alienation from mainstream society is only reinforced by denying imprisoned Aboriginal people the right to vote and could not be justified on the basis of the speculative policy justifications tendered by the government in support of prisoner disenfranchisement (see discussion above).

From the above analysis, it can be seen that the prohibition of racial discrimination expressed in international human rights law and constitutional provisions can assist in challenging the borders within the political community constructed through the coupling of deviancy and 'race'. Arguably, challenging prisoner disenfranchisement on the basis of racial discrimination may prove more effective than taking an approach in which deviancy alone is considered. In the American context, one writer has stated:

In the way Americans think about criminal justice, race provides the lens for perceiving the way our institutions go awry. We might not quite see the injustice of capital punishment, but we readily grasp the injustice of discriminatory application of the death penalty... And so it is with disenfranchisement as a sanction... The racial impact of the disenfranchisement means that we will finally take cognizance of an unjust institution—one that betrays a primitive conception of punishment and a deficient commitment to democratic voting.[131]

At present, this final step from the recognition of the discriminatory impact of disenfranchisement laws to questioning all disenfranchisement laws eludes most international legal and constitutional analyses.

5. Citizenship, deviancy, and 'social exclusion'

So far I have traced two intersecting borders of exclusion from membership of the political community (examined through the prism of the right to vote), namely deviancy and 'race'. In this final section, I consider a third overlapping border, namely poverty and 'social exclusion'.[132] According to the sociologist, Loïc Wacquant, historically the prison has been the means of controlling deviant and dependent populations, and today incarceration fulfils an analogous role in relation to groups rendered superfluous by the free market and the contraction of the welfare state, namely the working class and the poor African Americans of the cities. Poverty, he maintains, has become penalized. The prison warehouses and renders 'invisible'[133]

---

[129] *Sauvé (No 2)*, para 60.   [130] Ibid, para 202.

[131] G P Fletcher, 'Disenfranchisement as Punishment: Reflections on the Racial Uses of *Infamia*' (1998) 46(6) *UCLA L Rev* 1895, 1899–90.

[132] As argued by Margaret Somers, 'social exclusion' does not just mean poverty, rather it 'points to the consequences of poverty—exclusion from the mainstream of society' (Somers, *Genealogies of Citizenship*, 136).

[133] Wacquant refers to the 'invisibilization [sic] of...social "problems"'. Wacquant, *Punishing the Poor*, xxii and 288.

problem populations.[134] Wacquant's analysis is part of a broader examination of what he terms the 'new government of social insecurity' which regulates marginalized populations through the welfare and the penal systems. Social and penal policies he argues are 'two components of a single apparatus for the management of poverty'.[135] For the purposes of this chapter, Wacquant's analysis of the penalization of poverty points to the 'splint[ering] [of] citizenship along class lines'.[136] The universal rights of citizenship may be transformed into a privilege linked to perceptions of 'moral worth' (deserving and undeserving citizens) indexed to ethnicity and class, thereby undermining equal citizenship and democracy. Those who are considered morally deficient—evidenced by their 'unemployment, subemployment, and precarious work'[137] (and race)—lose their status as citizens—their right to have rights.

Margaret Somers also draws the link between a person's perceived 'market value' and the recognition of their rights of citizenship. With the rise of what Somers terms 'market fundamentalism', citizenship has become contractualized, an 'earned privileg[e] that [is] wholly conditional upon the ability to exchange something of equal value'.[138] The structurally unemployed become 'contractual malfeasants'.[139] 'Market value', she argues, has become the 'chief criterion for membership' and exacerbates pre-existing 'internal borders' such as those of race and class.[140] Those who are unable to fulfil the terms of the market contract (that is, who are unemployed or underemployed) are disqualified from full membership of the political community. Being socially excluded they are also excluded from membership of the political community and the enjoyment of the rights of citizenship. They become the 'internally stateless' superfluous population who are quarantined. According to Somers, when this market contractualism replaces a citizenship 'of rights based on inclusionary civil membership' the result has usually been some form of indentured labour or 'confinement to a poor/work house'.[141] Given the integral connection between social inclusion, full membership of the community, and the recognition of a person's citizenship rights, for Somers, Arendt's 'right to have rights' is 'the right to be fully included in a social and political community'.[142] Without both de jure and de facto membership, a citizen is unable to exercise any of the civil and political rights which they in principle hold. Recognition of rights (whether characterized as citizen or human rights) depends upon 'the foundational

---

[134] He maintains that the 'punitive turn' in the US and other 'advanced societies' (ibid, 287) is not a response to increased criminality but to increased 'social insecurity' arising from 'the fragmentation of wage labor and the destabilization of ethnoracial or ethnonational hierarchies' (ibid, 287). Wacquant's analysis is part of a broader examination of the neoliberal state's 'new government of social insecurity' which regulates marginalized populations through the welfare and the penal systems. Welfare is turned into 'workfare' (that is, the recipients of public aid must accept any job regardless of the pay and working conditions (ibid, 59)) while 'urban ills' are met with 'prisonfare' (ibid, 16–17).

[135] Ibid, 14.

[136] Ibid, 313.   [137] Ibid, 60.   [138] Somers, *Genealogies of Citizenship*, 3.

[139] Ibid.

[140] Ibid, 5. (This is not to exclude gender. See ibid, 46.) Somers argues that it therefore was not surprising that those who were most affected in the wake of Hurricane Katrina were the poor and African Americans (ibid, ch 2).

[141] Ibid, 117.

[142] Ibid, 58.

right to political and social membership'.[143] Those who are socially excluded are citizens in name only.

Clearly, Wacquant's and Somers' analysis is context specific[144] and their claims need to be viewed in light of their analytical frameworks. Wacquant, for example, acknowledges that in tracing still emerging patterns, he deliberately overstates the link between punishment and marginality,[145] and Somers emphasizes that her analysis deals with 'ideal-typical democratic and socially inclusive citizenship regimes'.[146] She is not making 'empirical claims about precise social entities'.[147] I draw on them here for the analytical link they make between recognition as an equal citizen and social inclusion. Particularly in Somers' work the 'common world', from which one is excluded and which exposes a person to superfluity, is not merely Arendt's public sphere of political equality but also the sphere of social inclusion. As noted above, Arendt notoriously distinguished the political sphere from the social sphere and restricted equality to the former, whereas today it is acknowledged that the dividing line between the two spheres is itself intensely political.[148] On Wacquant's and Somers' analysis, it is those who have been rendered socially and economically superfluous who are contained within the prison. Their consequential disenfranchisement seals and expresses their pre-existing exclusion from the community—in Somers' words, their internal statelessness. The recognition of one's rights does not merely turn on a robust conception of citizenship and political equality which counters citizenship being transformed into a privilege, but also on social inclusion, on a person's 'social standing'. The common world, exclusion from which renders a person superfluous and expendable (one instantiation of which is confinement to the prison), consists at least of the public and social spheres. The deviant who is to be disenfranchised—for whom citizenship is not a right but a privilege—may indeed be the member of the stigmatized ethnic minority but may also belong to the socially excluded. What is 'deviant behaviour' is linked to ethnicity and class (social status).

Of course one obvious and by no means novel conclusion from the above analysis is the importance of social and economic rights for political equality. Writers and advocates have long noted the inadequacy of purely formal political equality and the importance of securing economic, social, and cultural rights for political equality to be achieved.[149] International human rights law is at least in theory premised on the indivisibility of human rights—that is of civil and political rights on the one hand, and social, economic, and cultural rights on the other. However, when we turn to the prisoner disenfranchisement cases the substantive

[143] Ibid, 6.
[144] Wacquant's target is the 'new government of social insecurity' deployed by the US and other 'advanced societies' (Wacquant, *Punishing the Poor*, 287) including those in Western Europe, while Somers focuses on the US.
[145] Wacquant, *Punishing the Poor*, xix.
[146] Somers, *Genealogies of Citizenship*, 2.   [147] Ibid, 4.   [148] See Chapter 5.
[149] See Beetham, 'Human Rights and Democracy: A Multifaceted Relationship'; R Burchill, 'Democracy and the Promotion and Protection of Socio-Economic Rights' in M A Baderin and R McCorquodale (eds), *Economic, Social and Cultural Rights in Action* (Oxford: Oxford University Press, 2007) 361; and S Marks, *The Riddle of all Constitutions: International Law, Democracy, and the Critique of Ideology* (Oxford: Oxford University Press, 2000) 107.

citizenship—in particular, the enjoyment of social and economic rights—required for true political equality to be enjoyed recedes from view. The political equality which emerges is formal. As argued above this formal political equality—the mask of citizenship—is essential, but alone it is inadequate. This privileging of formal equality clearly flows at least in part from the right to vote being situated in human rights treaties which primarily deal with civil and political rights. However, it is also the product of a decontextualized analysis, a common criticism of human rights law. In the prisoner disenfranchisement cases discussed above we gain little insight into the potential relation between structural inequalities and disenfranchisement, between poverty and penality, or of the social circumstances of the prisoners. The 'serving prisoners' who are to be disenfranchised are a faceless, homogenous group in the cases. This decontextualized approach is to be contrasted with that of the Grand Chamber of the ECtHR in *DH v Czech Republic* (discussed above) where the court took into account the overall social context of the Roma population in examining whether they had been exposed to indirect discrimination.[150] In the context of prisoner disenfranchisement cases, this might involve the court taking into account the social context of serving prisoners when examining the legitimacy and proportionality of government disenfranchisement policies. There are hints of a more nuanced contextualized approach in *Sauvé (No 2)* in which McLachlin CJ noted that, to the extent that the disproportionate number of imprisoned Aboriginal people 'reflects factors such as higher rates of poverty and institutionalized alienation from mainstream society, penitentiary imprisonment may not be a fair or appropriate marker of the degree of individual culpability'.[151] International legal analyses of the rights and status of prisoners risk replicating Arendt's dichotomy of the political and social spheres. A more robust conception of political equality can be posited such that prisoner disenfranchisement is not necessarily 'viewed...as the first step toward rendering [those disenfranchised] civil and political outcasts, but as one of the final steps toward doing so'.[152]

Drawing links between social inclusion and political inclusion—and between social and economic rights and political and civil rights in the context of prisoner disenfranchisement—also raises the issue of the relation between prisoner disenfranchisement and forced prison labour. If prisoner disenfranchisement constitutes partial 'civil death' then prison labour has been said to entail 'social discrimination in the sense of exclusion from society'.[153] Throughout history, to be subjected to forced labour akin to slavery has meant disqualification from full membership of the political community: a slave is denied the right to vote. On this analysis, we can see a possible link, at least conceptually, between (forced) prison labour and the disenfranchisement of prisoners.[154] Prisoners' forced labour may reinforce their

---

[150] See para 182.   [151] *Sauvé (No 2)*, para 60.

[152] Lippke, 'The Disenfranchisement of Felons', 577.

[153] Unsuccessful argument of the applicants in *Twenty-One Detained Persons v Germany*, inter alia, Application No 3134/67, admissibility decision of the European Commission of Human Rights of 6 April 1968. (An application in relation to inadequate remuneration for work performed in detention which was declared inadmissible.)

[154] In the US context, the historic link between slavery, imprisonment, and disenfranchisement can also be drawn. See Ewald, 'Civil Death'.

inability to govern.[155] It is therefore striking to recall that hard labour imposed as a punishment for a crime is an exception to the prohibition of 'forced or compulsory labour' in the ICCPR.[156] Moreover, 'forced or compulsory labour' is defined so as to exclude prison labour not amounting to hard labour.[157] Even the 1930 ILO Forced Labour Convention[158] which requires states parties 'to suppress the use of forced or compulsory labour'[159] does not apply to the labour of convicted prisoners, provided that the 'work or service is carried out under the supervision and control of a public authority' and that the prisoner 'is not hired to or placed at the disposal of private individuals, companies or associations'.[160] That is, the Convention only protects prisoners in privately run prisons or where private entities employ or control prison labour.[161] It does not prohibit forced or voluntary labour for the benefit of the state[162] nor does it prohibit prisoners voluntarily accepting employment with private employers subject to guarantees such as the payment of normal wages.[163] In light of these and other international instruments, several writers have concluded that with certain qualifications, international law presumes 'that the state may exact forced or compulsory labour' from prisoners.[164] Yet, if the prisoner is equal in dignity with other citizens such that the fact of imprisonment alone cannot justify his disenfranchisement, then the forced labour of prisoners should also come into question. Of the international human rights bodies, to date the CESCR has been most vocal in challenging forced or compulsory prison labour as an abrogation of states' obligation to respect prisoners' right to work.[165] For the

---

[155] See K McBride, 'Hitched to the Post: Prison Labor, Choice and Citizenship' in A Sarat and P Ewick (eds), *Punishment, Politics and Culture* (Studies in Law, Politics and Society, Vol 30) (Amsterdam: Elsevier Ltd, 2004) 107.

[156] Art 8(3)(a) and (b).

[157] Art 8(3)(c)(i). See also ECHR, art 4(2) and (3)(a); ACHR, art 6(2).

[158] *Convention concerning Forced or Compulsory Labour* (Convention C29) Geneva, 28 June 1930, entered into force 1 May 1932.

[159] Art 1(1).

[160] Art 2(2)(c).

[161] C Fenwick, 'Private Use of Prisoners' Labor: Paradoxes of International Human Rights Law' (2005) 27(1) *Hum Rts Q* 249, 266–7. This leads Fenwick to conclude that prisoners who work in privately run prisons are actually better protected in international law than those in state run prisons. Contrast ICCPR, art 8(3)(c)(i) and ECHR, art 4(3)(a) which do not distinguish between prison labour for public authorities and for 'private entities'.

[162] Ibid, 276.

[163] See International Labour Conference, Report of the Committee of Experts on the Application of Conventions and Recommendations, Report III (Part IB), 'Eradication of Forced Labour' (Geneva: International Labour Office, 2007) para 59 and definition of 'forced or compulsory labour' in ILO Forced Labour Convention 1930 (C29), art 2(2)(c). Of course, in the case of prisoners, voluntary consent is difficult to establish.

[164] Fenwick, 'Private Use of Prisoners' Labor', 287 and G de Jonge, 'Still "Slaves of the State": Prison Labour and International Law' in D van Zyl Smit and F Dünkel (eds), *Prison Labour: Salvation or Slavery?: International Perspectives* (Oñati International Series in Law and Society) (Aldershot: Ashgate, 1999) 313, 320–30. Having said this, it is also argued that for many prisoners the issue is not compulsory labour, but the boredom of inactivity raising the question of prisoners' right to work (as opposed to being compelled to work). See D van Zyl Smit and F Dünkel, 'Conclusion: Prison Labour—Salvation or Slavery?' in van Zyl Smit and Dünkel, *Prison Labour: Salvation or Slavery?*, 335, 338–9.

[165] See CESCR, General Comment No 18, 'The Right to Work', adopted 24 November 2005, UN Doc E/C.12/GC/18 (6 February 2006) para 23 and CESCR, Concluding Observations for Estonia, E/2003/22 (adopted 29 November 2002) 68, 70 (para 496), 71 (para 518) (in relation to

HRC, it is a question of whether the labour is primarily aimed at prisoners' 'social rehabilitation'.[166] Arguably, where voluntary labour is integral to conceptions of citizenship, the citizenship of prisoners is undercut by international human rights principles that tolerate compulsory prison labour. Any conclusions on such a brief analysis can only be speculative, but the disjuncture is palpable between international law's increasing (albeit still circumscribed) recognition of the political rights of convicted prisoners on the one hand, and the toleration of compulsory labour (at least when controlled by public authorities) and tenuous recognition of prisoners' right to work on the other. From another perspective however, the toleration of at least partial disenfranchisement and of forced prison labour is perhaps apposite: the citizenship of the prisoner is that of the internal exile.

6. Conclusion

In this chapter I have examined the right to have rights as citizenship in the sense of membership of the political community, taking Arendt's conception of citizenship as the point of departure. For Arendt, humanity does not ground citizenship but citizenship grounds humanity such that human rights are held and protected by virtue of membership of the political community. It is in the instituted political community that equality of status is conferred and 'natural differences' subjugated. On an ideal-typical conception, rights are held and protected as equal citizens confer rights on one another with this equal status being held irrespective of personal distinctions. The citizen is the subject of rights. To be denied full membership of the political community is to be among the rightless. In so identifying the human with the citizen, and formulating humanity as citizenship, it becomes imperative that exclusions from full membership of the political community are foreclosed.

When we turn to international law, international legal approaches to the disenfranchisement of prisoners reveal that international law internalizes at least two conceptions of citizenship—citizenship as equality and citizenship as a privilege. On the one hand, citizenship is not a privilege to be earned, and thus imprisonment alone, deviancy, cannot justify disenfranchisement. On the other, the equality of citizenship is forgone if disenfranchisement is considered to be a proportionate measure. Consequently, the political equality posited by international law remains tenuous. The status of the prisoner within the sphere of the political community— his or her political place—remains insecure. If the right to have rights is citizenship, it is a precarious citizenship of potential internal exiles. The convicted prisoner

prisoners suffering penalties for refusing to perform forced or compulsory work). However, the Committee's questioning of forced labour is qualified by its also taking into account the Standard Minimum Rules for the Treatment of Prisoners (General Comment No 18, para 23 and fn 15) rule 71(2) of which provides that '[a]ll prisoners under sentence shall be required to work, subject to their physical and mental fitness as determined by the medical officer', and art 2 of the ILO Forced Labour Convention which is subject to the limitations discussed above.

[166] *Radosevic v Germany*, A/60/40 Vol II (views adopted 22 July 2005) 438, 443 (para 7.3). In relation to the ECHR, see *De Wilde v Belgium (No 1)* (1971) 1 EHRR 373, paras 89–90.

need not enjoy full membership of the political community. Yet is the relevant site of membership—relevant that is for the recognition of one's rights and status as a rights-bearer—merely the political community? At issue in the cases on prisoner disenfranchisement is exclusion from the political community, whereas Wacquant's and Somers' analysis suggests that full membership is indexed to political and social inclusion. To be in place is to be a member of (at least) the political and social community. While international human rights analyses are increasingly alive to the racialization of penality, legal analyses may exacerbate or conceal this double membership through a decontextualized approach and/or through privileging political and civil rights over social and economic rights in practice if not in theory. Finally, returning to Arendt, if the citizen is the subject of rights and the human is identified with the citizen, then to cease to be a citizen (however conceived) is to cease to be a rights-bearer. Citizenship, like nationality, cannibalizes humanity. It is such an analysis that in part prompts international human rights lawyers to articulate the right to have rights as humanity, an articulation to which I now turn.

4

The Right to have Rights as Humanity

If for Arendt, citizenship shapes and is the precursor to humanity, the claim examined in this chapter is that it is humanity which takes precedence: the human is the subject of rights. A person's 'place in the world' is that which international human rights law confers upon them—ideally as a bearer of fundamental rights irrespective of the legal status of nationality or citizenship,[1] or of a person's immigration status. Here the 'having' of the right to *have* rights is articulated in terms of entitlement to rights.[2] The basis of this entitlement, and even whether we can speak of entitlement, is of course intensely disputed.[3] On one approach, articulated by the IACtHR, humans possess fundamental rights by virtue of the unassailable attributes 'inherent' to 'human dignity'.[4] It is on the basis of a person's humanity that they are 'recognized' as a rights-holder. This has rightly been termed a more 'natural' or 'orthodox' conception of human rights.[5] A common characteristic of this conception is that human rights are not only inalienable entitlements, but those entitlements are expressed and positivized in international human rights law.[6] For others, entitlement to human rights flows purely from international human rights law: the law confers human rights and to that extent constitutes the individual a subject of human rights. Suffice it to say that this chapter explores the claim that 'humanity', as asserted in international human rights law, stands apart from and prevails over the rights of the citizen. In the words of one writer, '[w]hile international law scholars might claim that the right to a nationality is the right to have rights...the principles of human rights would maintain that being human

---

[1] In this chapter I use nationality and citizenship interchangeably in the sense of a legal status denoting membership of a state. However, for consistency and to emphasize that my primary focus is on a requisite status for right-bearing within the state, I use the terminology of citizenship except where treaty provisions or the context provide otherwise.

[2] J Donnelly, *Universal Human Rights in Theory and Practice* (2nd edn) (Ithaca: Cornell University Press, 2003) 9–10. See also discussion in M-B Dembour, *Who Believes in Human Rights?: Reflections on the European Convention* (Cambridge: Cambridge University Press, 2006) 243–7, 256.

[3] For an insightful analysis of four different approaches to human rights (the natural, deliberative, protest, and discourse 'schools' of human rights) see Dembour, ibid, 232–61.

[4] *Juridical Condition and Rights of Undocumented Migrants*, Advisory Opinion of the IACtHR of 17 September 2003, OC–18, Ser A, No 18, para 73. See also L Henkin *The Rights of Man Today* (London: Stevens & Sons, 1979) 3.

[5] Dembour, *Who Believes in Human Rights?*, 243–7, 253–6.   [6] Ibid, 256.

is the right to have human rights'.[7] International human rights law is said to have 'denationaliz[ed] protection'.[8]

The first section of this chapter briefly examines the individual as a subject of human rights in the international legal system. I then turn to the claim that international human rights norms have displaced citizenship as the legal status for entitlement to rights within states. This assertion I argue is put to the test by the institution of what might be termed 'internal borders' within states, namely the practice of interpreting human rights norms on the basis of a person's immigration status such that those whom a state has failed to exclude physically from its territory are nevertheless internally excluded. How human rights norms may on the one hand challenge, and on the other, affirm these internal borders, is examined in the context of the right to marry and the Migrant Workers Convention respectively. Finally, I explore the vexed issue of the human as the subject of rights when entitlement to an international human right has no purchase at the national level. This I examine from the perspective of the indefinite detention of stateless people.

1. The individual as the subject of human rights

In the preface to the first edition of *The Origins of Totalitarianism* Arendt asserted that anti-Semitism, imperialism, and totalitarianism had 'demonstrated that human dignity needs a new guarantee'.[9] While for Arendt this guarantee was to 'be found only in a new political principle',[10] and above all in the 'one right that transcends [a person's] various rights as a citizen: the right never to be excluded from the rights granted by his community',[11] for certain international lawyers, it is international human rights law which protects 'human dignity'. With the advent of international human rights law, individuals are recognized as holding human rights directly under international law. International human rights treaties not only impose obligations on state parties but confer rights on individuals. In this context, the individual is indeed the subject of rights. With limited exceptions, in the nineteenth century and the inter-war period, states alone were considered to hold rights under international law.[12] The treatment of individuals lay largely within the reserved domain of state sovereignty. Rules of international law for the benefit and protection of individuals imposed obligations on states without conferring rights on individuals, or limited

---

[7] D Weissbrodt, *The Human Rights of Non-Citizens* (New York: Oxford University Press, 2008) 81–2. See also M Manly and L van Waas, 'The Value of the Human Security Framework in Addressing Statelessness' in A Edwards and C Ferstman (eds), *Human Security and Non-Citizens: Law, Policy and International Affairs* (Cambridge: Cambridge University Press, 2010) 49, 66: '[w]hereas once it was held that *nationality* was the ticket to rights and protection, *humanity* or *human dignity* are now the basis for the enjoyment of most human rights' (original emphasis).

[8] *Case of the Yean and Bosico Children v The Dominican Republic*, judgment of the IACtHR of 8 September 2005, Ser C, No 130, separate opinion of Judge Cançado Trindade, para 7.

[9] H Arendt, *The Origins of Totalitarianism* (revised edn) (New York: Harcourt, [1973]) ix.

[10] Ibid.

[11] H Arendt, *The Burden of Our Time* (London: Secker and Warburg, 1951) 436–7.

[12] See K Parlett, *The Individual in the International Legal System: Continuity and Change in International Law* (Cambridge: Cambridge University Press, 2011), 13–26, 278–96.

any conferred rights to specified groups.[13] The changes wrought by international human rights law to the rights of non-nationals can perhaps best be seen when compared with the previous avenue of redress for wrongs to non-nationals, namely, state responsibility for injury to aliens. Whereas international human rights law posits rights which an individual holds by virtue of being human, in the law of state responsibility an injury to an alien is traditionally seen as an injury to the state of nationality.[14] In terms of states' obligations under human rights treaties, states are said to assume obligations not in relation to other states, but towards all individuals within their jurisdiction. They are obligations which apply irrespective of reciprocity.[15] The object and purpose of human rights treaties is 'the protection of the basic rights of individual human beings irrespective of their nationality, both against the State of their nationality and all other contracting States'.[16]

Some writers have gone further: the individual is not only a subject of human rights but the protection of those human rights and of 'humanity' per se is the overarching aim of the international legal system. Hersch Lauterpacht famously asserted that the law of nations is to be conceived as 'the universal law of mankind'.[17] The source of international law, he maintained, lies in natural law such that international law is 'indirectly under an obligation to the notion of inherent human rights'.[18] Not only is the individual a subject of international law who can hold fundamental rights apart from the law of the state,[19] but the state exists for the benefit of the individuals within it.[20] More recently, Judge Cançado Trindade of the ICJ

---

[13] Ibid, 338.

[14] *Mavrommatis Palestine Concessions (Greece v UK)* PCIJ Rep 1924, Ser A, No 2, 6, 12.

[15] HRC, General Comment No 15, 'The Position of Aliens under the Covenant', adopted 11 April 1986, UN Doc HRI/GEN/1/Rev.7 (12 May 2004) 140 (para 1). The implication of the non-reciprocal nature of human rights treaties has generated considerable debate in relation to the question of the effect of invalid reservations to human rights treaties. See ILC, 'Tenth Report on Reservations to Treaties', UN Doc A/CN.4/558 (1 June 2005) and UN Doc A/CN.4/558.Add.1 (14 June 2005) esp 19–21.

[16] *The Effect of Reservations on the Entry into Force of the American Convention on Human Rights (Arts. 74 and 75)*, Advisory Opinion of the IACtHR of 24 September 1982, OC–2/82, Ser A, No 2, paras 29–30. See also *Diallo Case (Republic of Guinea v Democratic Republic of the Congo)* ICJ, 2010 (30 November 2010), separate opinion of Judge Cançado Trindade, paras 83–84. The ICJ has also distinguished the obligations a state owes other states in the field of diplomatic protection from its obligations towards 'the international community as a whole'. These latter obligations—obligations *erga omnes*—are seen as those which touch on particularly important rights, such that 'all States can be held to have a legal interest in their protection'. See *Barcelona Traction Light and Power Co Ltd (Belgium v Spain)* (Second Phase) 1970 ICJ Rep 3, 32 (para 33). In the view of the ICJ, inter alia, these obligations derive from 'the principles and rules concerning the basic rights of the human person, including protection from slavery and racial discrimination' (para 34). Thus, respect for at least certain human rights is said to be an obligation owed by states to the international community as a whole. In the view of one writer, in contemporary international law '[f]reedom and welfare of individuals is a concern of the international community as a whole, and not only of the state of nationality'. See R Portmann, *Legal Personality in International Law* (Cambridge: Cambridge University Press, 2010) 268.

[17] H Lauterpacht, *International Law and Human Rights* (London: Stevens & Sons Ltd, 1950) 72.

[18] H Lauterpacht, 'The Law of Nations, the Law of Nature and the Rights of Man', *Transactions of the Grotius Society*, Vol 29, Problems of Peace and War, 1943, 1, 22.

[19] Lauterpacht, *International Law and Human Rights*, 4.

[20] For a reconceptualization of international legal personality from a natural law tradition which posits 'individual human beings [as] the *primary* legal persons in international law' see J E Nijman, *The Concept of International Legal Personality: An Inquiry into the History and Theory of International Law* (The Hague: Asser Press, 2004) 473 (original emphasis). Drawing on Arendt's concept of 'the

has conceived of contemporary international law as the age 'of a new *jus gentium*, focused on the rights of the human person'.[21] He states: 'the greatest legacy of the international legal thinking of the XXth century, to that of this new century, lies in the historical rescue of the human person as [a] subject of rights emanating directly from the law of nations (the *droit des gens*), as a true subject (not only "actor") of contemporary international law'.[22] Others, such as Anne Peters, have pointed to a global constitutional order in which international human rights serve as 'international constitutional rights'[23] and individuals are 'the primary international legal persons'.[24] A process is said to have begun (though by no means to have been completed) whereby 'humanity' is becoming the 'alpha and omega of sovereignty';[25] that is, 'state sovereignty has its source and *telos* in humanity, understood as the principle that the state must protect human rights, interests, needs, and security'.[26] It is argued that state sovereignty has 'legal value only to the extent that it respects human rights, interests, and needs'[27] thereby 'eliminat[ing] the basic antinomy between human rights and state sovereignty'.[28] One of the assumptions undergirding these accounts is that a 'humanized' account of international law protects the rights of the individual. International law is to be oriented towards the protection of the rights of the individual such that the individual need not be at the mercy of the protection afforded by the state.

Looking beyond international law, political theorists have advocated the emergence of 'global', 'world', or 'cosmopolitan' citizenship founded on the individual. While no single meaning can be attributed to these apparently oxymoronic terms, what is of interest is that they seek to exclude all possible exclusion, and that the human rights system is frequently and approvingly cited as fostering an emergent form of citizenship beyond the state. Jürgen Habermas, for example, posits a form of world citizenship derived in part from the normative framework of human rights. He supports a revised vision of Kant's cosmopolitan law, in the sense of establishing the legal status of individual subjects by 'granting them unmediated membership in the association of free and equal

right to have rights' Nijman argues that international legal personality is 'a natural right to political participation' (472). If a person's primary political community fails to provide the necessary conditions for the realization of the right, then its protection falls to the international community (457–73). For an 'individualistic conception' of international legal personality, see Portmann, *Legal Personality in International Law*, ch 7.

[21] *Diallo Case*, separate opinion, para 22. See also A A Cançado Trindade, *International Law for Humankind: Towards a New jus gentium* (2005) 316/317 *Recueil des Cours* (Leiden: Martinus Nijhoff Publishers, 2006).

[22] Ibid (*Diallo Case*), para 215.

[23] A Peters, 'Membership in the Global Constitutional Community' in J Klabbers, A Peters, and G Ulfstein, *The Constitutionalization of International Law* (Oxford: Oxford University Press, 2009) 153, 167–8. Note, however, that Peters and her co-authors do not provide a purely descriptive account of the process of constitutionalization. The authors' approach is 'in-between the strictly normative...and the strictly descriptive' (4).

[24] Ibid 157. See also ibid, 157–79. For Peters, Arendt's 'right to have rights' is the human right to international legal personality (ibid, 158–9).

[25] A Peters, 'Humanity as the Alpha and Omega of Sovereignty' (2009) 20(3) *EJIL* 513.

[26] Ibid, 543.   [27] Ibid, 514.   [28] Ibid, 543.

world citizens'.[29] Cosmopolitan theorists such as David Held argue that the cosmopolitan value of the equality of human beings is not a utopian ideal but is already embedded in the current system and institutions of the human rights regime.[30] Similarly, David Beetham states that in terms of standard-setting and monitoring, the human rights regime is cosmopolitan in being 'universalist in aspiration and global in its scope of operation'.[31]

The above accounts either present the international human rights regime as a crucial element in an emerging cosmopolitan world order, and/or as at least constituting the individual as a subject of human rights at the international level. Yet, we must be clear what we mean when we talk of the 'international human rights regime' or the 'international protection' of human rights. We have to ask 'where does international [human rights] law take place'[32] and what forms does the protection afforded by international law take? The international system of the protection of human rights is not dissociated from protection at the national level but points to the state as the site of its fulfilment. In terms of international enforcement, the international human rights regime is notoriously weak, as indeed theorists such as Beetham acknowledge.[33] '[I]nternational instruments and treaties of the International Law of Human Rights' may be cited as the only protection afforded 'the wretched of the earth'[34] and yet the 'views' of UN human rights treaty bodies in relation to individual communications are not legally binding on state parties.[35] Regional protection mechanisms

---

[29] J Habermas, *The Inclusion of the Other: Studies in Political Theory*, C Cronin and P De Greiff (eds) (Cambridge: Polity, 2002) 181. See also J Habermas, *The Postnational Constellation: Political Essays* (Cambridge: Polity, 2001).

[30] D Held, 'Law of States, Law of Peoples: Three Models of Sovereignty' (2002) 8(1) *Legal Theory* 1, 24–5. See also R Falk, 'The United Nations and Cosmopolitan Democracy: Bad Dream, Utopian Fantasy, Political Project' in D Archibugi, D Held, and M Köhler (eds), *Re-imagining Political Community* (Cambridge: Polity Press, 1998) 309, 316: 'cosmopolitan democracy' is not a 'utopian project' 'but is rooted in the evolving norms and patterns of practice in the life-world of political behaviour'.

[31] D Beetham, 'Human Rights as a Model for Cosmopolitan Democracy' in Beetham, *Democracy and Human Rights* (Cambridge: Polity, 1999) 136, 137. The work of these writers clearly also raises the issue of the relation between human rights and democratic politics. Paulina Tambakaki argues that while writers such as Held retain the language of citizenship and seek to reinvigorate democratic politics by recasting it in universalist terms, in doing so they nevertheless privilege human rights and undermine citizenship. Citizenship collapses into human rights. See P Tambakaki, *Human Rights, or Citizenship?* (Abingdon: Birkbeck Law Press, 2010) 48–57.

[32] See H Osofsky, 'Panel: Law and Geography' (2007) 5(2) *Santa Clara J Int L* 507, 521–4.

[33] Beetham, 'Human Rights as a Model for Cosmopolitan Democracy', 140.

[34] Judge Cançado Trindade, *Diallo Case*, separate opinion, para 236. While the *Diallo Case* before the ICJ is an example of a state party being held internationally responsible for violation of human rights in an international forum, as an individual, Mr Diallo did not have standing before the ICJ and thus remained reliant upon his state of nationality to vindicate his rights in his stead. Judge Cançado Trindade acknowledged that the mechanism for the protection of human rights in the case 'remains a strictly inter-State one, rather anachronistically' (para 21).

[35] The HRC maintains that while its views are non-binding they 'exhibit some important characteristics of a judicial decision'. General Comment No 33, 'The Obligations of States Parties under the Optional Protocol to the International Covenant on Civil and Political Rights', adopted 28 October 2008, UN Doc CCPR/C/GC/33 (5 November 2008) para 11. To try to enhance the enforcement of their decisions and concluding observations on state party reports, a number of the UN human rights treaty bodies have established follow-up procedures, including for example, the appointment of Follow-up Rapporteurs.

are notable exceptions to this.[36] The human rights system is premised on the state, the domestic sphere, being the primary site of the enforcement of human rights.[37] The state remains the primary sphere of right-bearing. Indeed, international human rights law is to be embedded within the law of the state. National law is to implement the international standard. Looking beyond questions of enforcement, the salient question for the purposes of this chapter is the content and scope of human rights norms. International human rights law may constitute the individual a subject of human rights but what does this subjectivity entail? What is the substance of the rights conferred? Who is the human of international human rights law and what is the place in the world (in the sense of the protection and quality of status) international human rights norms confer on the otherwise excluded such as undocumented migrants and the stateless within the state? In light of these questions, it is to the claim that international human rights law has displaced the legal status of citizenship as the basis of right-bearing within a state, and to the consequences of any such displacement, that I now turn.

2. The human transcends the citizen

According to some theorists, national citizenship is being transformed and the significance of the legal status of citizenship for the enjoyment of rights within a state diminished. It is claimed that 'humanity' is the basis on which a person has a 'place' within the state in the sense of being the basis of right-bearing. On examining the membership status of guest workers in Western nation states, Yasemin Soysal, for instance, concludes that citizenship in the contemporary world emphasizes 'universal personhood' rather than 'nationality'.[38] Citizenship is becoming 'postnational' in that long-term resident aliens of liberal democracies enjoy rights traditionally limited to citizens. Although the unit of membership continues to be the nation state, and thus responsibility for implementing individual rights rests with the state,[39] Soysal argues that the basis of membership today is universal personhood (human rights), with the legitimacy of those rights being derived from the 'transnational community'.[40] In Soysal's account, 'the individual transcends the citizen'—'universal personhood replaces nationhood; and universal human

---

[36] Eg ECHR, arts 34, 46 and ACHR, arts 44, 63.

[37] For example in the European context, the ECtHR has repeatedly emphasized that '[b]y virtue of Article 1 [of the Convention], the primary responsibility for implementing and enforcing the guaranteed rights and freedoms is laid on the national authorities. The machinery of complaint to the Court is thus subsidiary to national systems safeguarding human rights'. See *M S S v Belgium and Greece*, Application No 30696/09, judgment of the ECtHR of 21 January 2011 (Grand Chamber), para 287.

[38] Y N Soysal, *Limits of Citizenship: Migrants and Postnational Membership in Europe* (Chicago: University of Chicago Press, 1994) ch 8. See also K Rubenstein, 'Citizenship in a Borderless World' in A Anghie and G Sturgess (eds), *Legal Visions of the 21st Century: Essays in Honour of Judge Christopher Weeramantry* (The Hague: Kluwer Law International, 1998) 183, 193–4.

[39] See, for example, ibid (Soysal), 143.   [40] Ibid, 139–56.

rights replace national rights'.[41] Aspects of citizenship now enjoyed by citizens and non-citizens alike are those related to the person such as civil and social rights.[42]

Saskia Sassen also maintains that many 'microtransformations' are reshaping contemporary citizenship in such a manner that the 'distance' between the citizen and the state is being 'lengthen[ed]'.[43] The human rights regime is one element in this process. Others include the shrinking welfare state and the growing acceptance of dual and multiple nationality. In disassociating fundamental rights from citizenship, international human rights law not only provides the non-citizen with rights irrespective of citizenship status, but it also realigns national citizenship with international norms. Crucially for Sassen, the human rights regime is not an external regime, but instead is 'wired into national law and therewith transform[s] the right-bearing subject that is the citizen'[44] and contributes to the processes 'exploding' the boundaries of the legal status of citizenship.[45] On her analysis, the multiple transformations of the national institution of citizenship are blurring the distinction between the citizen subject and the alien subject, and leading to the emergence of new political subjects.

On its face, international human rights norms would seem to affirm the claim that individuals hold rights within states by virtue of their humanity rather than their citizenship status. The assumption of the international human rights system is that the rights contained in the various international human rights treaties are to be enjoyed by all who are within a state's jurisdiction.[46] With limited exceptions,[47] the obligations binding on states under international human rights law are to apply

---

[41] Ibid, 142.

[42] Ibid, 142–3. At the same time, Soysal recognizes that there is a dialectic between national sovereignty and universal rights—universal rights supplant those of the citizen and yet the nation state's authority is also affirmed in being the site for the realization of rights (ibid, 164–5). Moreover, the 'symbolic intensity' of the formal categories of 'alien and citizen' remains (ibid, 166).

[43] S Sassen, *Territory Authority Rights: From Medieval to Global Assemblages* (Princeton: Princeton University Press, 2006) 319. Sassen's work is not only concerned with postnational citizenship—that is with conceiving citizenship as an institution 'located partly outside the confines of the national' (305), but also with what she terms 'denationalized citizenship'. The latter remains focused on the national institutions of citizenship, but analyses how globalizing and denationalizing dynamics are transforming the meaning of the national. As the 'political power and the authority of the state have changed ... key features of the institution of citizenship—its formal rights, its practices, its subjective dimension—have also been transformed even when it remains centred on the national state' (306).

[44] Ibid, 320–1. See also 309.

[45] See S Sassen, 'The Repositioning of Citizenship and Alienage: Emergent Subjects and Spaces for Politics' (2005) 2(1) *Globalizations* 79, 88.

[46] The scope of application of human rights treaties is a contested issue. In the case of the ICCPR, states parties undertake 'to respect and to ensure to all individuals within [their] territory and subject to [their] jurisdiction the rights recognized' in the Covenant (art 2(1)). Whether the terms 'territory' and 'jurisdiction' are to be read conjunctively or disjunctively is disputed. This debate need not detain us here. For the position of the HRC, see HRC, General Comment No 31, 'The Nature of the General Legal Obligation Imposed on States Parties to the Covenant', adopted 29 March 2004, UN Doc CCPR/C/21/Rev.1/Add.13 (26 May 2004) para 10.

[47] Most notably political rights such as the right to vote and stand for election (see eg ICCPR, art 25). The right to freedom of movement within a state (ICCPR, art 12(1)) and to procedural guarantees in expulsion proceedings are limited to those lawfully residing in a state's territory (art 13). As discussed in Chapter 1, the right to enter a state is limited to one's 'own country' (art 12(4)). See also ICESCR, art 2(3) which permits developing countries, 'with due regard to human rights and their national economy', to determine the extent to which they guarantee the 'economic rights' recognized in the Covenant to 'non-nationals'. But see CESCR, General Comment No 20, 'Non-Discrimination in

irrespective of a person's citizenship, nationality, or migration status.[48] Thus, a fundamental principle of international human rights law is the principle of equality and non-discrimination. The ICCPR, for example, requires state parties to ensure and protect the Covenant rights of 'all individuals within [their] territory and subject to [their] jurisdiction...without distinction of any kind'.[49] This extends to discrimination on the grounds of the legal status of 'nationality' or 'citizenship'.[50] According to the HRC, the general rule is that each one of the rights of the ICCPR must be guaranteed 'without discrimination between citizens and aliens'.[51] They 'apply to everyone, irrespective of reciprocity, and irrespective of his or her nationality or statelessness'.[52] Even in the more contested area of economic and social rights, CESCR has affirmed that '[t]he Covenant rights apply to everyone including non-nationals, such as refugees, asylum-seekers, stateless persons, migrant workers and victims of international trafficking, regardless of legal status and documentation'.[53]

In addition to the requirement that treaty rights be enjoyed on a non-discriminatory basis, some treaties contain a general non-discrimination provision requiring states to ensure that all persons are 'equal before the law and are entitled without any discrimination to the equal protection of the law'; that is in relation to all national rights and not just those protected by the relevant treaty.[54] For example, while the ICCPR does not protect the right to a pension, differential enjoyment of accrued pension rights on the grounds of nationality will violate the requirement of equal protection before the law where the differential treatment cannot be justified.[55] In more recent treaties such as the ICRMW, 'nationality' is expressly listed as a prohibited ground of discrimination,[56] although as discussed below, 'immigration status' is strikingly omitted. Even where the terms of a treaty would appear to allow discrimination between citizens and non-citizens, as in article 1(2) of ICERD, these

Economic, Social and Cultural Rights, Art 2, para 2', adopted 18 May 2009, UN Doc E/C.12/GC/20 (2 July 2009) para 30.

[48] See, for example, *Juridical Condition and Rights of Undocumented Migrants*, esp para 118. Of course the rights which certain categories of non-nationals enjoy are supplemented by specific conventions: see the Refugee Convention; the 1954 Statelessness Convention; and the ICRMW. See also *Declaration on the Human Rights of Individuals Who are not Nationals of the Country in which they Live*, adopted by the UN General Assembly, 13 December 1985 without a vote, Resolution A/RES/40/144.

[49] Art 2(1).

[50] The HRC has acknowledged that the prohibition of discrimination on the ground of 'other status' in art 26 of the ICCPR (the right to the equal protection of the law) embraces 'nationality' and 'citizenship': see *Ibrahima Gueye & Ors v France*, UN Doc CCPR/35/D/196/1985 (views adopted 3 April 1989) para 9.4; *Adam v Czech Republic*, UN Doc CCPR/C/57/D/586/1994 (views adopted 23 July 1996) para 12.8; and *Karakurt v Austria*, UN Doc CCPR/C/74/D/965/2000 (views adopted 4 April 2002) para 8.4.

[51] HRC, General Comment No 15, para 2.

[52] Ibid, para 1. See also HRC, General Comment No 31, para 10: 'the enjoyment of Covenant rights is not limited to citizens of States Parties but must also be available to all individuals, regardless of nationality or statelessness, such as asylum seekers, refugees, migrant workers and other persons, who may find themselves in the territory or subject to the jurisdiction of the State Party'.

[53] CESCR, General Comment No 20, para 30.

[54] See eg ICCPR, art 26; *Broeks v Netherlands*, UN Doc CCPR/C/29/D/172/1984 (views adopted 9 April 1987); and HRC, General Comment No 18, 'Non-Discrimination', adopted 10 November 1989, UN Doc HRI/GEN/1/Rev.7 (12 May 2004) 148 (para 12). See also ECHR, Twelfth Protocol, art 1(1).

[55] *Ibrahima Gueye v France*, paras 9.4–9.5.   [56] Art 1(1).

provisions have been interpreted in light of states' non-discrimination obligations under general international law.[57] CERD has affirmed that 'human rights are, in principle, to be enjoyed by all persons'.[58] As an exception to the principle of equality, distinctions between citizens and non-citizens 'must be construed so as to avoid undermining the basic prohibition of discrimination'.[59] Of course, this is not to say that distinctions on the grounds of nationality or citizenship status are never permissible in international human rights law; it is a question of whether the difference in treatment can be objectively justified,[60] that is, it must pursue a legitimate aim and there must be a 'reasonable relationship of proportionality between the means employed and the aim sought to be realised'.[61] How these principles are interpreted in practice will clearly turn on the context, the particular right in question,[62] and the non-citizen's relation to the state, not to mention the standard of review adopted by the human rights court or supervisory body. In the opinion of the ECtHR, for example, 'very weighty reasons would have to be put forward before the court could regard a difference of treatment based exclusively on the ground of nationality as compatible with the Convention'.[63] Thus in one case, the court found that the differential enjoyment of pension rights solely on the basis of nationality, while pursuing the legitimate aim of protecting the state's economic system, could not be justified in the case of a permanently resident stateless woman who could not claim social security against any other state.[64] Leaving to one side the vexed issue of precisely when distinctions on the basis of nationality, citizenship, or immigration

[57] CERD, General Recommendation No 30, 'Discrimination against Non-Citizens', adopted 1 October 2004, 'Report of the Committee on the Elimination of Racial Discrimination', 64th and 65th sessions, UN Doc A/59/18 (Supp) (2004) 93, 94 (para 2).
[58] Ibid, 94 (para 3).
[59] Ibid, 94 (para 2).
[60] See *Juridical Condition and Rights of Undocumented Migrants,* paras 105, 119.
[61] See eg *Belgian Linguistics Case (No 2)* (1968) 1 EHRR 252, para 10; HRC, General Comment No 18, para 13; *Gillot et al v France,* UN Doc CCPR/C/75/D/932/2000 (views adopted 15 July 2002) paras 13.2, 13.17; and *Broeks v Netherlands,* para 13. See also UN Commission on Human Rights, 'Final Report of the Special Rapporteur on the Rights of Non-Citizens' (Special Rapporteur D Weissbrodt), UN Doc E/CN.4/Sub.2/2003/23 (26 May 2003) para 1 and CERD, General Recommendation No 30, 94 (para 4). As noted by Manly and van Waas, the fact that international human rights law permits justifiable distinctions between citizens and non-citizens, means that the provisions of the 1954 Statelessness Convention which 'guarantee stateless persons treatment on a par with nationals may still be of particular value, even in the modern human rights environment'. Manly and van Waas, 'The Value of the Human Security Framework in Addressing Statelessness', 68 (fn 70).
[62] Clearly in relation to non-derogable rights (such as the prohibition of torture) distinctions between nationals and non-nationals would never be permissible, while for some other rights denial 'would never be reasonable or proportionate' (eg freedom of thought, conscience, and religion). See J Fitzpatrick, 'The Human Rights of Migrants' in T A Aleinikoff and V Chetail (eds), *Migration and International Legal Norms* (The Hague: TMC Asser Press, 2003) 169, 173–4.
[63] *Gaygusuz v Austria* (1997) 23 EHRR 364, para 42. This approach was affirmed by the court in *Koua Poirrez v France* (2005) 40 EHRR 2, para 46 and *Andrejeva v Latvia* (2010) 51 EHRR 28, para 87. By contrast, the HRC does not treat distinctions on the basis of nationality as inherently suspect. See D Moeckli, *Human Rights and Non-Discrimination in the 'War on Terror'* (Oxford: Oxford University Press, 2008) 83.
[64] *Andrejeva v Latvia,* para 88. The applicant was a former national of Kazakhstan and the court took into account that there was 'no evidence that during the Soviet era there was any difference in treatment between nationals of the former USSR as regards pensions' (para 88).

status will be objectively and reasonably justified, international human rights law would seem to posit the human and not the citizen as the subject of rights.

3. Internal borders: humanity imperilled?

Yet the above account all too easily presumes that the legal status of citizenship has been supplanted by that of humanity. A counter-narrative, or at least one which challenges the optimism of postnational or denationalized citizenship, can also be told in which the universality of the subject of rights continues to be undercut by a person's citizenship or immigration status. Distinctions between citizens and non-citizens have generally been considered legitimate within the immigration context. However, what constitutes an 'immigration context'? For instance, is the preventive detention of irremovable foreign terrorist suspects[65] an immigration or a national security measure if nationals who also pose a threat to national security remain at liberty? Addressing such an issue, the ECtHR has affirmed that if seen as an immigration measure then 'a distinction between nationals and non-nationals would be legitimate'.[66] In the case in question, however, the impugned powers sought 'to avert a real and imminent threat of terrorist attack'[67] emanating from both nationals and non-nationals such that what was at issue was not immigration but national security. In discriminating unjustifiably between nationals and non-nationals, the measures derogating from the right to liberty were disproportionate and the derogation under article 15 of the ECHR invalid.[68] Consequently, the state was in violation of its obligations under article 5(1) of the Convention.

However, the question still presents itself: where does immigration control begin and end? A typical immigration context might be thought to concern the entry, residence, or expulsion of non-citizens—that is, their access to a state's territory. However, as I argue in this section, as states struggle to stem the flow of undocumented migrants, there is the temptation to shift border control to within their territory and institute 'internal borders' of varied forms including the interpretation and construction of human rights on the basis of immigration status.[69] In Chapter 1, I argued that borders are increasingly being 'exported', such that the experience of seeking entry into a third state may arise for some people while they are still at home. Although they are physically absent from the state into which they are seeking entry, they are legally present to the extent that immigration law is applied extraterritorially to deny their admission. My focus in this section is on the borders that may surface within a state's territory. In the words of Nevzat Soguk, a

---

[65] For example, if they face a real risk of being subjected to treatment contrary to art 3 of the ECHR in their state of nationality and no safe third country can be found.

[66] *A v United Kingdom* (2009) 49 EHRR 29 (Grand Chamber), para 186. See also *A v Secretary of State for the Home Department* [2004] UKHL 56; [2005] 2 AC 68.

[67] Ibid (*A v UK*).

[68] Ibid, para 190.

[69] In this section I draw on A Kesby, 'Internal Borders and Immigration Control: New Prospects and Challenges' [2010] 2 *European Human Rights Law Review* 176.

border can 'fold outward' and become a policy of external security control manifested in such measures as the interception of asylum seekers on the high seas. Alternatively, it can 'move inward' and take the form of 'a policy of [the] denial of rights to migrants and refugees'.[70] In the European context it has been argued that the rise in internal controls in European states is inversely related to diminishing control of external borders. Because the borders of the EU have proved difficult to control, states' focus has shifted to identifying those illegally within EU member states.[71] This may take the form of identity checks or differential access to welfare benefits. As immigration control increasingly takes place within states, it has been argued that it is no longer primarily directed at the regulation of entry into the territorial space, but into the social space; that is, into the rights and resources of society.[72] John Crowley, for example, argues that what is at stake is social, rather than territorial, namely integration into society. The aim is to ensure that a person though physically present in a state is socially absent.[73] Perhaps one of the most effective internal borders is that constructed through the legal status of 'illegality'. Catherine Dauvergne argues that, as globalizing forces assert pressure on national borders, migration law has become the 'last bastion of sovereignty'.[74] Migration laws 'make national borders meaningful for people' and are integral to constructing 'the community of insiders'.[75] However, as states are unable to assert complete control over who enters their territory, the status of being 'illegal' has become a crucial bordering process within states. She writes: '[t]he labelling of part of the population as "illegal" accomplishes this exclusion when the border itself does not'.[76] While immigration control is surfacing within states in the form of exclusion from the resources and entitlements of society, it is justified in terms of the state's right to regulate entry into its territory. In the human rights context this coupling of social exclusion and territorial control is expressed in terms of the construction of 'human rights' on the basis of immigration status. This throws into question assertions that 'humanity' is the right to have rights (and that citizenship as a legal status is becoming irrelevant for entitlement to rights). The rights of 'humanity'—here articulated as 'human rights'—are not hermetically sealed from the exclusionary practices of the border; rather, as cross-border people flows intensify, the enjoyment of rights within a state's territory may become linked to

---

[70] N Soguk, 'Border's Capture: Insurrectional Politics, Border-Crossing Humans, and the New Political' in P K Rajaram and C Grundy-Warr (eds), *Borderscapes: Hidden Geographies and Politics at Territory's Edge* (Minneapolis: University of Minnesota Press, 2007) 283, 285.

[71] D Bigo, 'Frontier Controls in the European Union: Who is in Control?' in D Bigo and E Guild (eds), *Controlling Frontiers: Free Movement Into and Within Europe* (Aldershot: Ashgate, 2005) 49, 70–1.

[72] See, for example, J Crowley, 'Where Does The State Actually Start? The Contemporary Governance of Work and Migration' in D Bigo and E Guild (eds), *Controlling Frontiers: Free Movement Into and Within Europe* (Aldershot: Ashgate, 2005) 140 and J Crowley, 'Locating Europe' in K Groenendijk, E Guild, and P Minderhoud (eds), *In Search of Europe's Borders* (The Hague: Kluwer Law International, 2003) 28.

[73] Crowley, 'Where Does The State Actually Start?, 151–2.

[74] C Dauvergne, *Making People Illegal: What Globalization Means for Migration and Law* (New York: Cambridge University Press, 2008) 184.

[75] Ibid, 17.

[76] Ibid.

immigration status bringing into sharp relief the complex issue of the relationship between international human rights law and a state's right to control the entry and residence of non-citizens. Here I am concerned with physical presence and legal absence (in the sense that territorially present non-citizens are denied, or limited in their enjoyment of, and perceived entitlement to, human rights).

Internal borders raise the issue of the dividing lines drawn by and within the law itself, both national and international human rights law. A complex interplay emerges between the territorial border and the limits—or boundaries—of the legal order. Are those who are fully 'within' the legal order only those who have lawfully negotiated the territorial border? As argued by Elspeth Guild, borders are not only those of protection separating outsiders physically from insiders but also 'the dividing line of legal orders'—the line between those who can fully benefit from the legal order (citizens in Guild's account) and those who though physically present are to be excluded from the legal order.[77] Guild argues that the border constructed 'around legal orders is for those who cannot be expelled'.[78] These borders surface within international human rights law and between it and national law. An example of a dividing line within a legal order (here the US's legal order) is explored by Linda Bosniak who has traced the ambivalence of US law to the significance of 'citizenship status' for entitlement to rights and benefits.[79] She notes that alienage—being a non-citizen—is a 'hybrid legal status'[80] subject to two distinct regulatory spheres. First, the sphere of 'borders, sovereignty and national community membership' which remains relatively unconstrained in the US context and which produces the status of aliens, and secondly, 'the world of social relationships among territorially present persons' in which aliens are 'at once indistinguishable from citizens' and the social group requiring the law's protection.[81] As argued by Bosniak, both spheres surface in the person of the non-citizen. He or she is at once subject to immigration control and 'the domai[n] of territorial personhood'[82] leading to the question as to which sphere is to prevail and when. Bosniak identifies two key responses in the US case law and academic writings. On the separationist model, exclusionary membership norms are regarded as legitimately applying at the state's border in regulating admission and community membership, but are considered to be irrelevant for the purposes of regulating relationships among 'territorially present persons'.[83] Once an alien is territorially present within a state, norms of 'personhood' and equality prevail. By contrast, on the convergence model, membership principles not only structure admission and exclusion policies at the border but the rights and benefits of aliens within the state's territory.[84] On the separationist model, immigration control largely concerns admission

---

[77] E Guild, 'The Foreigner in the Security Continuum: Judicial Resistance in the United Kingdom' in Rajaram and Grundy-Warr, *Borderscapes: Hidden Geographies and Politics at Territory's Edge*, 65, 69.

[78] Ibid.

[79] L Bosniak, *The Citizen and the Alien: Dilemmas of Contemporary Membership* (Princeton: Princeton University Press, 2006) ch 3.

[80] Ibid, 38.

[81] Ibid, 38.   [82] Ibid, 75.   [83] Ibid.

[84] Ibid, 48.

to the state's territory, while on the convergence approach it addresses membership issues which extend to the enjoyment of rights and benefits within the state's territory. When we turn to international human rights law, the border of the legal order with which I am concerned is primarily that which surfaces when a state's right to control the admission and residence of non-citizens shapes the interpretation and articulation of human rights enjoyed by non-citizens subject to a state's jurisdiction. In question is the relevance of the state's sovereign right to control the admission and residence of non-citizens to the enjoyment of the right in question (sections 4 and 5 below). A second border is that within national law dividing immigration law and international human rights law (section 6).

4. The undocumented migrant as the human: questioning internal borders

It is clear that internal borders pose a serious challenge to the claim that humanity is the right to have rights—that the enjoyment of rights within a state does not depend on immigration status. In this section, I take the right to marry as a case study of one context in which human rights law has been harnessed to challenge internal borders and reassert entitlement to the right irrespective of immigration status.

In *R (on the application of Baiai & Ors) v Secretary of State for the Home Department (Nos 1 and 2)*[85] the House of Lords held that a scheme established under section 19 of the Asylum and Immigration (Treatment of Claimants, etc) Act 2004 involved a disproportionate interference with the right to marry protected by article 12 of the ECHR. Section 19 was enacted to address the issue of marriages of convenience that are entered into for the purpose of circumventing the effect of UK immigration law. The section applies to civil marriages[86] where one party is subject to immigration control.[87] The key provision in the appeal, section 19(3), prohibits the superintendent registrar from entering in the marriage book notice of a marriage to which the section applies unless he or she is satisfied that the party subject to immigration control satisfies one of three conditions: that he has an entry clearance granted expressly for the purpose of enabling him to marry in the UK (section 19(3)(a)), or the written permission of the Secretary of State to marry in the UK (section 19(3)(b)), or falls within a class specified for the purpose of paragraph (c) by regulations made by the Secretary of State (section 19(3)(c)). The respondents to the appeal came within section 19(3)(b). At the heart of the appeal is the effect on

---

[85] [2008] UKHL 53; [2009] 1 AC 287 (hereafter '*Baiai* (HL)'). The following analysis draws on Kesby, 'Internal Borders and Immigration Control: New Prospects and Challenges'.

[86] That is, the section applies to marriages 'solemnised on the authority of certificates issued by a superintendent registrar under Part III of the Marriage Act 1949': Asylum and Immigration (Treatment of Claimants, etc) Act 2004, s 19(1). Marriages conducted according to the rites of the Church of England (governed by Part II of the Marriage Act) were therefore excluded which was held to be discriminatory in the courts below.

[87] A person is 'subject to immigration control' if they are not a European Economic Area national and they require leave to enter or remain in the UK under the Immigration Act 1971. See Asylum and Immigration (Treatment of Claimants, etc) Act 2004, s 19(4).

the right to marry of instructions issued by the Immigration Directorates which required that those wishing to obtain a 'Home Office certificate of approval' possess leave to enter or remain in the UK for six months or more and have at least three months of this leave remaining at the time of making the application.[88] The Secretary of State adduced evidence as to the advantages obtained by people subject to immigration control if they marry, and the high incidence of marriages of convenience amongst people subject to immigration control who have been granted less than six months leave to remain and have less than three months of that leave remaining.[89] The effect of the scheme is that those to whom it applies must travel overseas to marry.

The Secretary of State presented the case as a conflict between the right of individuals to marry and the right of the state to control its own immigration policy. On the Secretary of State's construction, the right to marry in article 12 of the ECHR is a qualified right, interference with which could be justified in the same way as interference with the right to family life under article 8(2) of the Convention. It was maintained that 'conditions on the right to marry that served the interests of an effective immigration policy were justifiable, provided that such measures satisfied the requirement of proportionality'.[90] The interpretation of article 12 proposed by the Secretary of State exemplifies the bordering process referred to by Crowley above, namely exclusion from society. According to Baroness Hale, '[d]enying to members of minority groups the right to establish formal, legal relationships with the partners of their choice is one way of setting them apart from society, denying that they are "free and equal in dignity and rights"'.[91] Such a denial of rights serves to filter and exclude those deemed to pose a risk to immigration policy, as also occurs at the physical border. Here however, the exclusionary (or bordering) process takes place within the state and in the form of exclusion from a key societal relation, namely marriage. The equality of status within the state is shaped, and undercut, by the imperatives of border control. By virtue of immigration status, a person's right to marry (in the state's territory), a right claimed on the basis of their 'humanity', is denied. A person does not appear in the state as a 'human' who has the right to marry but as a non-citizen subject to immigration control.

The House of Lords and subsequently, the ECtHR,[92] however disagreed with the Secretary of State's construction of the right. The starting point of analysis is not the legitimacy of the UK's immigration policy, but the scope of the right to marry, a right of a fundamental nature,[93] for '[t]he exercise of the right to marry gives rise to social, personal and legal consequences'.[94] Unlike the right to private life, the right to marry may not be qualified on grounds such as what is 'necessary in a democratic society' or the 'protection of the rights and freedoms of others' (see

---

[88] *Baiai* (HL), para 11.
[89] See *R (Baiai and Anor) v Secretary of State for the Home Department (Nos 1 and 2)* [2007] EWCA Civ 478, para 11.
[90] *Baiai* (HL), para 17.
[91] Ibid, para 44.
[92] *O'Donoghue & Ors v United Kingdom*, Application No 34848/07, judgment of the ECtHR of 14 December 2010.
[93] Ibid, para 84.   [94] Ibid, para 82.

art 8(2));[95] rather, the issue is whether an impugned interference with the right is arbitrary or disproportionate.[96] Any conditions imposed on the right to marry must not impair 'the essence of the right', namely the right to enter a *genuine* marriage.[97] Thus, national authorities would be entitled to impose conditions on the right of non-citizens to marry in order to identify and prevent marriages of convenience.[98] To require 'non-EEA nationals' to apply for a certificate of approval to marry was not 'inherently objectionable'.[99] The vice of the scheme lay in the absence of any investigation into the genuineness of the affected marriage: a blanket ban was imposed on the right to marry of those subject to immigration control, a position which constituted a disproportionate interference with the right to marry. The conditions imposed by the Immigration Directorates' Instructions, while relevant to immigration status, did not bear any relevance to the genuineness of a proposed marriage.[100] The right to enter a genuine marriage was not to be denied on the basis of immigration status.

The scheme was subsequently modified twice. The first amendment (second version of the scheme) provided that those with insufficient leave to enter or remain at the time of applying for a certificate of approval could be asked to submit further information to establish that their proposed marriage was genuine.[101] The second amendment (third version of the scheme) allowed those who did not have valid leave to enter or remain, who previously in the absence of exceptional circumstances had been refused a certificate of approval, to be treated in the same way as those who had limited but insufficient leave to qualify for a certificate.[102] All three versions were challenged before the ECtHR with the court finding that they each raised issues under article 12 as the decision to grant a certificate was not solely based on the genuineness of the proposed marriage. Under all three versions, applicants with 'sufficient' leave to remain were not required to prove the genuineness of their marriage.[103] Thus, the *Baiai* cases illustrate both the capacity (on the UK's approach) for internal borders to facilitate a denial of rights, such that the holding of a right (the right to marry) turns on possessing the requisite immigration status, and also how international human rights norms may be harnessed to assert humanity as the guarantor of, and basis of entitlement to, rights.

This is strikingly demonstrated when the above reasoning is applied to an 'illegal' resident's right to marry as was indeed the case for Mr Baiai. Although the case before the Lords solely concerned the compatibility of the section 19 scheme with article 12,

---

[95] Ibid, para 84.   [96] Ibid.
[97] Ibid, paras 82, 87–8. See also *Baiai* (HL), paras 16, 22.
[98] *O'Donoghue v United Kingdom*, para 87. See also *Baiai* (HL), para 22.
[99] Ibid (*O'Donoghue v United Kingdom*).
[100] Ibid, paras 88–9. (The court also noted that the fee imposed on applicants for a certificate of approval was sufficiently high to impair the right to marry especially as 'many persons who are subject to immigration control will either be unable to work in the United Kingdom, such as the second applicant, or will fall into the lower income bracket' (para 90).) See also *Baiai* (HL), para 30.
[101] Ibid (*O'Donoghue v United Kingdom*), paras 25, 48.   [102] Ibid, paras 26, 49.
[103] Ibid, para 88.

the judgments of Silber J[104] and the Court of Appeal,[105] considered whether the scheme disproportionately interfered with Mr Baiai's right to marry under article 12. Silber J adopted the reasoning of the Secretary of State: article 12 is a qualified right and in the case of 'illegal' immigrants, the 'balance' between the right to marry and effective immigration control must be struck in favour of the latter. His earlier conclusion[106] that the section 19 scheme infringes article 12 was said to hold only for non-nationals who have a right to enter and remain in the UK. In the opinion of Silber J, 'the fact that [Mr Baiai] was an illegal immigrant [was] of critical importance because to allow him to marry an EEA national, and thereby to obtain the right of residence in spite of the fact that he had entered the United Kingdom illegally, would undermine immigration policy'.[107] By contrast, on appeal, Buxton LJ identified the key issue as being the right to marry, not immigration control. The sole basis on which the Secretary of State had interfered with Mr Baiai's right to marry was the section 19 scheme and the vice of that scheme, namely that it inhibits marriages on the grounds of immigration status, applies equally to illegal entrants as to those with limited leave to remain.[108] On the approach of the House of Lords and the Court of Appeal, the focus is the proper construction of the right with immigration status being irrelevant to the enjoyment of the right in question. On the approach of Silber J and the Secretary of State, the right to marry is qualified by illegality of status. The ECtHR subsequently adopted an approach akin to that of Buxton LJ. The first and second versions of the scheme excluded all who did not possess valid leave to enter, including, for example, undocumented migrants. Such an 'automatic and indiscriminate restriction on a vitally important Convention right' was said to fall outside a state's margin of appreciation.[109] To impose such a blanket ban on those who fall within this category 'without any attempt being made to investigate the genuineness of the proposed marriages' impairs the very essence of the right to marry.[110]

Of course, the extent to which the scope of the enjoyment of a right may be limited on the basis of immigration status will depend on the right in question and the context in which it is to be enjoyed. As discussed in Chapter 1, the court's case law on article 8 (the right to respect for family and private life) which is subject to a balancing exercise, reveals humanity to be a potentially valuable but equally tenuous status. The right to family and private life may prevent a person from being removed from the place in which his or her 'web of relationships' is located, but there are no guarantees it will do so. Whether the right is infringed rests upon a delicate balance of factors. The point of the analysis above is that the right to marry cases signal the potential for international human rights norms to disassociate rights from citizenship and even immigration status. It is a question of

---

[104] *R (Baiai & Anor) v Secretary of State for the Home Department (No 2)* [2006] EWHC 1454 (Admin) (hereafter '*Baiai* (Silber J)').

[105] *R (Baiai and Anor) v Secretary of State for the Home Department (Nos 1 and 2)* [2007] EWCA Civ 478 (hereafter '*Baiai* (CA)').

[106] *R (Baiai & Anor) v Secretary of State for the Home Department* [2006] EWHC 823 (Admin).

[107] *Baiai* (Silber J), para 32.   [108] *Baiai* (CA), para 61.

[109] *O'Donoghue v United Kingdom*, para 89.

[110] Ibid. If a draft order before parliament is passed, then the certificate of approval scheme will effectively be abolished (see ibid, para 28 and Asylum and Immigration (Treatment of Claimants etc) Act 2004 (Remedial) Order 2010).

examining the significance of immigration status to the context and right in question. Citizenship and immigration status need no longer be a self-evident basis of differential treatment.

5. The borders of international human rights law

If cases such as *Baiai* suggest that internal borders may be challenged by international human rights law, this same law may also facilitate their imposition. In this section I explore the tension between immigration control and human rights which surfaces within international human rights law. An obvious example of this is the right to liberty and security of the person: immigration detention which conforms to the principles of legality and freedom from arbitrariness is not prohibited under international human rights law. Indeed, the ECHR specifically provides an exception to the right to liberty in the immigration context, namely, to prevent unauthorized entry into a country or where 'action is being taken with a view to deportation or extradition'.[111] While this right has been interpreted strictly by the HRC,[112] the ECtHR does not require that detention 'be reasonably considered necessary, for example to prevent [the non-citizen] committing an offence or fleeing'.[113] The 'border' of international human rights law, however, is perhaps most evident in relation to the rights of undocumented migrants under the Migrant Workers Convention. In the discussion below, I examine how within the framework of the Convention the undocumented migrant does not primarily appear—is not recognized—as the human of 'common humanity' whose rights are to be protected irrespective of immigration status, but as the transgressor of the national border thereby calling into question the right to have rights as humanity. As discussed by Dauvergne, in distinguishing between the rights of documented and undocumented migrants,[114] the ICRMW merely reinforces the paucity of the latter's rights under international human rights law and the primacy of state sovereignty over the rights of 'illegal' migrants.[115] Crucially, 'migration status' or more pertinently 'irregular or [un]documented migration status' is conspicuously absent from the prohibited grounds of discrimination.[116] While it is possible to interpret 'other status' to include irregular migrant status, the explicit reference to lack of status elsewhere in the Convention would, as argued by Dauvergne, suggest that the omission is to be read as a deliberate exclusion.[117] Moreover, under the Convention, it is domestic law which determines who is an 'illegal' migrant, while state parties are to take measures to detect and eradicate irregular migration and to

---

[111] Art 5(1)(f).

[112] *A v Australia*, UN Doc CCPR/C/59/D/560/1993 (views adopted 3 April 1997) para 9.2. According to the Committee, 'remand in custody could be considered arbitrary if it is not necessary in all the circumstances of the case, for example to prevent flight or interference with evidence'.

[113] *Chahal v United Kingdom* (1997) 23 EHRR 413 (Grand Chamber), para 112 and *Saadi v United Kingdom* (2008) 47 EHRR 17 (Grand Chamber), paras 72–3.

[114] Part III addresses the 'Human Rights of All Migrant Workers and Members of their Families' while Parts IV and V only address migrant workers in a 'documented or in a regular situation'.

[115] See Dauvergne, *Making People Illegal*, 22–8.

[116] Art 1(1). See ibid, 23.   [117] Ibid (Dauvergne).

eliminate the employment of undocumented migrants within their territory.[118] Crucially, the rights enjoyed by all migrant workers in Part III of the Convention including those 'in an irregular situation' largely parallel those already included in other human rights instruments.[119] Dauvergne thus concludes that it is through the law—not only national law but also international human rights law—that illegal status is constructed, rather than remedied.[120]

The ICRMW also perpetuates the exclusion of undocumented migrants from the public sphere. The undocumented migrant does not 'appear' in the state as the human in all the potential richness of that status—as a political, social, spiritual, productive being—but purely, by stark contrast, as a 'labourer'. Gregor Noll, for example, insightfully notes that the 'sphere' in which the undocumented migrant appears as a rights-holder under the Convention is limited to the private sphere of the *oikos*. She is the 'labourer' in the 'workplace' as opposed to the member of the *polis* and thus accorded human rights which enable her to survive in the labour market,[121] but denied the rights pertaining to the *polis* such as the right to start a trade union to 'free herself politically' from servitude.[122] On this account, the ICRMW amounts to a 'tributary transaction' between the South and the North[123] or in the words of Pheng Cheah a 'hospitality of calculative reason' in which international human rights law is tied and allied with 'economic globalization'.[124] The IACtHR's advisory opinion on the *Juridical Condition and Rights of Undocumented Migrants* in asserting that once an employment relationship has been established, a worker's rights must be recognized and guaranteed irrespective of his migration status,[125] merely affirms the human rights of the undocumented migrant as a worker.[126] On this articulation, human rights do indeed constitute the human as apolitical, social man who, to adopt an Arendtian idiom, is alienated from the world we hold in common with others in the political community. Human rights do not provide the undocumented migrant with a 'place in the world which makes opinions significant and actions effective'.[127] The 'human' of international human rights law is all too situated and particular—she is the pawn of the economic system. A person is 'recognized' by the law only as a labourer in terms of one human function: work.

Even where undocumented migrants are entitled to rights under international human rights law, deportability constrains the exercise of any human rights

---

[118] Art 68.
[119] Dauvergne, *Making People Illegal*, 25 and G Noll, 'Why Human Rights Fail to Protect Undocumented Migrants' (2010) 12(2) *European Journal of Migration and Law* 241, 256. The right to social security is an exception to this: art 27(1).
[120] Ibid (Dauvergne), 27–8.
[121] Noll, 'Why Human Rights Fail to Protect Undocumented Migrants', 260–4.
[122] Ibid, 264. Noll states that the ICRMW contains the right to join and take part in a trade union but not the right to start a trade union (art 26) (see 256).
[123] Ibid, 243 and 259–60.
[124] P Cheah, 'Necessary Strangers: Law's Hospitality in the Age of Transnational Migrancy' in A Sarat, L Douglas, and M M Umphrey (eds), *Law and The Stranger* (Stanford: Stanford University Press, 2010) 21, 58.
[125] Para 134. This, the court clarified, does not mean that the state or employers are obliged to employ undocumented migrants (para 135).
[126] Noll, 'Why Human Rights Fail to Protect Undocumented Migrants', 261.
[127] Arendt, *Origins*, 296.

which may be enjoyed. While under international human rights law a state may be required to guarantee certain rights such as the right to marry irrespective of immigration status (discussed above), this does not obviate a state's right to deport undocumented migrants. As noted by Gregor Noll, under international human rights law a state's jurisdiction is indivisible such that an undocumented migrant cannot engage a state's 'welfare jurisdiction' without also triggering its 'immigration jurisdiction'.[128] A state may owe human rights obligations to those under its jurisdiction, and that jurisdiction may be primarily territorial such that those physically present on a state's territory trigger a state's human rights obligations, but this jurisdiction is an 'all-or-nothing concept' embracing state powers which are for the individual's benefit and detriment.[129] The result, problematic both in its content and expression, is that the undocumented migrant does not 'appear' to the state as a 'human' to whom human rights obligations are owed, but as a deportable undocumented migrant. Over a person's humanity stands the film of the territorial border which colours that humanity. Noll writes: the capacity of undocumented migrants 'to appear in the *polis*, as the beneficiaries of... human rights obligations, is strictly limited to their being detainable and ultimately removable'.[130] At the national level, formal impediments in accessing legal remedies persist such as the common law rule that an employment contract is not binding when the worker is 'illegal'.[131]

In the end we are left with Bosniak's 'hybrid legal status' of alienage. The border is internalized into the human such that immigration status shapes the articulation of human rights: humanity and border control stand in constant tension.[132] Arguably, the very centrality of personhood/humanity to rights within a state, means 'humanity' has become the site of contestation over the border—humanity is the site of the border. By this I mean that the exclusions of the territorial or the externalized border shift to exclusions from human rights to be enjoyed within a state's territory. The exclusions of the 'territorial border' are internalized such that even though a person may be physically present, they are to be socially and legally absent through the denial of key rights or formal and practical impediments to their enjoyment—not least detection by the authorities and subsequent expulsion. They are taken up into humanity, here in the form of the posited universality of rights, but excepted out on the basis of immigration status. At times the internalization of the border within humanity may be resisted (as in the case of *Baiai*) and at others upheld, but the point is that the contest over the relevance of borders to rights within a state is ongoing and ever-shifting. In one case, human rights may facilitate the inclusion of the non-citizen within the legal space and in another reaffirm that he or she does not in fact belong to the community with a consequential diminution in

---

[128] Noll, 'Why Human Rights Fail to Protect Undocumented Migrants', 248.   [129] Ibid.
[130] Ibid, 250.
[131] See Dauvergne, *Making People Illegal*, 21; R Cholewinski, 'The Rights of Migrant Workers' in R Cholewinski, R Perruchoud, and E MacDonald (eds), *International Migration Law: Developing Paradigms and Key Challenges* (The Hague: TMC Asser Press, 2007) 255, 265; and R Cholewinski, *Study on Obstacles to Effective Access of Irregular Migrants to Minimum Social Rights* (Strasbourg: Council of Europe, 2005).
[132] See also Bosniak, *The Citizen and the Alien*, 140.

rights. I do not seek to resolve the tension between the convergence and separationist approaches outlined by Bosniak above, nor to present a solution to humanity's internalization of the border, but rather to highlight that humanity is not necessarily *the* answer to the question of exclusion from posited human rights, but a site of its contestation. Any attempt to fix the line separating 'citizens' rights' and 'human rights' will always evade grasp. It is contingent, constantly shifting, and contested. The relationship between a state's power to exclude (from rights and territory) and migrants' entitlement to rights on the basis of humanity is 'unstable'.[133]

This boundary to humanity cannot simply be overcome by erasing territorial borders. Even without territorial borders humanity would remain emplaced in the sense of being linked to a '*bounded* common interest' to cite Hans Lindahl.[134] Lindahl argues that all legislation, including that of international human rights law, is reflexive in that it is related to a 'self', a collective. Even within postnational legal orders premised on legal human rights enjoyed by all people in all places, such as those referred to by Habermas, or a constitutionalized legal order of 'humanity' posited by Peters, mentioned above, humanity remains 'bounded'. Lindahl writes: '[t]o posit and articulate human rights in a legal order is to *determine* the concept of humanity for legal purposes, to *limit* that which is germane from a politico-legal perspective as constituting *our* "common humanity"'.[135] Human rights cannot but constitute the legal protection of a particularized conception of humanity: as has long been noted, they cannot include without excluding[136] giving rise to contests over what constitutes 'humanity'.[137] There is a constant tension between the surface boundlessness or universality of 'humanity' and humanity's relation to a particular collective. Assertions of humanity can never be a panacea—a guarantee of inclusion in the community. The question of membership—where is the line between inside/outside, membership/exclusion—is not resolved by an appeal to humanity. Humanity, as articulated in international human rights law, is not the answer. 'Humanity' of international human rights law is never purely 'humanity', it is always, at least potentially, a bounded conception of humanity: the human of the border (whether that border is the territorial border or the border of humanity as conceived by a particular collective).

6. The border dividing national law and international human rights law: the human as the deportable alien

In the discussion so far, I have mapped two relationships between the border, immigration control, and human rights norms. On the first, international human rights

---

[133] Noll, 'Why Human Rights Fail to Protect Undocumented Migrants', 244.
[134] H Lindahl, 'A-legality: Postnationalism and the Question of Legal Boundaries' (2010) 73(1) *MLR* 30, 52 (original emphasis).
[135] Ibid, 52 (original emphasis).
[136] See, for example, ibid, 53.
[137] Similarly Lindahl argues that 'world citizenship' like all forms of citizenship 'is necessarily *emplaced* citizenship'. H Lindahl, 'Give and Take: Arendt and the *Nomos* of Political Community' (2006) 32(7) *Philosophy & Social Criticism* 881, 891 (original emphasis).

law stands apart from the border such that the human rights norm is to be enjoyed irrespective of immigration status. On the second, the border is incorporated into the norm or instrument such that entitlement to rights differs on the basis of immigration status. In both of these relationships, it is not in dispute that international human rights law applies in some form. The international norm is present and 'at work', though its content and scope may be disputed. In this final section, I examine the reversal of the first relationship: domestic immigration law stands apart from international human rights law such that it is solely domestic law which determines the rights of the non-citizen. The 'international norm' is displaced such that the question of the relationship between the international and the national barely surfaces. The 'border' of the law with which I am dealing here is the border between national immigration law and international human rights law as two distinct areas of law. In this context, the undocumented migrant is above all the deportable alien.

In principle, under international human rights law a stateless person who has entered a state 'unlawfully' is not to be indefinitely and arbitrarily detained. A stateless person possesses—in the sense of is entitled to—the right to be free from arbitrary detention.[138] As an exception to 'a most basic guarantee of individual freedom', a narrow interpretation of provisions restricting the right to liberty is to be adopted.[139] In order not to be arbitrary, detention should not exceed that reasonably required for the purpose of deportation.[140] The crucial question is whether 'action' is being taken with a view to deportation. Most evidently, deportation proceedings must be in progress, be prosecuted diligently,[141] and not be 'excessive' in duration.[142] There must be a 'reasonable prospect' of deportation.[143] Thus in one case, the Grand Chamber of the ECtHR found that the detention of foreign-national terrorist suspects did not fall within article 5(1)(f) of the ECHR as there was no evidence that there was 'any realistic prospect' of their being expelled without a real risk of being subjected to torture or to inhuman or degrading treatment contrary to article 3 of the Convention.[144] Moreover, one of the applicants was stateless and the government had failed to produce any evidence that another state

---

[138] See eg ICCPR, art 9(1); ECHR, art 5(1)(f); ACHR, art 7(1) and (3); ACHPR, art 6; and ArabCHR, art 14(1).

[139] See *Kurt v Turkey* (1998) 27 EHRR 373, para 122 and in the context of the ACHR, *Chaparro Álvarez and Lapo Íñiguez v Ecuador*, judgment of the IACtHR of 21 November 2007, Ser C, No 170, paras 52–3.

[140] *Mikolenko v Estonia*, Application No 10664/05, judgment of the ECtHR of 8 October 2009, paras 64–5.

[141] *Chahal v United Kingdom*, para 113. See also Ad hoc Committee of Experts on the Legal Aspects of Territorial Asylum, Refugees and Stateless Persons (CAHAR), 'Twenty Guidelines on Forced Return', CM(2005)40 final (4 May 2005), guideline 7.

[142] *Chahal v United Kingdom*, para 113. However, in that case detention for several years was deemed acceptable as 'considerations of an extremely serious and weighty nature' were involved such as national security and expulsion to torture (para 117). (See paras 113–17.)

[143] *Jalloh v The Netherlands*, Communication No 794/1998 (HRC), A/57/40 (Vol II) (views adopted 26 March 2002) 144, 148 (para 8.2).

[144] *A v United Kingdom*, para 167. In the case of two of the applicants, however, detention did fall within art 5(1)(f)—that is, action was being pursued with a view to deportation—as the authorities were trying to establish their nationalities and investigate the feasibility of removal to their countries of origin or to other countries (para 168).

was willing to accept him.[145] Thus, under international human rights law, at least in theory, a stateless person may not be consigned to the limbo of indefinite immigration detention. He is entitled to the right to be free from arbitrary detention. However, from decisions such as that of the High Court of Australia in *Al-Kateb v Godwin*[146] (discussed below) a different picture emerges: international law is displaced by national law. The sphere of rights to which the stateless person belongs is that determined by national law divorced from international law. National law unconstrained by international human rights norms determines who has—who is entitled to—the right to protection from indefinite detention.

Mr Al-Kateb was a stateless Palestinian who had lived for most of his life in Kuwait. In mid-December 2000, he arrived in Australia by boat without a passport or Australian visa. As an 'unlawful non-citizen', that is, a non-citizen who had entered Australia illegally, he was mandatorily detained under the Migration Act 1958.[147] On failing to secure refugee protection, he requested to be removed from Australia and returned to Kuwait or Gaza. The Migration Act required that he be removed 'as soon as reasonably practicable'[148] and kept in immigration detention in the meantime.[149] The authorities, however, were unable to secure his admission to another state. As a stateless person, Mr Al-Kateb was unable to obtain residency in a third country nor did he possess a 'right of return' to live in Gaza.[150] The judge at first instance determined that his removal from Australia was 'not reasonably practicable...as there [was] no real likelihood or prospect of removal in the reasonably

---

[145] Ibid, para 167. Keeping their detention 'under active review' was not 'sufficiently certain or determinative to amount to "action...being taken with a view to deportation"' (para 167). It was clear that the true reason for their detention was that they were suspected of being international terrorists and their presence in the UK was considered a threat to national security (para 171). Further guidance as to when a 'reasonable prospect' of removal no longer exists has been provided by the EU's Return Directive. See European Union, 'Directive 2008/115/EC of the European Parliament and of the Council of 16 December 2008 on Common Standards and Procedures in Member States for Returning Illegally Staying Third-Country Nationals', art 15. Art 15 allows for detention of a third country national subject to removal where there is a risk of absconding or the third country national hampers the removal process. Detention must be 'for as short a period as possible and only maintained as long as removal arrangements are in progress and executed with due diligence' (art 15(1)). However, a person must be released immediately '[w]hen it appears that a reasonable prospect of removal no longer exists for legal or other considerations or the conditions laid down in paragraph 1 no longer exist' (art 15(4)). Administrative detention pending deportation is time limited with an initial maximum period of six months being extendable by a further twelve months where the removal is likely to last longer due to a lack of cooperation by the third country national or 'delays in obtaining the necessary documentation from third countries' (art 15(6)). That is, administrative detention of up to eighteen months is permissible. See also *Proceedings concerning Kadzoev*, Case C–357/09PPU, ECJ [2010] QB 601 (Grand Chamber) concerning the interpretation of art 15(4)–(6) of the Returns Directive.

[146] *Al-Kateb v Godwin & Ors* (2004) 219 CLR 562; [2004] HCA 37.

[147] Section 189 of the Migration Act provides that '[i]f an officer knows or reasonably suspects that a person in the migration zone...is an unlawful non-citizen, the officer must detain the person'.

[148] Section 198(1) of the Migration Act requires an immigration officer to 'remove as soon as reasonably practicable an unlawful non-citizen who asks the Minister, in writing, to be so removed'. The officer is also obliged to remove the detainee once his protection visa proceedings have failed: see s 198(6).

[149] Section 196(1) of the Act requires an 'unlawful non-citizen', such as Mr Al-Kateb, to be kept in immigration detention until removed from Australia under s 198, deported, or granted a visa.

[150] *Al-Kateb v Godwin*, para 104.

foreseeable future'.[151] Under international human rights law, such a finding would render his continued detention arbitrary.

The majority of the High Court,[152] however, held that the Migration Act authorized the indefinite detention of an 'unlawful non-citizen' where there is no prospect of his or her removal in the foreseeable future. In domestic law, as an unlawful non-citizen, Mr Al-Kateb did not possess the right not to be arbitrarily detained. The majority reasoned that Mr Al-Kateb was required under the Migration Act to be detained until removed from Australia or granted a visa, notwithstanding that it was unlikely that he would be able to be removed in the reasonably foreseeable future. Detention, it was stated, is authorized until removal becomes reasonably practicable—and this did not require that that there be a 'real likelihood of removal in the reasonably foreseeable future'.[153] To do so would transform 'as soon as reasonably practicable' into 'soon'.[154] Detention was authorized under the Act for as long as the authorities had the purpose of removing him. In effect, the Minister and relevant officers could have the requisite purpose 'for the whole of a detainee's life'.[155] The 'law' to which Mr Al-Kateb was subject was national law, which here could not be read subject to principles of fundamental rights or to international law. Domestic law as it were displaced international law such that Mr Al-Kateb's status as a 'human'—as a subject of international human rights law—was irrelevant. According to the majority, as the provisions of the Migration Act were 'unambiguous', the statute could not be given a purposive construction or read 'subject to...an intention not to affect fundamental rights'.[156] The provisions required Mr Al-Kateb's indefinite detention 'notwithstanding that it is unlikely that any country in the reasonably foreseeable future will give him entry to that country'.[157] One judge maintained that it was 'heretical' to claim that the Australian Constitution had to be interpreted consistently with international law.[158] 'Rules' of international law, he argued, are of 'recent origin' such that to interpret the Constitution by reference to them would be to amend the Constitution.[159] '[D]esirable as a Bill of Rights may be, it is not to be inserted into [the] Constitution by judicial decisions drawing on international instruments that are not even part of the law of [Australia]'.[160] So long as the legislation is constitutionally valid, '[i]t is not for the courts...to determine whether the course taken by parliament is unjust or contrary to basic human rights'.[161] 'Tragic' as Mr Al-Kateb's position was acknowledged to be,[162] his appeal had to be dismissed. No special allowance could be made for the fact of Mr Al-Kateb's statelessness.[163]

Nor could the law be said to be punitive, and thus an unconstitutional exercise of judicial power, for it took its character from the purpose of detention namely

---

[151] Ibid, para 105.
[152] McHugh, Hayne, Callinan, and Heydon JJ.
[153] *Al-Kateb v Godwin*, para 232 (Hayne J).   [154] Ibid, para 237.
[155] Ibid, para 16 (a comment by Gleeson CJ, in the majority, stated in the context of teasing out the implications of the respondent's interpretation of the Act).
[156] Ibid, para 33 (McHugh J). See also para 241 (Hayne J); 298 (Callinan J).
[157] Ibid, para 33.
[158] Ibid, para 63 (McHugh J).   [159] Ibid, para 68.   [160] Ibid, para 73.
[161] Ibid, para 74   . [162] Ibid, para 31.   [163] Ibid, para 301.

to ensure the non-citizen was available for deportation or to prevent him or her from entering Australia or the Australian community.[164] As the purpose of the detention was non-punitive, indefinite detention (even for life) did not render the detention punitive and an unconstitutional exercise of judicial power. If indefinite detention is the result, 'it comes about because the non-citizen came to or remained in [Australia] without permission';[165] that is, as someone who did not possess the right to enter Australia, detention for the purpose of removal, up to and including indefinite detention, could not be said to be punitive. In the opinion of one judge, the choice was not one between 'detention and freedom': '[t]he detention to be examined is not the detention of someone who, but for the fact of detention, would have been, and been entitled to be, free in the Australian community'.[166] To hold that parliament cannot detain unlawful non-citizens pending deportation 'would mean that such persons, by their illegal and unwanted entry, could become de facto Australian citizens'.[167]

Thus, at the national level, a stateless man could legitimately be detained indefinitely—even for life. Any redress would need to be sought at the international level. In the words of one judge, parliament would need to answer to 'the international bodies who supervise human rights treaties'[168]—international bodies, it is to be recalled, which cannot enforce their opinions. The sphere of the rights of 'humanity', inflected here in the stateless person, is limited to the international level. Lawful presence or citizenship status and not humanity are the bases on which rights are recognized in national law. Humanity alone does not constitute a person as a subject of rights. Mr Al-Kateb was neither a citizen nor a 'lawful non-citizen' with the right to liberty and the right to enter. Nor was he the 'human'—the bearer of human rights (here the right to be free from arbitrary detention). As an unlawful non-citizen, Mr Al-Kateb could be 'legitimately treated as not being [a] full beare[r] of human rights'.[169] He was situated in the sphere in between international human rights law, of the rights of humanity (entailing freedom from arbitrary detention) on the one hand, and national law, the rights of the citizen and 'lawful non-citizen' on the other. Neither a citizen, a lawful entrant, nor a human. He is a superfluous subject who to borrow from Arendt is 'the kind that [is] put in concentration camps by [his] foes and in internment camps by [his] friends'.[170] From *Al-Kateb*, it is the citizen and lawful entrant who emerge as the subject of rights (at least of the right not to be arbitrarily detained).

Cases such as *Al-Kateb* affirm that '[m]ore than any other legal subject, the foreigner perches precariously on [the] borders [of national/international law], seeking entry *qua* human being into the normative terrain of human rights discourse, yet too often denied shelter under the rights of citizenship precisely because she

---

[164] Ibid, para 45 (McHugh J). See also para 255 (Hayne J).　[165] Ibid, para 268.

[166] Ibid, para 219 (Hayne J).

[167] Ibid, para 46 (McHugh J). See also para 262 (Hayne J); para 289 (Callinan J).

[168] Ibid, para 48 (McHugh J).

[169] D Dyzenhaus, *The Constitution of Law: Legality in a Time of Emergency* (Cambridge: Cambridge University Press, 2006) 165.

[170] H Arendt, 'We Refugees' in J Kohn and R H Feldman (eds), *The Jewish Writings* (New York: Schocken Books, 2007) 264, 265.

is not a citizen. Sometimes lucky, sometimes not'.[171] In one domestic system, her detention may be limited under the law,[172] in another indefinite.[173] The limits of 'humanity' in cases such as *Al-Kateb* have led writers such as Dauvergne to turn from international human rights law and place their hope in the 'rule of law'— namely a rule of law reconceived as 'unhinged' from the nation.[174] This is undeniably a creative approach, but it risks simply shifting the question of humanity to a new site of contestation. The point is that 'humanity' is an unmoored lifeboat in which the shipwrecked can be cast adrift.

7. Conclusion

The articulation of the right to have rights as humanity gives voice to the imperative that human rights are to be held irrespective of nationality or citizenship status. They are referable to the status of being human. For some international human rights lawyers and advocates, this necessity is encapsulated within international human rights law. The subject of human rights is not the national or the citizen, but the human. Rights are to be held by 'all individuals within [a state's] territory and subject to its jurisdiction...without distinction of any kind'.[175] Humanity is indeed a valuable status. International human rights norms may be invoked to challenge and dismantle internal borders, that is, attempts to construct human rights on the basis of immigration status, such that the right to marry is to be enjoyed by the citizen along with the undocumented migrant. A person's status as a rights-bearer need not be defined by their legal relation to the state of residence. Here international human rights norms stand apart from the imperatives of the territorial border and immigration control. Yet the place in the world humanity confers is far from stable: human rights norms cannot (leaving to one side whether they should not) erase the spectre of the territorial border and the significance of citizenship and immigration status for both entitlement to, and the enjoyment of, human rights. Indeed, as was argued in the context of the Migrant Workers Convention, international human rights law may internalize the exclusions of the border contributing to the construction of the 'illegal status' of the undocumented migrant worker. At present, the non-citizen remains a 'hybrid legal status'[176] at once inhabiting the sphere of humanity (the human as the subject of rights) and that of the border (the citizen or legal entrant as the subject of rights). Cases such as *Al-Kateb* reveal that the human is precariously balanced on the border between the international and the national: from the perspective of international law, he is

[171] A Macklin, 'The State of Law's Borders and the Law of States' Borders' in D Dyzenhaus (ed), *The Unity of Public Law* (Oxford: Hart Publishing, 2004) 173, 199.
[172] See *Zadvydas v Davis* (2001) 533 US 678.
[173] See further HRC, General Comment No 15, para 3.
[174] Dauvergne, *Making People Illegal*, 175–85. In relation to the rule of law, see also Dyzenhaus, *The Constitution of Law*.
[175] ICCPR, art 2(1).
[176] Bosniak, *The Citizen and the Alien*, 38.

recognized as the bearer of rights on the basis of humanity, and yet at the national level, reduced to the deportable alien and denied recognition as the subject of rights. Thus, humanity is not the answer to the right to have rights but the site of its contestation. If a person's entitlement to human rights is precarious, is it then a question of their claiming and enacting the rights they have been denied? Is the right to have rights best articulated in terms of the politics of human rights? This is the subject of Chapter 5.

5

The Right to have Rights as the Politics of Human Rights

How can a person 'have' rights when denied the requisite status on which entitlement is founded? Are human rights merely the rights of the rightless (the rights for example of the indefinitely detained stateless person) or of those who already have rights (the rights of the citizen) and thus meaningless? Thinking with and beyond Arendt, contemporary political philosophers have reinterpreted the right to have rights as the right to politics conceived as the rightless taking up, claiming, and enacting the rights they have been denied. It is not a question of being 'recognized' as a rights-bearer by virtue of a conferred legal or political status, but of demonstrating that one is a subject of rights. In this context, a 'place in the world' is not a given—that which is conferred by the law from above on the rightless—but that which the rightless create for themselves. They are not 'emplaced' but emplace themselves within the order from which they have been excluded thereby challenging the order's rules of inclusion. The focus in this chapter thus shifts to a more performative understanding of human rights and of the 'having' of the right to *have* rights. The analysis centres less on law and more on the claims of political philosophy as to how the right to have rights is to be interpreted.

Of the many writers engaged with the question of the right to have rights in the contemporary context, it is the work of Jacques Rancière which speaks most directly and comprehensively to the question of the 'having' of the right to have rights, which on his account is also the question of the 'subject' of rights.[1] If for Arendt, rights belong to a definite, predetermined subject (most notably the citizen, the subject-as-citizen) then for Rancière, rights are the rights of the ever-fluctuating subject of politics. This subject is neither apolitical man nor Arendt's citizen, but the subject who exists in the interval between identities—between man and the citizen—and plays one off against the other. Whoever engages in a polemic of putting inscribed rights to the test, of enacting denied equality, of invoking denied rights and building a case for their extension, is the subject of rights. A limitless spectrum of subjects thereby emerges. In this way, Rancière seeks to overcome exclusions from the subject of rights (section 2). Nevertheless,

---

[1] In particular J Rancière, 'Who is the Subject of the Rights of Man?' (2004) 103(2/3) *South Atlantic Quarterly* 297; *On the Shores of Politics*, L Heron (trans) (London: Verso, 1995); and *Disagreement: Politics and Philosophy*, J Rose (trans) (Minneapolis: University of Minnesota Press, 1999).

Rancière's account, I will argue, is not immune from exclusion (section 3). We are once again confronted with a constitutive limit on right-bearing. Moreover, we cannot simply escape from law into a Rancièrian politics of contestation and dissensus. Rancière's analysis may be instructive in pointing to the limits of national and international human rights law, but it does not absolve us from grappling with the thorny issue of the politics to be exercised within the law. Indeed, the 'having' of the right to have rights depends at least in part upon such engagement (section 4).

1. Arendt: the problem of the paradox of human rights

Cases such as *Al-Kateb v Godwin* discussed in Chapter 4[2] leave us with a seemingly inescapable dilemma: human rights, such as the right to liberty of the person, are either the rights of the rightless (those who may be indefinitely detained) or they are the rights of those who already 'have' rights, the citizen, or more broadly in *Al-Kateb*, the 'lawful non-citizen', thus affirming Arendt's analysis of what she terms the 'paradox' of human rights. The paradox she poses is that the rights of man are either the rights of abstract, unpoliticized man—the rights of those who have no rights—and thus a 'void' or nothing. Or they are the rights of the citizen—of those who already have rights—and therefore a tautology.[3] It will be recalled that for Arendt human rights are not a given flowing from an individual's abstract 'humanity' but an artefact associated with membership of a political community. As Arendt famously remarked: '[t]he world found nothing sacred in the abstract nakedness of being human'.[4] Stripped of the legal and political status of their former citizenship, and thus reduced to the status of 'a human being in general',[5] the stateless found themselves to have lost all human rights: to be rightless. The loss of their human rights coincided with their reduction to the very status for which human rights—those inalienable rights which are said to be independent of government—are supposed to provide. Arendt wrote:

The paradox involved in the loss of human rights is that such loss coincides with the instant when a person becomes a human being in general—without a profession, without a citizenship, without an opinion, without a deed by which to identify and specify himself—*and* different in general, representing nothing but his own absolutely unique individuality which, deprived of expression within and action upon a common world, loses all significance.[6]

Human rights for Arendt deal with 'an "abstract" human being', who exists nowhere.[7] They are a 'mere abstraction'.[8] The true subject of rights is the citizen.

---

[2] *Al-Kateb v Godwin & Ors* (2004) 219 CLR 562; [2004] HCA 37. See Chapter 4, section 6.
[3] Rancière, 'Who is the Subject of the Rights of Man?', 302.
[4] H Arendt, *The Origins of Totalitarianism* (revised edn) (New York: Harcourt, [1973]) 299.
[5] Ibid, 302.   [6] Ibid (original emphasis).   [7] Ibid, 291.
[8] Rancière, 'Who is the Subject of the Rights of Man?', 298.

2. Rancière: the subject of rights as the subject of politics

Are human rights then merely the rights of the rightless—a void—or the rights of the citizen and thus a tautology as Arendt suggests? To find a way out of this paradox, we must, Rancière insists, reconceive the subject of rights as the subject of politics, however, of a politics which differs fundamentally from that espoused by Arendt—a politics without borders of the political, and thus without predetermined limits of the subject of rights.

Both Rancière and Arendt can be interpreted as conceiving the right to have rights as the right to politics. However (at least on a Rancièrian approach to Arendt), Rancière and Arendt diverge as to who enjoys this right (who is entitled to engage in politics)—who is considered to be a speaking being who can claim rights. Rancière construes Arendt as confining politics to a predetermined sphere, the public sphere of political community,[9] such that those who are 'alienated' from it or denied access (who lack the requisite legal and political status) such as the stateless, are 'superfluous' and without a voice. Their 'bare life' cannot be 'political'; consequently their actions are ineffective. For Arendt, politics is the practice of a constituted subject–citizen: to be recognized as a speaking being one must be a participant in the community of equals. The speech and actions of non-citizens are without effect: they are not recognized. They have lost their place in the world in which opinions are significant and actions effective. They belong to the private, social sphere of 'necessity' and are unable to appear in the public sphere and claim rights. Thus, as noted above, for Arendt the paradox of human rights is that they are the rights of the unpoliticized, bare human being.[10] As stated by Andrew Schaap, on Arendt's approach, stateless people's struggle for human rights is not a political struggle as it consists in gaining the civil rights necessary to then participate in politics. In being 'deprived of public appearance', they are deprived of politics and unable to claim the right to have rights.[11] Theirs is a struggle for liberation and thus for 'social' and not 'political freedom'.[12]

For Rancière, politics is not confined to a sphere but is a 'process'.[13] He rejects all borders of politics—borders between the public and the private, the political and the social. Indeed, politics is about questioning any seemingly 'given' border between political and private life.[14] The subject of rights is not a fixed subject—one dependent upon a conferred legal and political status (Arendt's citizen)—but the ever-fluctuating subject of politics. This is not to deny that far more sympathetic readings of Arendt have been adopted by other theorists. Indeed, Arendt's concept of action has been invoked in support of a politics of human rights and of the rightless creating rights through democratic action and asserting a place for themselves

---

9 Ibid, 298–9.   10 Ibid, 298.
11 A Schaap, 'Enacting the Right to have Rights: Jacques Rancière's Critique of Hannah Arendt' (2011) 10(1) *European Journal of Political Theory* 22, 33, 39.
12 Ibid, 39 and Rancière, 'Who is the Subject of the Rights of Man?', 298.
13 Ibid (Rancière), 305.   14 Ibid, 303.

within the community.[15] As will be recalled, 'action' was one of Arendt's key polit-ical concepts. She argued that it is the means by which a person 'inserts' him- or herself into the world[16] and is the basis of political community. There are sug-gestions in Arendt's work that the *polis*—the political community—is not purely institutional; rather it emerges wherever the people 'ac[t] and spea[k] together' wherever they happen to be:[17] '[w]herever you go, you will be a *polis*'.[18] For the purpose of this chapter, however, I will be examining Rancière's rearticulation of the right to have rights and his approach to Arendt. The significance of Rancière's work lies in his grappling with the gap between statuses—between 'man' and the 'citizen'. Those writers who appropriate Arendt in favour of a politics of human rights, such as Étienne Balibar, do so by identifying man with the citizen in favour of a 'universal right *to politics*'.[19] As will be seen, the force of Rancière's work lies in his conception of politics as mediating between statuses.

Foundational to Rancière's analysis, and what makes it so attractive in light of cases such as *Al-Kateb*, is that the subjects of politics/of rights are the very peo-ple who lack the qualification and 'status' to hold rights. Rights are held by those who, though lacking all qualification to do so, take them up, claim, and enact them.[20] To be a subject of rights does not depend on possessing a predetermined legal status, the 'citizen' of constitutional texts or the particular 'human' of inter-national human rights law, or on being qualified to speak[21] as a citizen. Indeed, such predetermined 'roles' or parts do not constitute the subject of politics but of what Rancière terms the 'police'. What would usually be considered to consti-tute politics—such as 'the set of procedures whereby the aggregation and consent of collectivities is achieved, the organization of powers, the distribution of places and roles, and the systems for legitimizing this distribution'[22]—Rancière terms the 'police'. The 'police' is the order or logic which determines a party's share in the order—that is, who is recognized as a political actor, which activity is 'visible',[23] or what 'having a part' means. Rancière states that the police 'is an order of the visible and the sayable that sees that a particular activity is visible and another is not, that

[15] See, for example, É Balibar, *We, the People of Europe?: Reflections on Transnational Citizenship*, J Swenson (trans) (Princeton: Princeton University Press, 2004) 117–20; É Balibar, 'What is a Politics of the Rights of Man?' in É Balibar, *Masses, Classes, Ideas: Studies on Politics and Philosophy Before and After Marx* (New York: Routledge, 1994) 205; É Balibar, 'Is a Philosophy of Human Civic Rights Possible? New Reflections on Equaliberty' (2004) 103(2/3) *South Atlantic Quarterly* 311; and M Krause, 'Undocumented Migrants: An Arendtian Perspective' (2008) 7(3) *European Journal of Political Theory* 331. See further J D Ingram, 'What is a "Right to have Rights"? Three Images of the Politics of Human Rights' (2008) 102(4) *American Political Science Review* 401, 410–13. (Ingram draws on Arendt but argues we need to go beyond her.)

[16] H Arendt, *The Human Condition* (2nd edn) (Chicago: University of Chicago Press, 1998) 176–7.

[17] Ibid, 198.

[18] Ibid.   [19] Balibar, 'What is a Politics of the Rights of Man?', 212 (original emphasis).

[20] See also Engin Isin's work on 'acts of citizenship'. Isin, citing Arendt, Balibar, and Rancière, is concerned with 'those moments when, regardless of status and substance, subjects constitute themselves as citizens—or, better still, as those to whom the right to have rights is due'. E F Isin, 'Theorizing Acts of Citizenship' in E F Isin and G M Nielsen (eds), *Acts of Citizenship* (London: Zed Books, 2008) 15, 18.

[21] Rancière, *Disagreement*, 27.

[22] Ibid, 28.   [23] Ibid, 29.

this speech is understood as discourse and another as noise'.[24] For example, it is 'police logic' that construes the workplace as a 'private space' in which the worker's part is limited to that of remuneration for work and which excludes him or her from those who are 'visible' and can be heard in the 'public domain'.[25] In line with Rancière's erasure of the borders of politics, the 'police' is not to be confused with the 'state apparatus'; rather it refers to a logic which permeates all of social relations including relations in the private sphere.[26]

Rancière presents the police order as a regime of 'consensus', not in the sense that it is the outcome of deliberation, but in the sense of a regime in which there is no 'supplement', no 'surplus subjects', for each 'part' has its allocated role and place. Politics is the rupture of this logic by a surplus subject—a 'supplementary part'— 'the part of those who have no part'.[27] On a Rancièrian politics, the only qualification of the subject of politics, that is, of rights, is the fact of not belonging, of not being counted within the parts which are considered to constitute the community (what Rancière terms the 'miscount').[28] This supplementary part, this subject of politics, is above all the collective subject (the true *demos*) that emerges through collective action.[29] To adopt Rancière's terminology, politics is a process of 'political subjectivization'.[30] Thus, Rancière presents us with a novel conception of politics as the process by which these surplus subjects struggle 'to be seen and heard as speaking subjects within a social order that denies that they are qualified to participate in politics'.[31] Those 'who have no right to be counted as speaking beings make themselves of some account'.[32] As will be seen, it is a politics which consists in disrupting the ruling order by lodging a dispute. Politics take place when the 'configuration' of the police order is disrupted such that what 'has no place', 'had no business being seen' becomes 'visible'.[33] By contrast for Arendt, those who are not citizens, who do not belong to the community of equals remain invisible and 'have no place from which to be seen'.[34] They are the superfluous beings indefinitely detained in the camp and who remain 'without words'.

The place of Rancière's political subject—or more accurately of the process of subjectivization (of the emergence of a political subject)—is 'an interval or a gap',[35] an 'in-between',[36] the 'non-place' between man and the citizen. Clearly, Rancière's use of the 'non-place' is to be distinguished from my use of the 'non-place' in terms

[24] Ibid.   [25] Ibid.   [26] Ibid.
[27] Rancière, 'Who is the Subject of the Rights of Man?', 305.
[28] Rancière, *Disagreement*, 6.
[29] Rancière, 'Who is the Subject of the Rights of Man?', 304 and T May, *Contemporary Political Movements and the Thought of Jacques Rancière: Equality in Action* (Edinburgh: Edinburgh University Press, 2010) 12.
[30] Ibid (Rancière), 305.
[31] Schaap, 'Enacting the Right to have Rights', 30.
[32] Rancière, *Disagreement*, 27. See also J Rancière, 'Ten Theses on Politics' (2001) 5(3) *Theory and Event* (electronic journal), para 21. He writes: '[p]olitics is first and foremost an intervention upon the visible and the sayable'.
[33] Ibid (*Disagreement*), 29–30.
[34] Rancière, 'Ten Theses on Politics', para 26.
[35] J Rancière, 'Politics, Identification, and Subjectivization' (1992) 61 *October* 58, 62.
[36] Ibid, 61.

of the containment of non-nationals within their state of nationality discussed in Chapter 1. It is also to be distinguished from that employed by writers in other disciplines to refer to a particular, and usually negative conception of physical space. Most famously, Marc Augé has suggested that '[i]f a place can be defined as relational, historical and concerned with identity, then a space which cannot be defined as relational, or historical, or concerned with identity will be a non-place'.[37] In Augé's analysis, the non-place is the space of supermodernity[38]—of supermarkets and airport lounges—a 'fleeting', 'ephemeral' world of the 'solitary individua[l]'[39] and of the space of the traveller.[40] Non-places are characterized by the absence of relationship and identity. Others have referred to 'abject spaces' such as frontier zones and detention centres, spaces in which certain people are 'render[ed] ... as invisible and inaudible', that is as 'inexistent'.[41] Common to these conceptions is a correlation between physical space and absence of relationship: Augé's places of supermodernity are those where relationships between people are absent or minimal, while the 'abject' space of the detention centre has been termed the 'the spatial expressio[n] of the foreigner without legal status'.[42] Although there may certainly be a correlation between the physical space of the 'non-part' and their lack of voice—their exclusion from the order—the concept of the 'non-place' in Rancière's work, as in that of many other French writers, serves as a 'conceptual tool'[43] for critical thought, namely for thinking 'through whatever lies outside of the order that is actually in place'.[44] It is the 'non-place' between statuses and identities, between 'man' and the 'citizen', 'humanity and inhumanity, citizenship and its denial'.[45] It is the gap of inequality and the denial of what should be included. But this is a different conception of the gap or interval between statuses to that which emerges from the reasoning of the High Court of Australia in *Al-Kateb*. In that case, it will be recalled, a gap arose between the 'human' of the international human rights instruments who is to enjoy freedom from arbitrary detention, and Mr Al-Kateb's plight of indefinite detention. At the same time he was not a citizen or a 'lawful non-citizen'. He was neither the subject of human rights nor the subject-citizen. He was situated in the interval between the two statuses. On the reasoning of the High Court, in belonging to neither the human nor the citizen, he was able to be detained indefinitely: the gap between man and the citizen found

[37] M Augé, *Non-places: An Introduction to Supermodernity* (2nd edn) (London: Verso, 2008) 63.
[38] Supermodernity is characterized by 'excess' (ibid, 24) and 'overabundance'—namely, an 'overabundance of events', which Augé terms the '"acceleration" of history' (ibid, 23); 'spatial overabundance' (the shrinking of space) (see ibid, 25–9); and 'the individualization of references' (the rise of the individual) (ibid, 33) (see ibid, 29–32).
[39] Ibid, 63.
[40] Ibid, 70.
[41] E F Isin and K Rygiel, 'Abject Spaces: Frontiers, Zones, Camps' in E Dauphinee and C Masters (eds), *The Logics of Biopower and the War on Terror: Living, Dying, Surviving* (New York: Palgrave Macmillan, 2007) 181, 189.
[42] P Nyers, 'Abject Cosmopolitanism: The Politics of Protection in the Anti-Deportation Movement' (2003) 24(6) *Third World Quarterly* 1069, 1080.
[43] B Bosteels, 'Nonplaces: An Anecdoted Topography of Contemporary French Theory' (2003) 33(3/4) *Diacritics* 117, 119.
[44] Ibid, 118.
[45] Rancière, 'Politics, Identification, and Subjectivization', 61.

its physical expression in indefinite detention thereby seeming to confirm Arendt's analysis of the paradox of human rights—that human rights are the rights of the rightless or the rights of the citizen.

By contrast, for Rancière, the gap between man and the citizen is not an affirmation of the vacuity of human rights but is essential for a subject of rights, that is, of politics, to emerge. The non-place (the interval between identities, such as man and the citizen) is not characterized by the absence of relationship as per Augé or the rightlessness of man resulting in indefinite detention (*Al-Kateb*), but instead is the position from which the relationship of the excluded to the included is launched. The 'having' of the right to have rights turns on negotiating the relation between the 'non-place' (between statuses) and the 'place' (of visibility and political speech) such that what was invisible is seen. As will be discussed below, the 'non-place' is the site of a 'polemical demonstration'[46] by which the excluded group, the part with no part, comes to represent and stand in the place of the universal. Thus for Rancière the gap between man and the citizen does not demonstrate the 'illusion' of human rights such that man has to be collapsed into the citizen—the rights of man become the rights of the citizen as per Arendt; rather, it is in the very failure of human rights—in their exclusions—that their potential lies. The non-place is productive and integral to politics as it opens a space for political subjectivization which transforms the 'gap', the 'non-relationship', the void, into a relation. The gap between man and the citizen, which in *Al-Kateb* revealed the impotency of the law to protect the stateless from indefinite detention, is here transformed into the true site of politics and right-bearing. For this to be so, as noted above, Rancière contends that we must reconceive the subject of rights as the subject of politics. The seemingly superfluous subject who lies in between statuses of the man and the citizen—is paradoxically *the* subject of rights.

2.1 Lodging a dispute: asserting and verifying equality

Thus, on Rancière's account, politics is a particular 'mode of acting'[47] enacted by a subject who has 'no part' in the community and yet inserts itself into the order from which it has been excluded.[48] The subject of human rights is not he who possesses rights (the citizen on Arendt's account or the 'human' of international human rights law) but the collective subject who takes written declarations of human rights which posit equality (make equality visible)[49] and puts them to the test and enacts them. The gap, the non-relation, between statuses such as between the stateless and the human, and the stateless and the citizen, is identified and

---

[46] This is demonstrated by Bosteels' translation of a passage from the French version of *On the Shores of Politics* (*Aux bords du politique* 87) which Bosteels states is omitted from the English translation. Polemical statements 'allow not only the manifestation of a logical fissure which itself uncovers the tricks of social inequality. But they also allow the articulation of this fissure as a relation, by transforming the logical non-place into the place of a polemical demonstration'. Bosteels, 'Nonplaces', 133. See also Rancière, *Disagreement*, 89 discussed further below.
[47] Rancière, 'Ten Theses on Politics', Thesis 1.
[48] Rancière argues that Arendt's approach leaves us blind to those who have no part (ibid, para 26).
[49] Rancière, 'Who is the Subject of the Rights of Man?', 303.

brought into question through a polemical construction which sets inclusion and exclusion provocatively alongside one another.

That the site of the subject of rights is the interval between statuses is precisely what escapes Arendt (and also Giorgio Agamben) who, Rancière maintains, collapse the interval between man and the citizen and turn the subject of rights into the 'single', definite, permanent subject, rather than the fluctuating subject of Rancière's politics.[50] On Arendt's approach, the rights of man become the rights of the citizen, 'the rights attached to a national community as such':[51] 'man and the citizen are the same liberal individual enjoying the universal values of human rights embodied in the constitutions of our democracies'.[52] The source and the bearer of the rights are one and the same such that a person can only use the rights he or she formally possesses (which are declared in their name, for example in national law or international human rights law).[53] As the human in whose name rights are declared does not in practice enjoy rights, human rights (on Arendt's account) are the rights of the rightless or the rights of the citizen. For Rancière, a linear, simple relationship cannot be drawn between a subject of rights and the 'having' of rights (a subject of rights is he in whose name rights are articulated and who enjoys them); rather, the relationship is more complicated. Rancière states: 'the Rights of Man are the rights of those who have not the rights that they have and have the rights that they have not'.[54] One example he gives is Olympe de Gouges' famous statement during the French Revolution that 'if women are entitled to go to the scaffold, they are entitled to go to the Assembly'.[55] This provocative phrase opens to dispute who is included within the 'men' proclaimed to be 'born free and equal' in the Declaration of Rights,[56] and who is a citizen. It was clear that women were arbitrarily deprived of the rights the Declaration grants to all 'free and equal' men.[57] Yet in being sentenced to death on political grounds as 'enemies of the revolution', alongside men, the women showed that they were political beings[58]—that they had a part. By their actions, the women showed that the de jure right which was restricted to men could apply to women.[59] The consequence of de Gouges' polemical statement was that if women were equal with men at the point of death they had the right to equal political participation in the Assembly.[60] They demonstrated that they were deprived of the rights that they had under the Declaration of Rights (they did not have the rights that they had), and through their public action they enacted the rights denied them under the

[50] Ibid, 302. Rancière states that '[p]olitical demonstrations are...always of the moment and their subjects are always provisional' (Rancière, 'Ten Theses on Politics', para 25). There are only ever 'moments of community' (Rancière, *On the Shores of Politics*, 91). Todd May, however, has advocated institutionalizing Rancièrian equality (May, *Contemporary Political Movements*, ch 5).
[51] Rancière, 'Who is the Subject of the Rights of Man?', 298.
[52] Rancière, 'Politics, Identification, and Subjectivization', 63.
[53] Rancière, 'Who is the Subject of the Rights of Man?', 302.   [54] Ibid.
[55] Ibid, 303.   [56] Ibid.
[57] J Rancière, 'Democracy, Republic, Representation' (2006) 13(3) *Constellations* 297, 302 and J Rancière, 'Does Democracy Mean Something' in *Dissensus: On Politics and Aesthetics*, S Corcoran (trans) (London: Continuum, 2010) 45, 57.
[58] Rancière, 'Who is the Subject of the Rights of Man?', 303.
[59] Ingram, 'What is a "Right to have Rights"?', 412.
[60] Rancière, 'Who is the Subject of the Rights of Man?', 303–4.

Constitution and demonstrated that they had the rights the Constitution denied them (they had the rights that they had not).[61]

Here we see that for Rancière, the 'having' of the right to have rights is tied to 'political capacity' and the enactment of rights. Through the women's protest they 'demonstrated a political capacity'.[62] 'They showed that since they could enact [the rights they had been denied], they actually possessed them'.[63] The women thereby disputed 'the border separating bare life and political life'[64] and showed that women's 'bare life' was indeed political—they were citizens. The border of the political was challenged by 'playing [man/woman] off against citizen and citizen off against [man/woman]'.[65] On the first limb, 'man' of the Declaration is the political predicate exposing exclusions from citizenship under the Constitution. On the second limb, the women's acts of citizenship challenge the designation of 'woman' as bare life relegated to the private sphere.[66] This example shows that on Rancière's account, 'man' and 'citizen' are not the predetermined subject of rights but 'conflictual' or 'litigious' names—their meaning and extension is the subject of dispute.[67] Each term 'polemically plays the role of the universal that is opposed to the particular'.[68] Rancière terms this enacting 'scenes of dissensus'[69]—of disagreement—bringing two worlds together into a common world, the excluded and included, and asserting a place for the 'part with no part'. This dissensual politics takes the form of the 'twofold demonstration' discussed above.[70] It is not just a matter of highlighting a denial of inscribed rights but of 'put[ting] together the world where those rights are valid and the world where they are not'.[71] Rancière argues that legal texts and declarations of rights are crucial to this process as they make visible and point to a different social reality—that of an equality which displaces the prevailing inequality of social relations.[72] (But as will be discussed in section 4 below, for Rancière it was crucial that a political dispute not be reduced to a legal dispute.)

Thus we can see that the subject of rights emerges in the interval between two forms of rights—the inscription of a right and its verification—its being put to the test. Rancière argues that '[t]he subject of rights is the subject, or more accurately the process of subjectivization, that bridges the interval between two forms of the existence of those rights'.[73] First there are the written, declared rights which inscribe equality into a situation—which make equality 'visible'.[74] Secondly, 'the rights of man' are the rights of those who take up that inscribed equality and 'make something' of it and put it to the test. The process of subjectivization lies in the to and fro between these two forms of rights.[75] In so doing, a relationship is

[61] Ibid, 304.   [62] Rancière, 'Does Democracy Mean Something', 57.   [63] Ibid.
[64] Rancière, 'Who is the Subject of the Rights of Man?', 303.
[65] Rancière, 'Democracy, Republic, Representation', 301.   [66] Ibid, 301–2.
[67] Rancière, 'Does Democracy Mean Something', 56.
[68] Rancière, 'Democracy, Republic, Representation', 301.
[69] Rancière, 'Who is the Subject of the Rights of Man?', 304.   [70] Ibid.   [71] Ibid.
[72] Rancière, *On the Shores of Politics*, 48.
[73] Rancière, 'Who is the Subject of the Rights of Man?', 302.   [74] Ibid, 302–3.
[75] Rancière writes that '[t]he strength of those rights lies in the back-and-forth movement between the first inscription of the right and the dissensual stage on which it is put to test' (ibid, 305).

established where previously there was none: what Rancière terms 'bring[ing] the nonrelationship into relationship and giv[ing] place to the nonplace'.[76] Through polemical discourse the gap between statuses is expressed as a relation.[77] The nonplace is the 'place for a polemical construction'.[78]

The aim of connecting inscriptions of rights with their denial[79] is not to conclude that human rights are illusory and to be dismissed, that the subject of rights is rightless, which Rancière asserts is Arendt's approach, but to 'invent a new place' for rights[80]—to take up, build on, and enact inscribed rights (declared, written rights). Rights remain linked to the concept of universality but the universality does not lie in 'common humanity' as per certain received or orthodox accounts of international human rights law discussed in Chapter 4, or in the term citizen. It arises from the polemical discourse in the interval between man and the citizen which appeals from one to the other[81] and 'demonstrates' the consequences that follow from the polemical statement:[82] '[d]o we or do we not belong to the category of men or citizens or human beings, and what follows from this?'[83] It is in the linking of what belongs to what does not belong 'that common humanity argues for itself, reveals itself, and has an effect'.[84] Thus universality arises from a particular subject asserting and standing in the place of the universal by their discourse and action. As such, universality is always constructed locally through the particular.[85]

2.2 The assumption of equality

For Rancière there is no question of a top-down determination of political worth or subjecthood, nor even of emancipation from above by a sovereign power—rights are not conferred but claimed and enacted.[86] This is possible because on Rancière's account, the subject of politics/of rights is above all a 'speaking being',[87] and secondly and crucially, because he asserts that discourse proceeds on the assumption of equality between interlocutors. Indeed, it is precisely this assumption of equality which declarations of rights posit and 'make visible'. In speaking, the subject assumes equality between interlocutors and proceeds on the basis that the other can understand him.[88] To do this, the subject of politics must take equality as a given: an assumption

---

[76] Rancière, *Disagreement*, 89.
[77] Rancière, 'Politics, Identification, and Subjectivization', 60.   [78] Ibid.
[79] Rancière, 'Who is the Subject of the Rights of Man?', 304.
[80] Rancière, *Disagreement*, 89.
[81] Rancière, 'Politics, Identification, and Subjectivization', 63.   [82] Ibid, 60.
[83] Ibid.   [84] Rancière, *Disagreement*, 138.
[85] It is a matter of 'construct[ing] locally the place of the universal, the place for the demonstration of equality' (Rancière, 'Politics, Identification, and Subjectivization', 63). Rancière states that politics is 'the art of the local and singular construction of cases of universality' (Rancière, *Disagreement*, 139).
[86] See also B Honig, *Democracy and the Foreigner* (Princeton: Princeton University Press, 2001) in which Honig drawing on Rancière argues that the 'practice of taking rights and privileges rather than waiting for them to be granted by a sovereign power is...a quintessentially democratic practice' (99). See also 100–1.
[87] Rancière, *On the Shores of Politics*, 51.
[88] Ibid.

of equality (and not inequality) forms the starting point of discourse.[89] Rancière writes: '[t]his means starting from the point of view of equality, asserting equality, assuming equality as a given, working out from equality, trying to see how productive it can be and thus maximizing all possible liberty and equality'.[90] Equality is then to be verified, and demonstrated in each case. The attraction of Rancière's work in this respect is that it is not a precondition of acting that equality is recognized by the other (as per one approach to Arendt's work where institutionalized equality enables political action); rather it is assumed and then demonstrated.

2.3 The limitless and open spectrum of the subject of rights

In terms of a rearticulation of the right to have rights, the strength of Rancière's analysis lies in there being no permanent subject of rights. Rights can be taken up by a limitless spectrum of subjects—what has been termed the 'openness of human subjectivity'.[91] There is no man of the rights of man; nor is there need for such a man for the rights of man are the rights of those political subjects who put prescribed rights to the test.[92] Our conception of who is a subject of rights is transformed from a closed subject identified with the citizen, or the human of international human rights law, to an unrestricted and open subject. Included in this spectrum, Rancière argues, are the 'clandestine immigrants' in transit zones. 'These rights are theirs when they can do something with them to construct a dissensus against the denial of rights they suffer.'[93] Legally and territorially prescribed equality and rights evident in *Al-Kateb* are put into question as action proceeds on the basis of assumed, and not instituted equality.[94] This assumed equality is then demonstrated through action. On Rancière's account, the stateless would emerge as a subject of rights as they demonstrate the gap between the inscription of equality and universality in international human rights instruments and their indefinite detention (they do not have the rights they have under international law) and secondly, as they by their action exercise the rights of citizens the law denies them (that they have the rights they do not have). That is, they are to demonstrate that they are indeed a part of the community—that their bare life is not apolitical life of rightless man, but political life which can claim and enact rights. I return to the complex question of how they are to perform denied rights in section 3 below.

2.4 The contingency of the present order

As the subject of rights emerges, the people not only expose a grievance but begin the process of addressing it by their discourse and action.[95] This process of

---

[89] Ibid, 51–2.   [90] Ibid.

[91] P K Rajaram and C Grundy-Warr, 'Introduction' in P K Rajaram and C Grundy-Warr (eds), *Borderscapes: Hidden Geographies and Politics at Territory's Edge* (Minneapolis: University of Minnesota Press, 2007) ix, xxiii.

[92] Rancière, 'Who is the Subject of the Rights of Man?', 305.   [93] Ibid, 305–6.

[94] See Schaap, 'Enacting the Right to have Rights', 34–5 and Rajaram and Grundy-Warr, 'Introduction', xxviii: 'politics is about the questioning of the border that would restrict the meaning of what it is to be human within a territorial frame'.

[95] Rancière, *On the Shores of Politics*, 97.

subjectivization thereby 'shifts a body from the place assigned to it or changes a place's destination. It makes visible what had no business being seen, and makes heard as discourse where once there was only place for noise; it makes understood as discourse what was once only heard as noise'.[96] The police order is disrupted in that we are made to see something new—a new political subject—and a new way of viewing the order. The worker, undocumented migrant, stateless person, etc emerge as political subjects[97] and thereby reconfigure the community's 'field of experience'—the shared meanings and perception of what is a given within the order.[98] As with all politics, there are no guarantees that the claims asserted by the 'part with no part' will be accepted. The claims and actions of the subject of rights present the police order with a choice: either to 'ratify' the presupposed and enacted equality and act accordingly or to admit that they do not believe in equality (and consequently must amend declared expressions of equality in declarations of rights and legal instruments).[99] The 'odds are stacked against change'.[100] It may happen later if at all.[101] On a Rancièrian politics, the point is that the actions of the 'part with no part' prefigure and demonstrate another 'world' in which their 'argument counts as an argument'.[102] Their dissensus carries the 'potential of moving towards something new'.[103] In disrupting the police order, the subject of politics shows the contingency of that order.[104]

Though not referring to Rancière, this dynamic and potential can be seen in the work of Hans Lindahl. He refers to political acts which disrupt the legal order by contesting the legal boundary between legality and illegality and pointing to the possibility of 'alternative ways of drawing legal boundaries'.[105] Such acts, he argues, are a-legal in that they 'disrupt a legal order by revealing *another legality*, other possibilities of drawing the distinction between legality and illegality in the legal order they contest'.[106] These acts reveal that what is legal may be illegal and vice versa and posit a different collective than the collective in whose name the existing legal border is drawn. They thereby point to the contingency of legal orders. Take the example of economic migrants in Europe.[107] On one construction, their presence within, and participation in, the common market is illegal. However, Lindahl argues that from another perspective, economic migrants can draw on the Treaty of Rome to point to a different legality which takes into account the common global market to which the European polity and the economic migrants belong. This is because while distinguishing between the internal and external market, the

[96] Rancière, *Disagreement*, 30. See also Honig, *Democracy and the Foreigner*, 101.
[97] Rancière, 'Ten Theses on Politics', para 23.   [98] Rancière, *Disagreement*, 35.
[99] Rancière, *On the Shores of Politics*, 47 and May, *Contemporary Political Movements*, 20–1.
[100] Ibid (May), 41.   [101] Eg Honig, *Democracy and the Foreigner*, 100.
[102] Rancière, 'Ten Theses on Politics', para 24.
[103] M Gunneflo and N Selberg, 'Discourse or Merely Noise? Regarding the Disagreement on Undocumented Migrants' (2010) 12(2) *European Journal of Migration and Law* 173, 189.
[104] See May, *Contemporary Political Movements*, 10.
[105] H Lindahl, 'A-legality: Postnationalism and the Question of Legal Boundaries' (2010) 73(1) *MLR* 30, 43.
[106] H Lindahl, 'Border Crossings by Immigrants: Legality, Illegality, and A-legality' (2008) 14(2) *Res Publica* 117, 125 (original emphasis).
[107] Ibid, 124–6.

Treaty of Rome includes both within a common global market thereby indirectly acknowledging that 'the realization of the internal market is part and parcel of the realization of a common global market'.[108] In holding the European polity to this claim, economic migrants' presence and labour within the internal market is not illegal but 'a-legal': they point to the potential legality of acts which otherwise might be construed as illegal and the possible illegality of the polity's distinction between the internal and external markets.[109]

2.5 The agency of Rancière's politics v biopolitics

From the above discussion it can be seen that Rancière's account shifts our focus from the power of the state and its institutions to the agency of the excluded. It is a question of the excluded group emancipating themselves by taking up declared rights, enacting them, and demonstrating their equality. This entails 'proving' to themselves and to the other that they belong to a 'common world',[110] and can demonstrate 'the legitimacy of [their] actions within it'.[111] We are not here confronted with the 'omnipotent sovereign of liberal imagination',[112] an account of human rights which reinforces the idea of the power of the sovereign state and which leads to a 'programmatic' and 'predictable' politics.[113] Nor does Rancière take us into the quagmire of Agamben's biopolitics of the state of exception in which politics is impossible and '[a]ny kind of claim to rights or any struggle enacting rights is…trapped from the very outset in the mere polarity of bare life and state of exception'.[114] Life here is not entirely governed.

Rancière's surplus subjects (the part of the non-part) are not 'bare life' caught in the state of exception, but instead the subjects of politics who 'burrow into the apparatuses and technologies of exclusion in order to disrupt the administrative routines, the day-to-day perceptions and constructions of normality'.[115] One cited example of a Rancièrian politics of dissensus is the 'sans-status' Algerian movement in Quebec of 2002, which sought to resist the deportation of those 'non status' Algerians whose applications for refugee status had been rejected.[116] The movement called attention to

---

[108] Ibid, 126.   [109] Ibid.   [110] Rancière, *On the Shores of Politics*, 49.
[111] Ibid, 50. See also M F N Franke, 'The Unbearable Rightfulness of Being Human: Citizenship, Displacement, and the Right to not have Rights' (2011) 15(1) *Citizenship Studies* 39, 49–51.
[112] A Orford, 'Biopolitics and the Tragic Subject of Human Rights' in E Dauphinee and C Masters (eds), *The Logics of Biopower and the War on Terror: Living, Dying, Surviving* (New York: Palgrave Macmillan, 2007) 205, 223.
[113] Ibid.
[114] See Rancière, 'Who is the Subject of the Rights of Man?', 301. Rancière writes that Agamben leaves us in the 'ontological trap' in which the equation of politics and power is presented as our 'ontological destiny' (ibid, 301–2). See also W Walters, 'Acts of Demonstration: Mapping the Territory of (Non-)Citizenship' in E F Isin and G M Nielsen (eds), *Acts of Citizenship* (London: Zed Books, 2008) 182. Walters argues that focusing on 'acts of citizenship' and approaches that grapple with the 'strategic and agonistic character of contemporary border crossings' may 'mov[e] us beyond Agamben's preoccupation with mechanisms of capture' (184). At the same time, Walters cautions that privileging 'acts of citizenship' as an 'analytical strateg[y]' (193) may sideline a politics in which subjects are not seeking to be identified as citizens (193–204).
[115] Nyers, 'Abject Cosmopolitanism', 1089.
[116] See May, *Contemporary Political Movements*, 29–45 and Nyers (ibid), 1082–90.

their plight and demanded the regularization of their status and an end to their deportation.[117] Crucially, it was a movement led by the *sans-status* themselves and which
proceeded on the assumption of equality. They did not hide or 'accept their status as
marginal. Although they were, quite literally, a part of Canadian society that had no
part, they did not accept the state's refusal to give them a part.'[118] They met publicly
thereby acting as though they were already Canadian citizens and not 'illegals' living
under the threat of imminent deportation. The presupposition of equality shaped their
relation to Canadian society and to one another.[119] Through the collective action of the
movement, a subject of politics, a collective 'we' emerged such that previously 'disparate
individuals' struggling to avoid deportation 'recognized themselves as part of a larger
whole'.[120] This collective was a fleeting subject in that it existed only for the duration of
the movement itself.[121] But in this fleeting subject of politics emerging, what was taken
as a given in the social order shifted. Todd May writes that through the movement, the
'not previously identifiable' *sans-status* became 'identifiable', and then were identified
with, by at least some Québécois.[122] For some, the refugees ceased to be those denied
the status of full citizenship and were recognized as people such as themselves 'seeking
to create lives for themselves'.[123] The very emergence of the movement—in making
seen what was previously invisible—and in transgressing the 'shared meanings' of the
'given police order'[124] demonstrated that the refugees belonged to a 'shared world'[125]
which Canadian society previously could not see.[126] In this consists democratic politics
on Rancière's account. As it turned out, in this instance, the claims of the 'part with no
part' were acknowledged. The federal and state governments acted on the movement's
demands and agreed to a new procedure for revisiting the files of the *sans-status* which
led to the status of many being regularized.[127]

3. The limits of Rancière's subject of rights

To summarize the foregoing discussion, Rancière articulates the right to have rights
as the 'rightless' engaging in dissensual politics and enacting and claiming rights.
Here the subject of rights is the ever-fluctuating subject of politics. Rights do not
belong to, nor are possessed by, the human or the citizen such that only the person
in whose name they are declared may enact and enjoy them, rather the subject of
rights is the limitless political actor who takes up declared rights and enacts them.
Thus, on Rancière's approach, there are no predetermined exclusions from the subject of rights but a limitless spectrum of rights-bearers. Yet Rancière's account of
the political subject is necessarily exclusionary. A politics of dissensus relies upon

---

[117] Ibid (May), 34.   [118] Ibid, 35.   [119] Ibid, 35–6.   [120] Ibid, 39.
[121] Ibid.   [122] Ibid, 40.   [123] Ibid, 39.   [124] Ibid, 41.
[125] Rancière, 'Ten Theses on Politics', para 24.
[126] To require political change in order for a movement to be democratic May argues, is to go beyond
Rancière, for democratic politics on Rancière's account rests on a presupposition of equality and not on
the response of those against whom it is asserted (May, *Contemporary Political Movements*, 41).
[127] Ibid, 42. For another example of a Rancièrian politics of dissensus see Gunneflo and Selberg,
'Discourse or Merely Noise?'.

discourse and action. His conception of politics presumes a capacity to engage in polemical discourse and enact the equality and rights which have been denied. This brings us to the limits and weaknesses of Rancière's account. It is a matter of the subject of rights proving that they have a right to the equality they are demanding.[128] As discussed above, whether a person 'has' rights depends on their ability to assert their competence and membership of the common world and 'prove the legitimacy of [their] action within it'.[129] Rancière writes: 'Hannah Arendt posits as the primary right the right to have rights. We might add that rights are held by those who can impose a rational obligation on the other to recognize them.'[130] This does not mean that the other will in fact recognize the obligation, but that the subject has proved the necessity of their rights being recognized.[131] Strikingly, Rancière argues that those who claim that 'the other cannot understand them, that there is no common language, lose any basis for rights of their own to be recognized'.[132] By failing to act on the assumption of equality, they in effect forfeit their right to have rights. If for Arendt, human rights are the 'rights of those who have no rights',[133] the rights of abstract man, then on Rancière's account, this is equally true of those who are unable to enact rights. They are left with the first limb of the polemical discourse; that is they are arbitrarily denied the rights posited by human rights declarations (they do not have the rights that they have) but they are unable to perform the denied rights and demonstrate that they in fact do belong to the community: they are not only denied the rights that they have; but they do not 'have' the rights that they are denied.

As argued by Christopher Watkin, in grounding the presumption of equality on a capacity to speak and understand one's interlocutor, Rancière 'risks excluding from his account those who do not have the capacity to militate for their equal treatment in the manner he prescribes for the *sans-part*'.[134] This incapacity may be internal to the person such as those suffering from 'extreme old age' or 'congenital disease'. Of course, as Watkin notes, Rancière is not asserting that everyone possesses equal intelligence; rather his point is that we need to see what can emerge when the excluded act from the premise of equality. Yet, as Watkin argues, even if the assumed equality is not contradicted, 'that still does not help those unable to seize their assumed equality in the way Rancière prescribes, for they have no means in his account of doing anything about their inequality'.[135] Those least able to defend themselves, remain without a voice. The strength of Rancière's approach (the limitless subject of politics) is also its weakness for the very focus on action and enacting rights privileges being able to assert one's voice and perpetuates the exclusion of those unable to do so.

If the inability to seize assumed equality may result from factors internal to the 'part with no part' they may also be externally imposed. Is it feasible, for example, to expect a politics of dissensus to take place within the confines and social isolation

---

[128] Rancière, *On the Shores of Politics*, 49.   [129] Ibid, 50.   [130] Ibid.
[131] Ibid, 49–50.   [132] Ibid, 50.
[133] Rancière, 'Who is the Subject of the Rights of Man?', 298.
[134] C Watkin, 'More Equal Than Others: On Thinking Equality Today', 5 (unpublished article on file with the author).
[135] Ibid.

of an immigration detention centre and the enervating predicament of indefinite detention? If we take the issue of the indefinite detention of stateless people, is the right to have rights to be interpreted such that the onus lies upon the detained to emancipate themselves? Is a collective subject to emerge from isolated individuals in immigration detention; that is in a detention centre operating according to what has been termed a logic of 'halting the ability to enact rights' and of 'strategies of silencing such as geographical and social isolation'?[136] Without necessarily adopting a biopolitical approach, we can still recognize the extent to which such techniques constrain politics. What form would any such dissensual politics take? Detained stateless people may be able to show that in national law they have not the rights that they have under international law, but how do they then verify their equality? How can they demonstrate the citizenship they are denied and 'prove' to themselves and to the other that they belong to a 'common world' within which their actions are legitimate, that is, that their 'bare life' is not that of the victim to be detained, but political life? Examples cited by some commentators include the detainees suturing their eyelids and lips. 'The act of suturing (along with the hunger strike that results) is an act by which the nonspeaking abject transforms his very own body (his own "bare life") into an act of resistance.'[137] Through such actions, those who were rendered invisible are said to assert their presence within the community. This is modest emancipation to be sure. It may consist of making visible what was once unseen but any presence within the community thereby achieved is tenuous at best: they may resist but more often than not remain the indefinitely detained non-part of isolated individuals.

4. Rancière and human rights law

4.1 The limits of human rights law

The preceding analysis has examined the strengths and weaknesses of Rancière's articulation of the right to have rights in terms of dissensual politics. Let me now turn from Rancière's dissensual politics proper, to consider how his analysis might shed light on the limits of international and domestic human rights law. On Rancière's approach, we are alerted to the potential pacifying and objectifying effect of international human rights law. When human rights cease to be considered as political capacities which the rightless take up and enact themselves, they become the rights of common humanity whose humanity is defined by the legal expert. The subject of human rights is transformed from the subject of politics into the 'wordless victim'.[138] The 'human', he argues, ceases to be a litigious name (that invoked in a dispute) and becomes the 'bare' human. There is no division within the community between those who are counted and those who have no part, rather

---

[136] Isin and Rygiel, 'Abject Spaces: Frontiers, Zones, Camps', 189.
[137] Ibid. See also K Rygiel, 'Bordering Solidarities: Migrant Activism and the Politics of Movement and Camps at Calais' (2011) 15(1) *Citizenship Studies* 1.
[138] Rancière, *Disagreement*, 126.

all are included within 'common humanity'.[139] Humanity is speechless and its rights are 'in the hands of the international community police'[140]—conferred from above (of which 'humanitarian intervention' is but the most extreme example).[141] Rancière asserts that the subject of rights cannot emerge when rights are handed over to the legal expert to be asserted on behalf of the 'part with no part'.

For Rancière, a legal dispute is a caricature of a political dispute such that transferring a dispute to the judicial sphere 'dives[ts] politics of its job'[142]—the political dispute is transformed into 'a matter for expert knowledge'.[143] Legal approaches to human rights are part of what he terms the politics of consensus.[144] They are part of the ruling order (the police order) which the 'part with no part' is seeking to disrupt with a politics of dissensus. The political wrong of which Rancière is speaking—the miscount of the community—cannot be reduced to a juridical wrong to be addressed by the law in that the 'irreconcilability of the parties antedates any specific dispute'.[145] The force of this is seen when we consider undocumented migrants. Their exclusion from the community cannot be remedied by any one legal case. Conferring the right to marry on undocumented migrants contests internal borders of society and of the law[146] but it leaves in place their assigned role—their classification—as the illegal, that is as a group defined in relation to the border with all the consequences such a characterization entails. The point of political subjectivization on Rancière's account is for the subject of politics (for example, undocumented migrants) to 'creat[e] [their] own name' and 'divorc[e] [themselves] from any of the characteristics associated with [them] by the police order'.[147] Thus any attempt to reduce democratic politics to global citizenship construed in terms of the international protection of human rights (briefly discussed in Chapter 4) is inimical to a Rancièrian politics of dissensus.[148]

When we turn to international and domestic human rights law, examples can certainly be found in support of Rancière's critique. In international human rights law subjectivity is conferred from above in that the scope and content of rights is determined by states who conclude the requisite international treaties and by the legal experts who interpret them.[149] The subject of rights may become the subject of the law[150] in that subjecthood is spoken into being through legal texts and limited to legally conferred rights. The rights held are determined by states and legal experts speak on behalf of the 'victim'. The ruling order of states and borders is not disrupted rather the stateless and undocumented migrants are further inscribed into it. Consider the right not to be arbitrarily detained in international human rights law, briefly discussed in Chapter 4. Whether a stateless person 'has'—in

[139] Ibid, 124–5.   [140] Ibid, 127.
[141] See Rancière, 'Who is the Subject of the Rights of Man?', 306–9.
[142] Rancière, *Disagreement*, 110.   [143] Ibid, 109.
[144] See also C Douzinas, *Human Rights and Empire: The Political Philosophy of Cosmopolitanism* (Abingdon: Routledge-Cavendish, 2007) 107–10.
[145] Rancière, *On the Shores of Politics*, 97.
[146] See Chapter 4.   [147] May, *Contemporary Political Movements*, 13.
[148] See further P Tambakaki, *Human Rights, or Citizenship?* (Abingdon: Birkbeck Law Press, 2010) ch 4.
[149] See Douzinas, *Human Rights and Empire*, 180.
[150] See further C Douzinas, *The End of Human Rights: Critical Legal Thought at the Turn of the Century* (Oxford: Hart, 2000), ch 9.

the sense of is the bearer of—the right not to be arbitrarily detained, turns on the articulation and interpretation of the right to liberty and then its implementation in domestic law and practice. The litigious dispute arising from the stateless person existing in the interval between the human and the citizen is transformed into a technical examination of whether the detention conforms to the principles of legality and freedom from arbitrariness. Where the stateless person does not in fact enjoy the right not to be arbitrarily detained, the problem is said to lie in inadequate state implementation of the right. This is not the case of humanity arguing for itself but of others deciding the rights of humanity. In the opinion of one scholar, international human rights law 'regards individuals as an object on which to bestow or recognize rights, not as agents from whom emanates the power to do such bestowing'.[151] It is partly due to the passivity of the 'protection' international human rights law affords that some advocates of the rights of non-citizens are attracted to the concept of human security. Inter alia, a security framework is aimed at the protection and empowerment of individuals such that people are able 'to act on their own behalf—and on behalf of others'.[152] '[E]mpowerment... implies that migrants be permitted to associate and organise to represent their shared interests, to form trade unions, to represent the rights of themselves and their families, and to speak up against fraud, abuse and exploitation'.[153] Yet others have sought to endow the individual with agency by reconceiving international legal personality in terms of the right to political participation. For example, Janne Nijman has proposed that international legal personality be articulated in terms of the right to have rights, namely as 'the capacity to speak and act, and, in a broader sense, the capacity to be a political participant, with a natural right to such participation'.[154] She argues that where the state amply represents the interests and rights of its citizens that personality resides in the state and the state is 'the legitimate representative of its citizens at the international level with the authority to pursue their interests'.[155] If the state fails or oppresses its people then international

---

[151] J H H Weiler, 'The Geology of International Law—Governance, Democracy and Legitimacy' (2004) 64 *ZaöRV* 547, 558.

[152] Commission on Human Security, *Human Security Now* (New York, 2003) 11 cited in A Edwards and C Ferstman, 'Humanising Non-Citizens: The Convergence of Human Rights and Human Security' in A Edwards and C Ferstman (eds), *Human Security and Non-Citizens: Law, Policy and International Affairs* (Cambridge: Cambridge University Press, 2010) 3, 33.

[153] Ibid, 44. Edwards and Ferstman argue that in applying a human security framework '... the perception of non-citizens may... be modified within security discourse from "non-persons" or "outsiders" to being full and equal human beings; a shift that can only be positive for their protection and empowerment'. (Ibid, 46)

[154] J E Nijman, *The Concept of International Legal Personality: An Inquiry into the History and Theory of International Law* (The Hague: Asser Press, 2004) 469. The aim here is to prevent what Nijman terms a 'civic death' (471). She writes: '[International Legal Personality] forms the *cords* between the individual human being and the universal human society, and because of it, the international community and international law must guarantee the right to have rights, the right to political participation, i.e., the right to speak out and raise one's *voice*' (473) (original emphasis). Anne Peters also advocates a form of transnational citizenship based on the right to political participation in global governance such that individuals are not passive but 'active international legal subjects'. A Peters, 'Membership in the Global Constitutional Community' in J Klabbers, A Peters, and G Ulfstein, *The Constitutionalization of International Law* (Oxford: Oxford University Press, 2009) 153, 300–2.

[155] Ibid (Nijman), 468.

legal personality returns to the citizens of the state and the international community must '*open up* its institutions and law...to *include* these human beings' and thereby affirm their personality.[156] For Rancière, however, politics is not to be relegated to the state as the individual's representative or to the 'international community', but to be enacted by subjects in a myriad of local sites of contestation.[157]

Returning to human rights, on Rancière's account, the role of the law is limited to declarations of written rights which make equality 'visible' within the society and become a platform for the politics of dissensus. The sphere of contestation is not the law itself. Rather than allowing for the gap between man and the citizen to be maintained—for surplus subjects to emerge—the law, Rancière contends, is continually expanded to embrace each new group which emerges. Law and fact coincide. That is, human rights lose their symbolic and political potential[158] and come to restate reality rather than be an element in its transformation. There are no surplus subjects and thus, Rancière asserts, no politics as each individual belongs to humanity: humanity becomes 'a whole that is equal to the sum of its elements'.[159] The post-war history of international human rights law attests at least in part to this latter point as international treaties and instruments proliferate and embrace an ever-expanding array of rights and groups. The vulnerability of stateless people for example has been said to derive in part from the paucity of international instruments dealing with their plight.

4.2 The emancipatory potential of human rights law

Yet in wanting to overcome the closure of the definite subject of human rights (of the subject as the citizen or the human) and the pacifying and objectifying impulse of international human rights law, Rancière fails to harness the emancipatory potential within the law—that within the law action, disruption, and potential alternative ways of constructing the world are possible.[160] In seeking to subvert

---

[156] Ibid (original emphasis).

[157] Both Rancière and Arendt reject the idea of 'world politics'. According to Arendt, globalizing processes have produced humanity as a 'factual', though not as a political, reality. (Arendt, *The Human Condition*, 248–57). She did not consider that the answer was to be found in the establishment of world government. In her words, 'one sovereign force ruling the whole earth' would be a 'forbidding nightmare of tyranny' and spell the end of politics, as it would promote the unity of a single opinion, whereas '[p]olitical concepts are based on plurality, diversity and mutual limitations' ('Karl Jaspers: Citizen of the World?' in H Arendt, *Men in Dark Times* (London: Cape, 1970) 81). Similarly, for Rancière, 'globalization' does not usher in the 'reign of the universal', for politics, is 'always local and occasional'. Politics is always the local instantiation of the universal: '[t]he reign of globalization is not the reign of the universal. It is the opposite'. For Rancière there is no 'world politics'. There is 'world police' but not 'world politics' (Rancière, *Disagreement*, 139).

[158] See further Douzinas, *The End of Human Rights* and S Pahuja, 'Rights as Regulation: The Integration of Development and Human Rights' in B Morgan (ed), *The Intersection of Rights and Regulation: New Directions in Sociolegal Scholarship* (Aldershot: Ashgate, 2007) 167.

[159] Rancière, *Disagreement*, 125. International human rights law for Rancière is part of the 'consensus system' which 'announced a world beyond the demos, a world made up of individuals and groups simply showing common humanity' (124–5).

[160] For the emancipatory potential of a critical approach to international law, see S Marks, *The Riddle of all Constitutions: International Law, Democracy, and the Critique of Ideology* (Oxford: Oxford University Press, 2000) 121–46.

approaches which restrict the right to have rights to a predetermined subject (the citizen with a legal and political status in the community, the lawful entrant, or the human of international human rights treaties, etc), Rancière overstates the agency of the 'part with no part' and understates the emancipatory potential of the law. If the 'part with no part' are to 'have' rights (not just in the sense of enacting them but of their rights being recognized in law thus militating against outcomes upholding their indefinite detention) then alongside dissensual politics and the enactment of rights (to the extent the excluded are able) the choices within the law must be exploited. While the political wrong of which Rancière is speaking—the miscount of the community—cannot be reduced to a juridical wrong to be addressed by the law,[161] we cannot simply escape from the law into a Rancièrian 'politics', for the law is part of the dispute. The law need not be reduced to making equality 'visible' in a 'political dispute' for the tension between 'politics' and 'police' plays out within the law calling for engagement. The law may indeed be part of the ruling order, Rancière's 'police', but it can also be about establishing relationships. Law can be conceived relationally—not in the Arendtian sense of the law's 'ability to open and establish a political space in which acting together can be realized'[162]— but in the sense of establishing relationships where previously there were none, of seeking to establish a relationship between, on the one hand, a particular conception of humanity posited by the law and, on the other, the excluded claimants. In other words, it is a matter of the claimant 'constructing locally the place of the universal' and linking what belongs to what does not belong (to paraphrase Rancière). Consider the case of *N v United Kingdom*[163] before the ECtHR in which the majority and minority judgments can be taken as indicative of a muted consensual and dissensual logic respectively. The case concerned the expulsion of an HIV sufferer to her country of nationality, Uganda. It was accepted that if she were deprived of the medication she had received in the UK for the past nine years, her condition would deteriorate rapidly and 'she would suffer ill-health, discomfort, pain and death within a few years'.[164] The case law of the court has consistently recognized that the prohibition of torture, inhuman or degrading treatment in article 3 of the ECHR is absolute in nature, and extends to prohibiting expulsion where there is a real risk of a person being subjected to treatment contrary to article 3 if expelled. Strikingly, in *N v UK* however, the majority failed to refer to the 'absolute' nature of the prohibition in article 3 and introduced a balancing argument into its reasoning. In the words of the majority, 'inherent in the whole of the Convention is a search for a fair balance between the demands of the general interest of the community and the requirements of the protection of the individual's fundamental rights'.[165] While article 3 was held to be fundamentally important in the Convention, it does not impose an obligation on contracting states to alleviate medical, social, and economic disparities between states by providing 'free and

---

[161] Rancière, *On the Shores of Politics*, 97.

[162] See C Volk, 'From *Nomos* to *Lex*: Hannah Arendt on Law, Politics, and Order' (2010) 23(4) *LJIL* 759, 776.

[163] (2008) 47 EHRR 39 (Grand Chamber) (hereafter '*N v UK*').

[164] Ibid, para 47.

[165] Ibid, para 44.

unlimited health care' to non-nationals who do not possess the right to reside in their jurisdiction. To hold otherwise would, in the majority's opinion, impose too great a burden on the contracting states.[166] The case is presented by the majority as an attempt inappropriately to extend state parties' obligations beyond that of the protection of civil and political rights to those of a social or economic nature.[167] If however, we turn to the minority judgment[168] a different picture emerges as exclusion and inclusion are placed side by side. The minority contrasts the court's affirmation of the absolute nature of the prohibition in recent cases of expulsion to torture (such as *Saadi v Italy*)[169] with the balancing exercise in *N v UK*. Article 3 is either absolute or it is not, with budgetary and policy considerations being irrelevant to the determination.[170] In the minority's reasoning we hear echoes of the 'part with no part's' dissensual claim: do we or do we not belong to the human whose protection against ill-treatment is absolute, and what follows from this? Either the court has to concede that the border of human rights—the limits of inclusion—is drawn along economic lines thus giving up any pretence as to the 'fundamental nature' of article 3 rights; or it must adhere to the absolute nature of the right. If the latter, then 'what follows'? Reactionary government responses and intensified external border control? Most likely. Yet at the same time, another muted logic is asserted: human rights are about the protection of the most vulnerable wherever they are located—even if they are on 'our doorstep'. But beyond this, implicit in a finding of the absolute nature of article 3 would be the provocative challenge of asking why medical treatment is not available in the state of origin. A complex and uncomfortable question to be sure, but one which if governments, the international human rights regime, individuals, etc are compelled to address may be far more transformative of the international order than the status quo of protecting states from a perceived avalanche of medical immigrants. By no means do I imply here that this is to be equated with a dissensual Rancièrian politics for the rightless do not speak directly nor do they engage in the second step of acting so as to verify their rights. Nevertheless, I would argue that their voice neither is, nor should be, entirely absent from the analysis.

The point is that the law can never entirely erase surplus subjects for there is always a non-part seeking to become a part and lodge a dispute as to who is the human of human rights. If law is part of the construction of the order (for example, of Rancière's 'police order') then that order can be disrupted from within. As with the case of Rancière's politics, there are no guarantees that the outcome of human

---

[166] Ibid. (To date, the court has only found that removal would violate art 3 on the ground of the applicant's ill-health in the case of *D v United Kingdom* (1997) 24 EHRR 423 concerning the proposed removal of an AIDS patient, whose illness had reached a critical stage, to a state whose medical facilities could not provide for his needs and where he had no close relatives. See *N v UK*, paras 32–4.)

[167] Eg ibid (*N v UK*).

[168] Joint dissenting opinion of Judges Tulkens, Bonello, and Spielmann.

[169] (2009) 49 EHRR 30 (Grand Chamber).

[170] *N v UK*, 'joint dissenting opinion', paras 7–8. They also maintained that the court's reasoning 'ignor[ed] the social dimension of the integrated approach adopted by the Court' in *Airey v Ireland* (1979–80) 2 EHRR 305 ('joint dissenting opinion', para 6).

rights cases will be emancipatory and result in a reconfiguration of the ruling order. Indeed, to use Rancière's terminology it is far from certain that an 'egalitarian logic' as opposed to a 'police logic' will prevail.[171] Human rights may at times remain that of the prevailing order of consensus such that in Costas Douzinas' words we are left with the 'non-part'—'the living, dying rather, proof' of the 'impossibility' of human rights,[172] or they may disrupt it from within such that we hear albeit fleeting echoes of another order in which the non-part asserts its voice as a part.

4.3 The politics of practice

Finally, let me turn to what has been termed the politics of the practice of law of which the above analysis is but an example. It will be recalled that Rancière argued that the subject of rights emerges in the gap between statuses. The interval in which a politics (though admittedly not a Rancièrian politics of dissensus) is possible also surfaces within the legal sphere. Bridging the 'gap' between legal rules and principles and the outcome of a case is what has been termed the 'politics' of the 'practice of law'.[173] Choices are made in international and domestic practice as to the interpretation of rights, the relationship between national and international law, and where the borders of the legal community lie as we saw in Chapter 4. Clearly, this is a different conception of 'politics' to that developed by Rancière. It is indeed practised by the 'experts' but recognizes their/our responsibility for outcomes. It is not a matter of lawyers applying 'the law' but grappling with the question 'which law?'.[174] In the words of Martti Koskenniemi, '[t]he question remains always: what kind of (or whose) law, and what type of (and whose) preference?'.[175] In cases such as *Al-Kateb* choices are being made as to the construction of the Migration Act—can it be read subject to fundamental rights—the relationship between international and national law, the content and conception of the rule of law,[176] and of the role of the judge. Whether detained stateless people will be recognized as 'having' the right not to be arbitrarily detained turns on such decisions. Choices are made here as to the borders of the law—as to the scope and subject of the right not to be arbitrarily detained. In the words of David Dyzenhaus, the difference between the majority and minority judges in *Al-Kateb* 'boils down to a view of legal authority, constructed around a view of who is the proper subject of the law's protection, who is in the legal community and who is out'.[177] He contrasts McHugh J's 'constitutional positiv[ist]' stance of understanding 'law as a matter of rules with a determinate content, fixed in time at the moment of their enactment', to Kirby's conception of law which 'includes principles'.[178] On the majority's approach, the law is impotent to protect against

---

[171] Rancière, *Disagreement*, 32.   [172] Douzinas, *Human Rights and Empire*, 108.

[173] Here I am drawing on M Koskenniemi, *From Apology to Utopia: The Structure of International Legal Argument* (Cambridge: Cambridge University Press, 2005). See, 'Epilogue', 601.

[174] Thanks also to Jan Klabbers for raising this point in relation to a differently conceived Chapter 5.

[175] M Koskenniemi, 'The Politics of International Law—20 Years Later' (2009) 20(1) *EJIL* 7, 17.

[176] D Dyzenhaus, *The Constitution of Law: Legality in a Time of Emergency* (Cambridge: Cambridge University Press, 2006) 92–7.

[177] Ibid, 92.   [178] Ibid, 95.

what, as noted in Chapter 4, is conceded to be the 'tragic'[179] plight of Mr Al-Kateb, and yet this outcome is at least in part the product of the legal analysis adopted. Responsibility is abjured for the 'tragic' outcome. It is said that parliament is to be held responsible for laws permitting indefinite detention and 'must answer to the electors, to the international bodies who supervise human rights treaties to which Australia is a party and to history'.[180] Al-Kateb is to look to the electors to change the government or to international bodies who supervise Australia's international law obligations. Change lies in the hands of others. For his interstitial status to change, he must rely on the action of others. In light of such decisions, the dissensual politics of Rancière is hardly surprising. If Mr Al-Kateb is to enjoy rights, it is up to him and other similarly placed stateless people to constitute themselves as the subject of rights and by their actions insert themselves into the community from which they have been excluded. Nevertheless, Rancière too easily relegates legal disputes to the consensual domain of the ruling order. We cannot escape from 'law' into 'politics' but must grasp the political choices within the law itself and decide 'which law' is to be applied. The point here is not to present an overarching theory as to how these choices are to be made, but the more modest argument of pointing to the potential within the law itself. Whether in Rancière's 'politics of dissensus' or in the legal sphere, the 'having' of rights turns on how we approach the gap, the non-place.

5. Conclusion

Taking Rancière as my guide in this chapter, I have explored the right to have rights in terms of the politics of human rights—of the rightless taking up, claiming, and enacting rights. I have argued that the lure of this approach lies in its empowerment of those formally denied the status from which entitlement to rights is deemed to flow. The person in whose name rights are declared and the person who exercises and enacts rights need not be the same. As the subject of rights is transformed into the subject of politics, we are presented with a limitless spectrum of rights-bearers. It is not a matter of looking to whether one has the requisite status—the qualification to hold rights (whatever status society deems is necessary)—but of constituting oneself a rights-bearer. The subject of rights ceases to be the passive victim on whom rights are conferred from above—whose place in the world is given—and becomes the speaking being acting on a presumption of equality and asserting and creating his or her place in the world. However, a foundation of rights still emerges—the having of the rights to have rights is not without exclusion even in Rancière's account. While Rancière tries to go beyond rights depending on a given status, he cannot overcome exclusion. On a performative understanding of rights we are still confronted with the need to legitimate who is the subject of rights, namely the subject who speaks, who makes claims to equality, and enacts equality. Those most vulnerable in society—those most in need of a voice and to

---

[179] *Al-Kateb v Godwin*, para 31.
[180] Ibid, para 48.

become a part—are precisely those who are often unable to take up and assert their voice. Rancière, I thus argued, overstates the agency and capacity of those who are entrusted with their own emancipation. Rancière's politics of dissensus provides a powerful guardrail against marginalizing the voices of those who have no part, but its limits and shortcomings must also be acknowledged. Moreover, if the rightless are to 'have' rights then there is no escaping engaging with the emancipatory potential (and limits) of the law itself for the law is integral to the dispute/miscount/exclusion of which the rightless suffer. Having come to the limits of nationality, citizenship, humanity, and politics, how are we to understand the meaning of the 'right to have rights'? Where then does this journey through the various modalities of the right to have rights leave us?

Conclusion

I began this investigation by asking how different and at times competing conceptions of the right to have rights might shed light on right-bearing in the contemporary context, and in particular on concepts and relationships central to the protection of human rights in public international law. Each articulation examined in Chapters 1 to 5 was shown to capture an aspect of right-bearing in the current international legal system, and to privilege a particular subject of rights. It was also seen how international law facilitates, and yet also impedes, the constitution of the most vulnerable and marginalized as rights-holders, such that their status as rights-bearers remains tenuous, their place in the world precarious. Faced with contested and competing conceptions of the right to have rights, how then is the right to have rights to be understood? What is the significance of this intriguing concept for international legal thought and practice today? Is it a question of yet again reconceiving the subject of rights, or is the problem more fundamental, such that the very approach to the question of the right to have rights needs to be rethought?

1. The right to have rights and the problem of naming

In the foregoing analysis, each articulation of the right to have rights privileges a particular subject of rights—either the national of public international law (Chapters 1 and 2), the citizen of the political community (Chapter 3), the human of international human rights law (Chapter 4), or the subject of politics (Chapter 5). It names a basis of right-holding—a bearer of rights—and accords those rights to a placeholder for 'x' (as in the phrase 'the rights accorded to x'). In part, the foregoing analysis has demonstrated the veracity of each posited subject. Equally, each basis of right-bearing or conception, each placeholder, was shown to be problematic insofar as it was exclusionary (whether as conceived in international law or in political thought and practice). Each placeholder draws a boundary of right-bearing, excluding those who do not (either literally or metaphorically) fall within its borders—whether the stateless (Chapters 1 and 2), the 'undeserving' citizen (Chapter 3), the undocumented migrant (Chapter 4), or those unable to enact and claim rights (Chapter 5).

Is the answer to the right to have rights then to be found in reconceiving nationality, citizenship, humanity, and dissensual politics? In part the analysis did indeed seek to draw out the limits of present conceptions in international law (and to a lesser extent political thought) and suggest how the given articulations of the right to have rights could be reoriented along more emancipatory lines, for example:

from formal to substantive nationality: an enduring conception of nationality in international law characterizes nationality as a passive and formal legal status pertaining to questions of international public order. Nationality stands apart from citizenship (in particular from the rights of citizenship within a state and from citizenship as connoting political and substantive membership) (Chapters 1 and 2). Not only may international law thereby fail to capture statelessness as a potential condition of rightlessness (with all the attendant implications for the protection of the rights of stateless people), but when a passive and public order conception of nationality prevails, a politics of formal membership is fostered which sidelines inequalities within and between nationalities;

from a tenuous citizenship to a citizenship of equality: in international legal analyses two conceptions of citizenship emerge, namely citizenship as a privilege to be earned, and citizenship as a status of equality conferred on all without differentiation (Chapter 3). Consequently the political equality posited by international law remains tenuous with the disenfranchisement of prisoners being attenuated but not prohibited;

from a bordered humanity to contesting the borders of humanity: the posited 'universal' humanity of international human rights law can collapse into humanity of the border such that those who have transgressed a state's territorial borders, whether undocumented migrants or stateless people, are excluded from either the scope or enjoyment of human rights (Chapter 4). Thus the 'humanity' of international human rights law always harbours a tendency to become a bounded conception of humanity: the human of the border (whether that border is the territorial border or the border of humanity as conceived by a particular collective);

and (to a lesser extent) from dissensual politics to the emancipatory potential of the politics within the law: alongside a Rancièrian dissensual politics, the choices within the law must be exploited (Chapter 5).

Although I advocated pushing international law beyond its current conceptions—of not being satisfied with present conceptions of nationality, citizenship, humanity, or of politics—the answer to the right to have rights does not lie in incrementally tinkering with the different placeholders in order to nudge them towards some notional horizon of perfection, nor of seeking a further holy grail placeholder that will succeed where all the others fail. My argument is not simply to state that the way forward lies in these or any other reconceptualizations. This would repeat the inevitable problem of exclusion, and if the excluded minority were smaller than before, it would not for that reason alone—and should not for that reason alone—be any more acceptable. While we are not to be complacent about any given placeholder, it is not a matter of merely setting them against each other in order to engineer some competition to find the most emancipatory reformulation. And this is for the very good reason that it is in seeking to give a single answer to the question of the right to have rights that difficulties surface.

The problem lies in the naming of the placeholder itself, because no one place-holder, no one positive determination of, and basis for, right-bearing (nor for that matter sphere of right-holding) can bear the weight of the right to have rights without collateral exclusionary damage. And yet there is a tendency for any given placeholder to fill the frame of the right to have rights in a totalizing gesture so as to subsume competing placeholders and exacerbate, rather than palliate the vulnerability of those who fall outside its scope. It is here that the relationships between nationality, citizenship, humanity, and politics traced throughout our analysis help to illuminate the underlying weaknesses of any given articulation of the right to have rights and point to a new understanding for the purposes of international law. To combat statelessness, for example, by advocating the confer-ral of a right to a nationality is essential, but may exacerbate the vulnerability of those who inevitably fall through the net of nationality. The subject of human rights becomes the national, and humanity disappears into nationality. As was seen in Chapter 2, nationality may not only be a 'requirement for the exercise of specific rights' but also become a precondition for there being a subject of rights per se. To be denied the legal status of nationality is to be denied human rights. Humanity alone is deficient. Another example of the posited placeholder filling the frame of the right to have rights is Arendt's identification of the citizen and the human such that the subject of human rights is the citizen: to be excluded from the political community is to be rightless (Chapter 3). Then again, invoca-tions of international human rights law may at times have the opposite effect, namely, the human subsumes the citizen such that the agency of the political status of citizenship is reduced to the passive condition of being a rights-bearer (Chapters 4 and 5).

Nevertheless, there were hints throughout the chapters of the possibility and importance of these concepts and discourses at times sitting alongside one another in a mutually affirming or productive relationship. Consider, for example, how the political status of citizenship—having a voice as an equal in a political commu-nity founded on plurality (to adopt Arendt's conception)—may help to minimize exclusions from the legal status of nationality, along with all the consequences this has for the protection of human rights (Chapter 2). A further example is seen in Rancière's work in that the gap between man and the citizen is put to productive use by the excluded who assert, claim, and enact the rights they have been denied (Chapter 5). A means has to be found for citizenship, nationality, humanity, and dissensual politics all to play to their strengths, without exposing the vulnerable at their limits. What we need is not one final and definitive crossword-filling answer to the problem of the right to have rights, but quite to the contrary a way of precisely delegitimating any hastily given answer when it reaches the limits of its helpfulness. The placeholder does not, in fact, need to be named. It needs to be un-named.

2. Un-naming the placeholder: the right to have rights as a gesture of delegitimation

What if naming the placeholder—identifying *the* right to have rights—is the problem and not the solution? That is, the problem is more fundamental than any particular placeholderish name. It lies in naming the placeholder per se. Here we come to the heart of my understanding of the right to have rights. The right to have rights must stand as a delegitimating gesture: it is the means of delegitimating any one conception of right-bearing and of opening a space in which citizenship, nationality, humanity, politics, along with other useful but limited placeholders, can be held together such that no one conception (with all its exclusions and insufficiencies) trumps the others and absolutizes its own shortcomings. As I explain further below, the right to have rights forms the function of un-naming the placeholder such that no one basis or sphere exhaustively fills our vision of right-holding. To be clear, then, my understanding of the right to have rights diverges from, and goes beyond, Arendt's articulation of the right to have rights as citizenship.

If we do not un-name the placeholder, the tendency is for the right to have rights to be reduced to one particular and limited conception of the subject. The subject becomes the national (Chapters 1 and 2), the subject as the citizen (Chapter 3), the subject of international human rights law with all its exclusions and contradictions (Chapter 4),[1] or the subject of dissensual politics (Chapter 5). Each has their good, useful, and necessary place but, if considered alone, each brokers irreducible exclusion and fails some of the most vulnerable. And this includes conceptions of humans rights which go beyond international human rights law and extol their utopian ends, that they are ultimately always to come and a call for unrealized justice,[2] for we are still left with human rights filling the horizon of the right to have rights.

Let me clarify what I am not saying. While a given context may call for strategic decision-making and advocating in terms of a certain placeholder—the right to a nationality, membership of a political community, rights held by virtue of humanity (however conceived), the politics of human rights...—it would be a profound misunderstanding of my position to reduce it to a pick and mix exercise between nationality, citizenship, humanity, and politics (or any other named placeholder). This would miss the point of the right to have rights as a delegitimating move—of preventing any placeholder filling the field of right-bearing. If the condition of possibility of both x and y (say the rights of the national and the rights of the human) is other (the right to have rights) then this delegitimates the absolutization of any single conception of rights.

---

[1] This is not to imply, however, that there is only one conception of the human in international human rights law. Competing logics coexist within international human rights law. (see Chapter 4)

[2] See C Douzinas, *The End of Human Rights: Critical Legal Thought at the Turn of the Century* (Oxford: Hart, 2000).

It is helpful to explain the importance of this distinction with a brief excursus through the thought of one final philosopher: Jean-Luc Nancy.[3] A fundamental distinction is made in Nancy's thought between 'sense' and 'signification'. Whereas signification is 'determinate sense' (the mathematical significations of a Galileo or a Descartes, for example), sense is 'the coming of a possible signification' (what is left unsaid, unmeasured, by modernity's significations).[4] Sense always exceeds signification, but it is also sense that makes signification possible in the first place. Whereas in signification a system of meanings closes in on itself, sense is the opening which precedes, makes possible, and crucially exceeds all signification.[5] As one writer has put it, 'the "call" of sense is a call not to foreclose sense in signification, but a call to "resist installation, calculation, domination etc" '.[6] Our concern here however is not with sense and signification as such, but with the way in which the relation between them can help us to approach the right to have rights in a more helpful way. For my purposes, sense is to signification as the right to have rights is to any of its appropriations or articulations: the right to have rights opens the condition of possibility of right-holding and exceeds—and de-absolutizes—any one conception of the subject of rights. It thus serves as a constant foreclosure of the foreclosure of different conceptions of the subject of rights, a Nancean dis-enclosure of any totalizing conception of rights, and a stone in the shoe of any reductive conceptualization apt to forget its own contingency. As the opening and condition of possibility of all placeholders, the right to have rights cannot itself be theorized, reduced to a principle, or to a particular right. I am not advocating the development of a new principle or norm of international law or of a new 'right to rights'. But let us be clear: to refuse to advocate such a development should not be seen as a failure. That is the point, the whole point of its necessity. If the right to have rights is to add to our analysis of the different placeholders, it cannot itself be put to productive use as a new right or norm. And yet this is why it is essential: its value lies in its resistance to any final value, in its excess, its opening of a horizon which can never be filled, and therefore its frustration of any attempt to lock down the subject of rights to any one formulation. It is not a matter of holding up one conceptualization of the right to have rights as the answer, but of recognizing the limitations of each and ensuring no individual conception—with all its weaknesses and exclusions—definitively prevails. The right to have rights is neither citizenship, nationality, humanity, nor politics but beyond and the condition of possibility of them all. Similarly, it is not a matter of finding one sphere or context of right-bearing, one 'place' (territory of the state; political community; place constituted through political action . . .). If the right to have rights un-names and delegitimates

---

[3] I am indebted to Christopher Watkin for drawing my attention to Nancy's work and to the relevance of the distinction between 'sense' and 'signification' for the right to have rights.

[4] J-L Nancy, *L'Oubli de la philosophie* (Paris: Galilée, 1986) 14 cited and translated in C Watkin, *Phenomenology or Deconstruction?: The Question of Ontology in Maurice Merleau-Ponty, Paul Ricoeur and Jean-Luc Nancy* (Edinburgh: Edinburgh University Press, 2009) 138, 160 (fn 13).

[5] J-L Nancy, *The Sense of the World*, J S Librett (trans) (Minneapolis: University of Minnesota Press, 1997) 10 and ibid, 138.

[6] Watkin, *Phenomenology or Deconstruction?*, 140, 161 (fn 22).

any given placeholder, it equally constitutes the 'non-place' to any posited 'place'. Not in the sense of Rancière's non-place between statuses which forms the site of political subjectivization (Chapter 5), but rather as a gesture to the inadequacy of any given place; that is, as a means of displacing any posited sphere of right-holding from filling the field of the places of the right to have rights.

The contribution of the right to have rights is that of a call to embed its own delegitimating gesture within the law, against the law, opening the law to a recognition of its own exclusions. It is the constant reminder that the posited appropriation of right-bearing might be otherwise; that there is a remainder that the given articulation does not embrace. As a condition of possibility its contribution is most evident in its absence. For when this opening is erased, our analyses, advocacy, and invocations of international law take the particular appropriation of the right to have rights as the horizon of possibility, stunting the very emancipation which is sought.

References

Adjami, M and Harrington, J, 'The Scope and Content of Article 15 of the Universal Declaration of Human Rights' (2008) 27(3) *Refugee Survey Quarterly* 93

Adler, H G, *Der verwaltete Mensch: Studien zur Deportation der Juden aus Deutschland* (Tübingen: Mohr, 1974)

Amerasinghe, C F, *Diplomatic Protection* (Oxford: Oxford University Press, 2008)

Antaki, M, 'The Critical Modernism of Hannah Arendt' (2007) 8(1) *Theoretical Inq L* 251

Arendt, H, '"The Rights of Man" What are They?' (1949) 3(1) *Modern Review* (New York) 24

——, *The Burden of Our Time* (London: Secker and Warburg, 1951)

——, 'Statelessness' lecture, 1955, Hannah Arendt Papers, The Library of Congress (Series: Speeches and Writings File, 1923–1975, nd)

——, 'Reflections on Little Rock' (1959) 6(1) *Dissent* 45

——, 'Karl Jaspers: Citizen of the World?' in H Arendt, *Men in Dark Times* (London: Cape, 1970) 81

——, *The Origins of Totalitarianism* (revised edn) (New York: Harcourt, [1973])

——, *Eichmann in Jerusalem: A Report on the Banality of Evil* (revised and enlarged edn) (Harmondsworth: Penguin, 1976)

——, *On Revolution* (London: Penguin Books, 1990)

——, 'On the Nature of Totalitarianism: An Essay in Understanding' in H Arendt, *Essays in Understanding 1930–1954: Formation, Exile, and Totalitarianism*, J Kohn (ed) (New York: Schocken Books, 1994) 328

——, 'A Reply to Eric Voegelin' in H Arendt, *Essays in Understanding 1930–1954: Formation, Exile, and Totalitarianism*, J Kohn (ed) (New York: Schocken Books, 1994) 401

——, *The Human Condition* (2nd edn) (Chicago: University of Chicago Press, 1998)

——, *The Promise of Politics* (New York: Schocken Books, 2005)

——, *The Jewish Writings* (New York: Schocken Books, 2007)

—— and K Jaspers, *Hannah Arendt, Karl Jaspers: Correspondence, 1926–1969*, L Kohler and H Saner (eds), R Kimber and R Kimber (trans) (New York: Harcourt Brace Jovanovich, 1992)

Augé, M, *Non-places: An Introduction to Supermodernity* (2nd edn) (London: Verso, 2008)

Balibar, É, 'The Nation Form: History and Ideology' in É Balibar and I Wallerstein, *Race, Nation, Class: Ambiguous Identities* (London: Verso, 1991) 86

——, 'What is a Politics of the Rights of Man?' in É Balibar, *Masses, Classes, Ideas: Studies on Politics and Philosophy Before and After Marx* (New York: Routledge, 1994) 205

——, *Politics and the Other Scene*, C Jones, J Swenson, and C Turner (trans) (London: Verso, 2002)

——, 'Europe as Borderland', The Alexander von Humboldt Lecture in Human Geography, University of Nijmegen, 10 November 2004, <http://socgeo.ruhosting.nl/colloquium/Europe%20as%20Borderland.pdf> accessed 30 March 2011

——, 'Is a Philosophy of Human Civic Rights Possible? New Reflections on Equaliberty' (2004) 103(2/3) *South Atlantic Quarterly* 311

——, *We, the People of Europe?: Reflections on Transnational Citizenship*, J Swenson (trans) (Princeton: Princeton University Press, 2004)

——, '(De)Constructing the Human as Human Institution: A Reflection on the Coherence of Hannah Arendt's Practical Philosophy' (2007) 74(3) *Social Research* 727

Bardonnet, D, 'Les frontières terrestres' (1976) 153 *Hag R* 9

Batchelor, C, 'Statelessness and the Problem of Resolving Nationality Status' (1998) 10 (1/2) *IJRL* 156

Bauböck, R, 'Citizenship and Migration—Concepts and Controversies' in R Bauböck (ed), *Migration and Citizenship: Legal Status, Rights and Political Participation* (Amsterdam: Amsterdam University Press, 2006) 15

Beetham, D, *Democracy and Human Rights* (Cambridge: Polity, 1999)

Benhabib, S, *The Reluctant Modernism of Hannah Arendt* (Oxford: Rowman & Littlefield Publishers, 2000)

——, *The Rights of Others: Aliens, Residents and Citizens* (Cambridge: Cambridge University Press, 2004)

Bernstein, R J, 'Hannah Arendt on the Stateless' (2005) 11(1) *parallax* 46

Bhabha, J, 'Arendt's Children: Do Today's Migrant Children have a Right to have Rights?' (2009) 31(2) *Hum Rts Q* 410

Bigo, D, 'Frontier Controls in the European Union: Who is in Control?' in D Bigo and E Guild (eds), *Controlling Frontiers: Free Movement Into and Within Europe* (Aldershot: Ashgate, 2005) 49

Blomley, N, *Law, Space, and the Geographies of Power* (New York: Guilford Press, 1994)

——, Delaney, D, and Ford, R T (eds), *The Legal Geographies Reader: Law, Power, and Space* (Oxford: Blackwell, 2001)

Boll, A M, *Multiple Nationality and International Law* (Leiden: Martinus Nijhoff Publishers, 2007)

Bosniak, L, 'Multiple Nationality and the Postnational Transformation of Citizenship' (2001) 42(4) *Va J Int'l L* 979

——, *The Citizen and the Alien: Dilemmas of Contemporary Membership* (Princeton: Princeton University Press, 2006)

Bossuyt, M, *Guide to the 'Travaux Préparatoires' of the International Covenant on Civil and Political Rights* (Dordrecht: Martinus Nijhoff Publishers, 1987)

Bosteels, B, 'Nonplaces: An Anecdoted Topography of Contemporary French Theory' (2003) 33(3/4) *Diacritics* 117

Brownlie, I, 'The Relations of Nationality in Public International Law' (1963) 39 *BYIL* 284

Brysk, A, and Shafir, G (eds), *People Out of Place: Globalization, Human Rights, and the Citizenship Gap* (New York: Routledge, 2004)

Burchill, R, 'Democracy and the Promotion and Protection of Socio-Economic Rights' in M A Baderin and R McCorquodale (eds), *Economic, Social and Cultural Rights in Action* (Oxford: Oxford University Press, 2007) 361

Butenschøn, N A, 'Citizenship and Human Rights: Some Thoughts on a Complex Relationship' in M Bergsmo (ed), *Human Rights and Criminal Justice for the Downtrodden: Essays in Honour of Asbjørn Eide* (Leiden: Brill, 2003) 555

Caloz-Tschopp, M-C, *Les sans-Etat dans la philosophie d'Hannah Arendt: Les humains super-flus, le droit d'avoir des droits et la citoyenneté* (Lausanne: Payot Lausanne 2000)

Cançado Trindade, A A, *International Law for Humankind: Towards a New jus gentium* (2005) 316/317 *Recueil des Cours* (Leiden: Martinus Nijhoff Publishers, 2006)

Canovan, M, *Hannah Arendt: A Reinterpretation of Her Political Thought* (Cambridge: Cambridge University Press, 1994)

Chan, J M, 'The Right to a Nationality as a Human Right' (1991) 12(1) *Human Rights Law Journal* 1

Cheah, P, 'Necessary Strangers: Law's Hospitality in the Age of Transnational Migrancy' in A Sarat, L Douglas, and M M Umphrey (eds), *Law and The Stranger* (Stanford: Stanford University Press, 2010) 21

Chetail, V, 'Freedom of Movement and Transnational Migrations: A Human Rights Perspective' in T A Aleinikoff and V Chetail (eds), *Migration and International Legal Norms* (The Hague: TMC Asser Press, 2003) 47

Cholewinski, R, *Study on Obstacles to Effective Access of Irregular Migrants to Minimum Social Rights* (Strasbourg: Council of Europe, 2005)

——, 'The Rights of Migrant Workers' in R Cholewinski, R Perruchoud, and E MacDonald (eds), *International Migration Law: Developing Paradigms and Key Challenges* (The Hague: TMC Asser Press, 2007) 255

Cotter, B, 'Hannah Arendt and "The Right to have Rights"' in A F Lang and J Williams, *Hannah Arendt and International Relations: Reading across the Lines* (New York: Palgrave Macmillan, 2005) 95

Cresswell, T, *In Place/Out of Place: Geography, Ideology, and Transgression* (Minneapolis: University of Minnesota Press, 1996)

Crowley, J, 'Locating Europe' in K Groenendijk, E Guild, and P Minderhoud (eds), *In Search of Europe's Borders* (The Hague: Kluwer Law International, 2003) 28

——, 'Where Does The State Actually Start? The Contemporary Governance of Work and Migration' in D Bigo and E Guild (eds), *Controlling Frontiers: Free Movement Into and Within Europe* (Aldershot: Ashgate, 2005) 140

Dauvergne, C, *Making People Illegal: What Globalization Means for Migration and Law* (New York: Cambridge University Press, 2008)

Dembour, M-B, *Who Believes in Human Rights?: Reflections on the European Convention* (Cambridge: Cambridge University Press, 2006)

Demleitner, N V, 'Preventing Internal Exile: The Need for Restrictions on Collateral Sentencing Consequences' (1999) 11(1) *Stan L & Pol'y Rev* 153

——, 'US Felon Disenfranchisement: Parting Ways with Western Europe' in A C Ewald and B Rottinghaus (eds), *Criminal Disenfranchisement in an International Perspective* (New York: Cambridge University Press, 2009) 79

Donnelly, J, *Universal Human Rights in Theory and Practice* (2nd edn) (Ithaca: Cornell University Press, 2003)

Donner, R, *The Regulation of Nationality in International* Law (2nd edn) (Irvington-on-Hudson, New York: Transnational Publishers, 1994)

Douzinas, C, *The End of Human Rights: Critical Legal Thought at the Turn of the Century* (Oxford: Hart, 2000)

——, *Human Rights and Empire: The Political Philosophy of Cosmopolitanism* (Abingdon: Routledge-Cavendish, 2007)

Dyzenhaus, D, *The Constitution of Law: Legality in a Time of Emergency* (Cambridge: Cambridge University Press, 2006)

Easton, S, *Prisoners' Rights: Principles and Practice* (Abingdon: Routledge, 2011)

Edwards, A and Ferstman, C, 'Humanising Non-Citizens: The Convergence of Human Rights and Human Security' in A Edwards and C Ferstman (eds), *Human Security and Non-Citizens: Law, Policy and International Affairs* (Cambridge: Cambridge University Press, 2010) 3

Equal Rights Trust, *Unravelling Anomaly: Detention, Discrimination and the Protection Needs of Stateless Persons* (London: Prontaprint Bayswater, 2010)

Ersbøll, E, 'The Right to a Nationality and the European Convention on Human Rights' in S Lagoutte, H Sano, and P Scharff Smith (eds), *Human Rights in Turmoil: Facing Threats, Consolidating Achievements* (Leiden: Martinus Nijhoff Publishers, 2006) 249

Ewald, A C, ' "Civil Death": The Ideological Paradox of Criminal Disenfranchisement Law in the United States' (2002) *Wis L Rev* 1045

——, 'Introduction' in A C Ewald and B Rottinghaus (eds), *Criminal Disenfranchisement in an International Perspective* (New York: Cambridge University Press, 2009) 1

Faist, T, 'The Fixed and Porous Boundaries of Dual Citizenship' in T Faist (ed), *Dual Citizenship in Europe: From Nationhood to Societal Integration* (Aldershot: Ashgate, 2007) 1

——, 'Introduction: The Shifting Boundaries of the Political' in T Faist and P Kivisto (eds), *Dual Citizenship in Global Perspective: From Unitary to Multiple Citizenship* (Basingstoke: Palgrave Macmillan, 2007) 1

Falk, R, 'The United Nations and Cosmopolitan Democracy: Bad Dream, Utopian Fantasy, Political Project' in D Archibugi, D Held, and M Köhler (eds), *Re-imagining Political Community* (Cambridge: Polity Press, 1998) 309

Fenwick, C, 'Private Use of Prisoners' Labor: Paradoxes of International Human Rights Law' (2005) 27(1) *Hum Rts Q* 249

Fisher, D, Martin, S, and Schoenholtz, A, 'Migration and Security in International Law' in T A Aleinikoff and V Chetail (eds), *Migration and International Legal Norms* (The Hague: TMC Asser Press, 2003) 87

Fitzpatrick, J, 'The Human Rights of Migrants' in T A Aleinikoff and V Chetail (eds), *Migration and International Legal Norms* (The Hague: TMC Asser Press, 2003) 169

Fletcher, G P, 'Disenfranchisement as Punishment: Reflections on the Racial Uses of *Infamia*' (1998) 46(6) *UCLA L Rev* 1895

Foucher, M, *Fronts et frontières: un tour du monde géopolitique* (Paris: Fayard, 1988)

Fox, G H, 'The Right to Political Participation in International Law' (1992) 17(2) *Yale J Int'l L* 539

Franke, M F N, 'The Unbearable Rightfulness of Being Human: Citizenship, Displacement, and the Right to not have Rights' (2011) 15(1) *Citizenship Studies* 39

Garner, J W, 'Recent German Nationality Legislation (1936) 30(1) *AJIL* 96

Goodwin-Gill, G, *International Law and the Movement of Persons Between States* (Oxford: Clarendon Press, 1978)

—— and McAdam, J, *The Refugee in International Law* (3rd edn) (Oxford: Oxford University Press, 2007)

Grant, S, 'The Legal Protection of Stranded Migrants' in R Cholewinski, R Perruchoud, and E MacDonald (eds), *International Migration Law* (The Hague: TMC Asser Press, 2007) 29

Guild, E, 'The Foreigner in the Security Continuum: Judicial Resistance in the United Kingdom' in P K Rajaram and C Grundy-Warr (eds), *Borderscapes: Hidden Geographies and Politics at Territory's Edge* (Minneapolis: University of Minnesota Press, 2007) 65

Gunneflo, M and Selberg, N, 'Discourse or Merely Noise? Regarding the Disagreement on Undocumented Migrants' (2010) 12(2) *European Journal of Migration and Law* 173

Habermas, J, *The Postnational Constellation: Political Essays* (Cambridge: Polity, 2001)

——, *The Inclusion of the Other: Studies in Political Theory*, C Cronin and P De Greiff (eds) (Cambridge: Polity, 2002)

Hannum, H, *The Right to Leave and Return in International Law and Practice* (Dordrecht: Martinus Nijhoff, 1987)

Harvey, C and Barnidge, R, 'Human Rights, Free Movement, and the Right to Leave in International Law' (2007) 19(1) *IJRL* 1

Held, D, 'Democracy and Globalization' in D Archibugi, D Held, and M Köhler (eds), *Re-imagining Political Community* (Cambridge: Polity Press, 1998) 11

——, 'Law of States, Law of Peoples: Three Models of Sovereignty' (2002) 8(1) *Legal Theory* 1

Henkin, L, *The Rights of Man Today* (London: Stevens & Sons, 1979)

Higgins, R, 'The Right in International Law of an Individual to Enter, Stay in and Leave a Country' (1973) 49(3) *International Affairs* 341

Holder, J and Harrison, C (eds), *Law and Geography*, Current Legal Issues 5 (Oxford: Oxford University Press, 2003)

Honig, B, *Democracy and the Foreigner* (Princeton: Princeton University Press, 2001)

Hull, E A, 'Our "Crooked Timber": Why is American Punishment so Harsh?' in A C Ewald and B Rottinghaus (eds), *Criminal Disenfranchisement in an International Perspective* (New York: Cambridge University Press, 2009) 136

Independent International Fact-Finding Mission on the Conflict in Georgia, Vol II, September 2009, <http://www.ceiig.ch/Report.html> accessed 31 March 2011

Ingram, J D, 'What is a "Right to have Rights"? Three Images of the Politics of Human Rights' (2008) 102(4) *American Political Science Review* 401

International Law Association, 'Final Report on Women's Equality and Nationality in International Law' (2000) 69 *Int'l L Ass'n Rep Conf* 248

——, 'Final Report on Diplomatic Protection of Persons and Property' (2006) 72 *Int'l L Ass'n Rep Conf* 353

International Law Commission, 'Nationality, including Statelessness' (Special Rapporteur M O Hudson), UN Doc A/CN.4/50 (21 February 1952) in *Yearbook of the International Law Commission 1952*, Vol II, 3

——, 'Report on the Elimination or Reduction of Statelessness' (Special Rapporteur R Córdova) (30 March 1953) in *Yearbook of the International Law Commission,* 1953, Vol II, 167

——, 'First Report on Diplomatic Protection' (Special Rapporteur J Dugard), UN Doc A/CN.4/506 (7 March 2000)

——, 'Tenth Report on Reservations to Treaties' (Special Rapporteur A Pellet), UN Doc A/CN.4/558 (1 June 2005)

——, 'Third Report on the Expulsion of Aliens' (Special Rapporteur M Kamto), UN Doc A/CN.4/581 (19 April 2007)

Isin, E F, 'Theorizing Acts of Citizenship' in E F Isin and G M Nielsen (eds), *Acts of Citizenship* (London: Zed Books, 2008) 15

—— and Rygiel, K, 'Abject Spaces: Frontiers, Zones, Camps' in E Dauphinee and C Masters (eds), *The Logics of Biopower and the War on Terror: Living, Dying, Surviving* (New York: Palgrave Macmillan, 2007) 181

Ispahani, L, 'Voting Rights and Human Rights: A Comparative Analysis of Criminal Disenfranchisement Laws' in A C Ewald and B Rottinghaus (eds), *Criminal Disenfranchisement in an International Perspective* (New York: Cambridge University Press, 2009) 25

Jagerskiold, S, 'The Freedom of Movement' in L Henkin (ed), *The International Bill of Rights: The Covenant on Civil and Political Rights* (New York: Columbia University Press, 1981) 166

Jennings, R, *General Course on Principles of International Law* (1967) 121 *Recueil des Cours* 452

—— and Watts, A (eds), *Oppenheim's International Law* (9th edn) (Harlow: Longman, 1992)

Johns, F (ed), *International Legal Personality* (Farnham: Ashgate, 2010)

Jones, M, 'The Nottebohm Case' (1956) 5(2) *ICLQ* 230

Jonge (de), G, 'Still "Slaves of the State": Prison Labour and International Law' in D van Zyl Smit and F Dünkel (eds), *Prison Labour: Salvation or Slavery?: International Perspectives* (Oñati International Series in Law and Society) (Aldershot: Ashgate, 1999) 313

Juss, S, 'Free Movement and the World Order' (2004) 16(3) *IJRL* 289

Kelsen, H, *General Theory of Law & State* (New Brunswick: Transaction Publishers, 2006)

Kesby, A, 'The Shifting and Multiple Border and International Law' (2007) 27(1) *OJLS* 101

——, 'Internal Borders and Immigration Control: New Prospects and Challenges' [2010] *European Human Rights Law Review* 176

——, 'International Law and the Right to have Rights' in *Select Proceedings of the European Society of International law*, Vol 2, 2008 (Oxford: Hart, 2010) 133

Klabbers, J, 'Possible Islands of Predictability: The Legal Thought of Hannah Arendt' (2007) 20(1) *LJIL* 1

Koskenniemi, M, *From Apology to Utopia: The Structure of International Legal Argument* (Cambridge: Cambridge University Press, 2005)

——, 'The Politics of International Law—20 Years Later' (2009) 20(1) *EJIL* 7

Krause, M, 'Undocumented Migrants: An Arendtian Perspective' (2008) 7(3) *European Journal of Political Theory* 331

Kunz, J L, 'The Nottebohm Judgment' (1960) 54(3) *AJIL* 536

Lauterpacht, E and Bethlehem, D, 'The Scope and Content of the Principle of *Non-Refoulement*: Opinion' in E Feller, V Türk, and F Nicholson (eds), *Refugee Protection in International Law: UNHCR's Global Consultations on International Protection* (Cambridge: Cambridge University Press, 2003) 87

Lauterpacht, H, 'The Law of Nations, the Law of Nature and the Rights of Man', *Transactions of the Grotius Society*, Vol 29, Problems of Peace and War, 1943, 1,

——, *An International Bill of the Rights of Man* (New York: Columbia University Press, 1945)

——, *International Law and Human Rights* (London: Steven & Sons Ltd, 1950) 347

——, 'Foreword to the First Edition' in P Weis, *Nationality and Statelessness in International Law* (2nd edn) (Alphen aan den Rijn: Sijthoff & Noordhoff, 1979) xi

Lefebvre, H, *The Production of Space*, D Nicholson-Smith (trans) (Oxford: Blackwell Publishing, 1991)

Lessing, H, *Das Recht der Staatsangehörigkeit und die Aberkennung der Staatsangehörigkeit zu Straf- und Sicherungszwecken* (Lvgdvni Batavorvm: E J Brill, 1937)

Lindahl, H, 'Give and Take: Arendt and the *Nomos* of Political Community' (2006) 32(7) *Philosophy & Social Criticism* 881

——, 'Border Crossings by Immigrants: Legality, Illegality, and A-legality' (2008) 14(2) *Res Publica* 117

——, 'In Between: Immigration, Distributive Justice and Political Dialogue' (2009) 8(4) *Contemporary Political Theory* 415

——, 'A-legality: Postnationalism and the Question of Legal Boundaries' (2010) 73(1) *MLR* 30

Lippke, R L, 'The Disenfranchisement of Felons' (2001) 20(6) *Law and Philosophy* 553

Lyon, D, 'Filtering Flows, Friends and Foes: Global Surveillance' in M B Salter (ed), *Politics at the Airport* (Minneapolis: University of Minnesota Press, 2008) 29

McAdam, J, *Complementary Protection in International Refugee Law* (Oxford: Oxford University Press, 2007)

McBride, K, 'Hitched to the Post: Prison Labor, Choice and Citizenship' in A Sarat and P Ewick (eds), *Punishment, Politics and Culture* (Studies in Law, Politics and Society, Vol 30) (Amsterdam: Elsevier Ltd, 2004) 107

McDougal, M S, Lasswell, H D, and Chen, L, 'Nationality and Human Rights: The Protection of the Individual in External Arenas' (1973) 83(5) *Yale LJ* 900

McGregor, L, 'Legal Routes to Restoring Individual Rights at Guantánamo Bay: The Effectiveness of *habeas corpus* Applications and Efforts to Obtain Diplomatic Protection' in A Edwards and C Ferstman (eds), *Human Security and Non-Citizens: Law, Policy and International Affairs* (Cambridge: Cambridge University Press, 2010) 560

Macklin, A, 'The State of Law's Borders and the Law of States' Borders' in D Dyzenhaus (ed), *The Unity of Public Law* (Oxford: Hart Publishing, 2004) 173

——, 'Who is the Citizen's Other? Considering the Heft of Citizenship' (2007) 8(2) *Theoretical Inq L* 333

Manby, B, *Struggles for Citizenship in Africa* (London: Zed Books, 2009)

Manly, M and van Waas, L, 'The Value of the Human Security Framework in Addressing Statelessness' in A Edwards and C Ferstman (eds), *Human Security and Non-Citizens: Law, Policy and International Affairs* (Cambridge: Cambridge University Press, 2010) 56

Manza, J and Uggen, C, *Locked Out: Felon Disenfranchisement and American Democracy* (Oxford: Oxford University Press, 2006)

Marks, S, *The Riddle of all Constitutions: International Law, Democracy, and the Critique of Ideology* (Oxford: Oxford University Press, 2000)

Martin, D A, 'The Authority and Responsibility of States' in T A Aleinikoff and V Chetail (eds), *Migration and International Legal Norms* (The Hague: TMC Asser Press, 2003) 31

May, T, *Contemporary Political Movements and the Thought of Jacques Rancière: Equality in Action* (Edinburgh: Edinburgh University Press, 2010)

Moeckli, D, *Human Rights and Non-Discrimination in the 'War on Terror'* (Oxford: Oxford University Press, 2008)

Nafziger, J, 'The General Admission of Aliens Under International Law' (1983) 77(4) *AJIL* 804

Nancy, J-L, *The Sense of the World*, J S Librett (trans) (Minneapolis: University of Minnesota Press, 1997)

Nesiah, V, 'Placing International Law: White Spaces on a Map' (2003) 16(1) *LJIL* 1

Neuman, G L, 'The Resilience of Nationality' (2007) 101 *Am Soc'y Int'l L Proc* 97

Newman, D, 'Boundaries' in J Agnew, K Mitchell, and G Toal (eds), *A Companion to Political Geography* (Oxford: Blackwell Publishing Ltd, 2003) 123

Nijman, J E, *The Concept of International Legal Personality: An Inquiry into the History and Theory of International Law* (The Hague: Asser Press, 2004)

Noll, G, 'Why Human Rights Fail to Protect Undocumented Migrants' (2010) 12(2) *European Journal of Migration and Law* 241

Nowak, M, *UN Covenant on Civil and Political Rights CCPR Commentary* (Kehl am Rhein: N P Engel, 1993)

Nyers, P, 'Abject Cosmopolitanism: The Politics of Protection in the Anti-Deportation Movement' (2003) 24(6) *Third World Quarterly* 1069

Orentlicher, D F, 'Citizenship and National Identity' in D Wippman (ed), *International Law and Ethnic Conflict* (Ithaca: Cornell University Press, 1998) 296

Orford, A, 'Biopolitics and the Tragic Subject of Human Rights' in E Dauphinee and C Masters (eds), *The Logics of Biopower and the War on Terror: Living, Dying, Surviving* (New York: Palgrave Macmillan, 2007) 205

Osiel, M, *Mass Atrocity, Ordinary Evil, and Hannah Arendt: Criminal Consciousness in Argentina's Dirty War* (New Haven: Yale University Press, 2001)

Osofsky, H, 'Panel: Law and Geography' (2007) 5(2) *Santa Clara J Int L* 507

Owens, P, *Between War and Politics: International Relations and the Thought of Hannah Arendt* (Oxford: Oxford University Press, 2007)

Pahuja, S, 'Rights as Regulation: The Integration of Development and Human Rights' in B Morgan (ed), *The Intersection of Rights and Regulation: New Directions in Sociolegal Scholarship* (Aldershot: Ashgate, 2007) 167

Panhuys (van), H F, *The Rôle of Nationality in International Law: An Outline* (Leiden: Sijthoff, 1959)

Parekh, S, 'A Meaningful Place in the World: Hannah Arendt on the Nature of Human Rights' (2004) 3(1) *Journal of Human Rights* 41

Parlett, K, *The Individual in the International Legal System: Continuity and Change in International Law* (Cambridge: Cambridge University Press, 2011)

Peters, A, 'Humanity as the Alpha and Omega of Sovereignty' (2009) 20(3) *EJIL* 513

——, 'Membership in the Global Constitutional Community' in J Klabbers, A Peters, and G Ulfstein, *The Constitutionalization of International Law* (Oxford: Oxford University Press, 2009) 153

Pickens, J A, 'Special Project—The Collateral Consequences of a Criminal Conviction' (1969) 23(5) *Vand L Rev* 929

Portmann, R, *Legal Personality in International Law* (Cambridge: Cambridge University Press, 2010)

Prescott, V and Triggs, G D, *International Frontiers and Boundaries: Law, Politics and Geography* (Leiden: Martinus Nijhoff Publishers, 2008)

Rajaram, P K and Grundy-Warr, C, 'Introduction' in P K Rajaram and C Grundy-Warr (eds), *Borderscapes: Hidden Geographies and Politics at Territory's Edge* (Minneapolis: University of Minnesota Press, 2007) ix

Rancière, J, 'Politics, Identification, and Subjectivization' (1992) 61 *October* 58

——, *On the Shores of Politics*, L Heron (trans) (London: Verso, 1995)

——, *Disagreement: Politics and Philosophy*, J Rose (trans) (Minneapolis: University of Minnesota Press, 1999)

——, 'Ten Theses on Politics' (2001) 5(3) *Theory and Event* (electronic journal)

——, 'Who is the Subject of the Rights of Man?' (2004) 103(2/3) *South Atlantic Quarterly* 297

——, 'Democracy, Republic, Representation' (2006) 13(3) *Constellations* 297

——, 'Does Democracy Mean Something' in *Dissensus: On Politics and Aesthetics*, S Corcoran (trans) (London: Continuum, 2010)

Redman, R, Brown, D, and Mercurio, B, 'The Politics and Legality of Prisoner Disenfranchisement in Australian Federal Elections' in A C Ewald and B Rottinghaus (eds), *Criminal Disenfranchisement in an International Perspective* (New York: Cambridge University Press, 2009) 167

Rubenstein, K, 'Citizenship in a Borderless World' in A Anghie and G Sturgess (eds), *Legal Visions of the 21st Century: Essays in Honour of Judge Christopher Weeramantry* (The Hague: Kluwer Law International, 1998) 183

—— and Adler, D, 'International Citizenship: The Future of Nationality in a Globalized World' (1999) 7(2) *Ind J Global Legal Stud* 519

Rygiel, K, 'Bordering Solidarities: Migrant Activism and the Politics of Movement and Camps at Calais' (2011) 15(1) *Citizenship Studies* 1

Salter, M B, 'The Global Airport: Managing Space, Speed, and Security' in M B Salter (ed), *Politics at the Airport* (Minneapolis: University of Minnesota Press, 2008) 1

Sassen, S, 'The Repositioning of Citizenship and Alienage: Emergent Subjects and Spaces for Politics' (2005) 2(1) *Globalizations* 79

——, *Territory Authority Rights: From Medieval to Global Assemblages* (Princeton: Princeton University Press, 2006)

Schaap, A, 'Enacting the Right to have Rights: Jacques Rancière's Critique of Hannah Arendt' (2011) 10(1) *European Journal of Political Theory* 22

Shachar, A, *The Birthright Lottery: Citizenship and Global Inequality* (Cambridge, Massachusetts: Harvard University Press, 2009)

Sloane, R, 'Breaking the Genuine Link: The Contemporary International Legal Regulation of Nationality' (2009) 50(1) *Harv Int'l LJ* 1

Soguk, N, 'Border's Capture: Insurrectional Politics, Border-Crossing Humans, and the New Political' in P K Rajaram and C Grundy-Warr (eds), *Borderscapes: Hidden Geographies and Politics at Territory's Edge* (Minneapolis: University of Minnesota Press, 2007) 283

Sohn L B and Buergenthal, T (eds), *The Movement of Persons across Borders*, A Part of the Joint Project on the Governing Rules of International Law of The American Society of International Law, The John D and Catherine T MacArthur Foundation, Studies in Transnational Legal Policy No 23, The American Society of International Law, October 1992

Sokoloff, C, 'Denial of Citizenship: A Challenge to Human Security', prepared for Advisory Board on Human Security, February 2005

Somers, M R, *Genealogies of Citizenship: Markets, Statelessness, and the Right to have Rights* (New York: Cambridge University Press, 2008)

Soya, E W, *Postmodern Geographies: The Reassertion of Space in Critical Social Theory* (London: Verso, 1989)

Soysal, Y N, *Limits of Citizenship: Migrants and Postnational Membership in Europe* (Chicago: University of Chicago Press, 1994)

Spiro, P, 'Dual Nationality and the Meaning of Citizenship' (1997) 46(4) *Emory L J* 1411

——, 'Mandated Membership, Diluted Identity: Citizenship, Globalization, and International Law' in A Brysk and G Shafir (eds), *People Out of Place: Globalization, Human Rights, and the Citizenship Gap* (New York: Routledge, 2004) 87

——, 'Dual Citizenship: A Postnational View' in T Faist and P Kivisto (eds), *Dual Citizenship in Global Perspective: From Unitary to Multiple Citizenship* (Basingstoke: Palgrave Macmillan, 2007) 189

——, *Beyond Citizenship: American Identity After Globalization* (New York: Oxford University Press, 2008)

Tambakaki, P, *Human Rights, or Citizenship?* (Abingdon: Birkbeck Law Press, 2010)

Thym, D, 'Respect for Private and Family Life under Article 8 ECHR in Immigration Cases: A Human Right to Regularize Illegal Stay?' (2008) 57(1) *ICLQ* 87

Tiburcio, C, *The Human Rights of Aliens under International and Comparative Law* (Hague: Martinus Nijhoff Publishers, 2001)

Torpey, J, *The Invention of the Passport: Surveillance, Citizenship and the State* (Cambridge: Cambridge University Press, 2000)

Uggen, C, Van Brakle, M, and McLaughlin, H, 'Punishment and Social Exclusion: National Differences in Prisoner Disenfranchisement' in A C Ewald and B Rottinghaus (eds), *Criminal Disenfranchisement in an International Perspective* (New York: Cambridge University Press, 2009) 59

United Nations, 'A Study of Statelessness', UN Doc E/1112;E/1112/Add.1 (August 1949)

United Nations Commission on Human Rights, 'Final Report of the Special Rapporteur on the Rights of Non-Citizens' (Special Rapporteur D Weissbrodt), UN Doc E/CN.4/Sub.2/2003/23 (26 May 2003)

United Nations Fact-Finding Mission on the Gaza Conflict, 'Human Rights in Palestine and other Occupied Arab Territories', UN Doc A/HRC/12/48 (25 September 2009)

Vandova, V, 'Protection of Non-Citizens against Removal under International Human Rights Law' in A Edwards and C Ferstman (eds), *Human Security and Non-Citizens: Law, Policy and International Affairs* (Cambridge: Cambridge University Press, 2010) 495

Villa, D R, 'Introduction: The Development of Arendt's Political Thought' in D Villa (ed), *The Cambridge Companion to Hannah Arendt* (Cambridge: Cambridge University Press, 2002) 1

Volk, C, 'From *Nomos* to *Lex*: Hannah Arendt on Law, Politics, and Order' (2010) 23(4) *LJIL* 759

Waas (van), L, *Nationality Matters: Statelessness under International Law* (Antwerp: Intersentia, 2008)

Wacquant, L, 'From Slavery to Mass Incarceration' (Jan/Feb 2002) (13) *New Left Review* 41

——, *Punishing the Poor: The Neoliberal Government of Social Insecurity* (Durham: Duke University Press, 2009)

Waldron, J, 'Participation: The Right of Rights' in *Law and Disagreement* (Oxford: Clarendon Press, 1999) 232

Walters, W, 'Acts of Demonstration: Mapping the Territory of (Non-)Citizenship' in E F Isin and G M Nielsen (eds), *Acts of Citizenship* (London: Zed Books, 2008) 182

Watkin, C, 'More Equal Than Others: On Thinking Equality Today', 5 (unpublished article on file with the author)

——, *Phenomenology or Deconstruction?: The Question of Ontology in Maurice-Merleau-Ponty, Paul Ricoeur and Jean-Luc Nancy* (Edinburgh: Edinburgh University Press, 2009)

Weiler, J H H, 'The Geology of International Law—Governance, Democracy and Legitimacy'(2004) 64 *ZaöRV* 547

Weis, P, 'The United Nations Convention on the Reduction of Statelessness, 1961' (1962) 11(4) *ICLQ* 1073

——, *Nationality and Statelessness in International Law* (2nd edn) (Alphen aan den Rijn: Sijthoff & Noordhoff, 1979)

Weissbrodt, D, *The Human Rights of Non-Citizens* (New York: Oxford University Press, 2008)

—— and C Collins, 'The Human Rights of Stateless People' (2006) 28(1) *Hum Rts Q* 245

Wilson, R J, 'The Right to Universal, Equal, and Non-Discriminatory Suffrage as a Norm of Customary International Law: Protecting the Prisoner's Right to Vote' in A C Ewald and B Rottinghaus (eds), *Criminal Disenfranchisement in an International Perspective* (New York: Cambridge University Press, 2009) 109

Winder, M A, 'Disproportionate Disenfranchisement of Aboriginal Prisoners: A Conflict of Law that Australia should Address' (2010) 19(2) *Pac Rim L & Pol'y J* 387

Young-Bruehl, E, *Hannah Arendt: For Love of the World* (2nd edn) (New Haven: Yale University Press, 2004)

Yovel, J, 'Imagining Territories: Space, Place, and the Anticity' (1 January 2010), University of Haifa Faculty of Law Legal Studies Research Paper, <http://ssrn.com/abstract=950895> accessed 30 March 2011

Zilbershats, Y, *The Human Right to Citizenship* (Ardsley: Transnational Publishers, 2002)

Zyl Smit (van), D and Dünkel, F, 'Conclusion: Prison Labour—Salvation or Slavery?' in D van Zyl Smit and F Dünkel (eds), *Prison Labour: Salvation or Slavery?: International Perspectives* (Oñati International Series in Law and Society) (Aldershot: Ashgate, 1999) 335

Index